AN INTRODUCTION TO SEVENTEENTH CENTURY FRANCE

AN INTRODUCTION TO EIGHTEENTH CENTURY FRANCE

By Professor John Lough

TWENTIETH CENTURY FRENCH TRANSLATION PASSAGES

Selected by Professor John Lough and Muriel Lough, Ph.D.

(In Preparation)

AN INTRODUCTION TO NINETEENTH CENTURY FRANCE

By Professor John Lough and Muriel Lough, Ph.D.

An Introduction to Seventeenth Century France

by

JOHN LOUGH, M.A., PH.D.

Professor of French in the University of Durham

LONGMANS

LONGMANS, GREEN AND CO. LTD
London and Harlow

Associated companies, branches and representatives throughout the world

First published 1954
Eighth (revised) impression 1969

SBN 582 36052 8 paper edition
SBN 582 31395 3 cased edition

Made and printed by offset in Great Britain by
William Clowes and Sons, Limited, London and Beccles

PREFACE TO THE FIRST EDITION

THE word *Introduction* in the title of this book is meant to be taken literally. It is addressed mainly to those who, in schools and universities or outside them, approach seventeenth century France through the great works of its literature. The first six chapters are devoted to a sketch of the social and political background of the age, illustrated by numerous passages in the original French from well-known literary works as well as from less familiar sources. Apart from a brief epilogue on the period of decline of the reign of Louis XIV, the rest of the book is concerned with the literary background of the age, in particular the relationship between men of letters and their public and its influence on the development of both language and literature in seventeenth century France. In a word, the book attempts to depict the main social and political developments of the age and the setting in which so many varied masterpieces were produced.

While the chapters on social and political history are merely a synthesis of available knowledge, illustrated by selections from contemporary documents, the pages on the literary background are the fruit of several years' research, most of which has not yet been published in full detail. Throughout the book the aim has been to set forth the material in a simple and straightforward manner which, if it does not always do justice to the great complexity of the facts, is essential in an *Introduction.* Since only a very minimum of general knowledge of the period could be taken for granted, and since space is severely limited, only the salient points of the themes treated here could be touched upon. Moreover, an *Introduction* must of necessity cover only a restricted field. To bring in the philosophical, religious and scientific background of the age would have required a much larger volume; and reasons of space have made it impossible to offer an outline of the history of French literature or the other arts in this period.

A considerable place has been given to quotations from all

manner of seventeenth century French sources, since nothing brings one closer to the atmosphere of the age. In selecting these passages, care has been taken to avoid too technical a vocabulary, and while a reasonable knowledge of French has been assumed, odd technical terms and those words which have since become obsolete or changed their meaning are explained in footnotes. Spelling and punctuation have been modernized throughout.

Much care has been taken in the choice of the illustrations which will, it is hoped, help to bring to life this absorbing period in the history of French civilization. The aim of the author has been to produce the sort of book which would have been useful to him, had it been available, when he first began to study the great writers of the Classical Age. Inevitably it falls short of his ideal. Yet it is hoped that, with all its failings, the book will assist towards a better understanding of life and literature in seventeenth century France.

Cambridge, 1952 J.L.

A NOTE TO THE SECOND EDITION

ANOTHER reprint has provided an opportunity to make a number of additions and corrections, particularly in the Introduction and the opening chapter. Some recently published works have been added to the suggestions for further reading.

Durham, 1969 J.L.

CONTENTS

ACKNOWLEDGMENTS

Photographs of Nos. 8, 13, 28, 29, 36, 39, 40, 41, 42 are by Alinari; Nos. 5, 15, 22 by Braun & Co.; No. 9 by Bulloz; Nos. 20, 26 by Caisse Nationale des Monuments Historiques, Paris; Nos. 11, 12, 21, 23, 24, 27, 32, 50, 53, 54 by Giraudon; Nos. 1-4, 10, 14, 16-19, 30, 33, 34, 35, 38, 43, 44, 48, 49, 51 by W. F. Mansell; No. 25 by Commissariat Général au Tourisme, and No. 37 by Photographie Aérienne and Aerofilms Library; graphs on pages 19, 21, 22 by S.E.V.P.E.N. (Paris).

ILLUSTRATIONS

MAPS AND DIAGRAMS

INTRODUCTION

If one looks at a map of seventeenth century France, it does not appear at first sight very different from a map of modern France. By 1700 the country was almost as large as it is

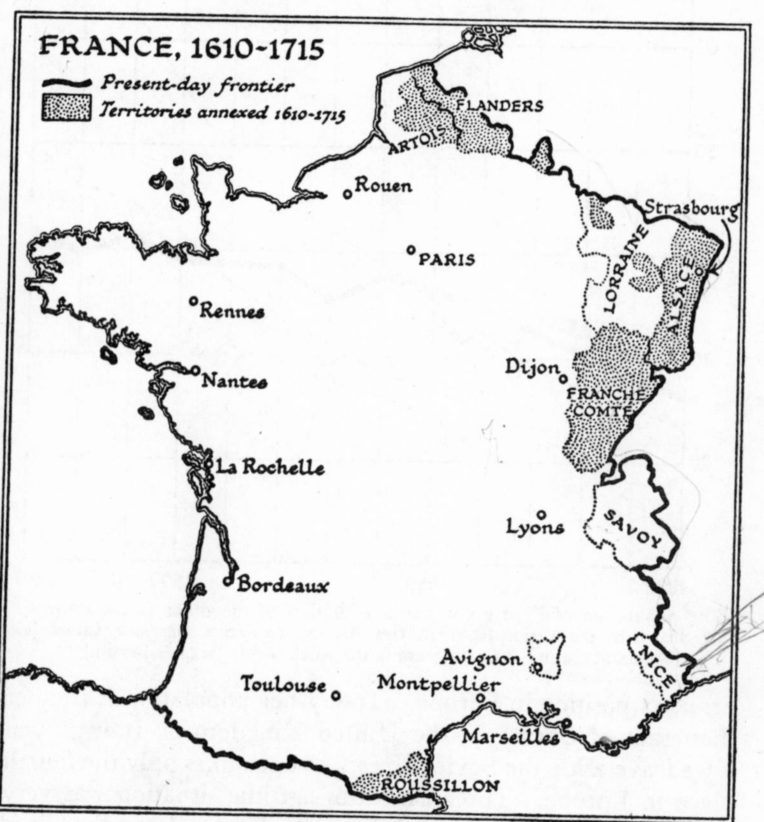

today. In the course of the seventeenth century she had added to her territory the provinces of Franche-Comté and Alsace in the east, Artois and a strip to the east of it in the north-east, and Roussillon in the south. The only significant changes we notice concern Lorraine, added in the eighteenth century, and Savoy and Nice, added in the nineteenth.

At the end of the seventeenth century the population within that slightly smaller area was less than half what it is today—some 18 or 20 millions against the present figure of 50 millions. Yet the mere recital of these figures masks a striking change in

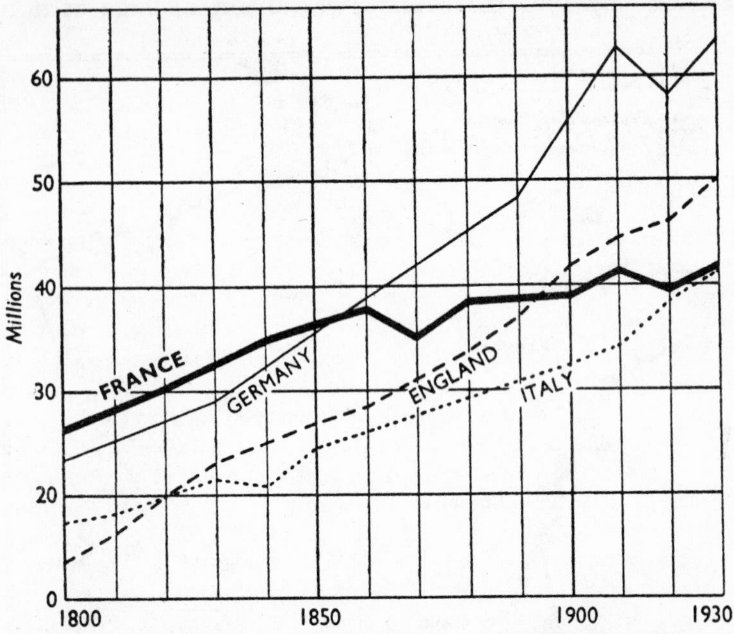

The population of France compared with that of the other Great Powers. (Redrawn by permission from Charles Morazé, *La France Bourgeoise*, Librairie Armand Colin. The diagram is the work of M. Jacques Bertin.)

France's position in Europe. Today her population is smaller than that of Germany, the United Kingdom or Italy; even if we leave aside the Soviet Union, she occupies only the fourth place in Europe. Three centuries ago the situation was very different. Europe was much less densely populated than it is now, and Germany and Italy were merely loose associations of states, each with a total population much inferior to that of France. Politically the most unified state on the Continent, France was numerically by far the strongest power in Europe.

Her only rival was the House of Austria with its heterogeneous possessions which formed a population block of some 20 millions; but she towered above the 5 millions of Spain and England, or even the 14 millions of Russia.

Not only was France politically unified and relatively densely populated. She was also richest in natural resources, thanks to her fertile soil and varied climate. In contemporary writings the wealth of the country is a constant subject for pride, as we see, for instance, in the old-fashioned style of the following passage addressed to Louis XIII and his mother the Regent, in 1615:

> Vos Majestés possèdent un grand état, agréable en assiette,[1] abondant en richesses, fleurissant en peuples, puissant en bonnes et fortes villes, invincible en armes, triomphant en gloire. Son territoire est capable pour le nombre infini de ses habitants, sa fertilité pour leur nourriture, son affluence de bétail pour leur vêtement; pour l'entretien de leur santé et le contentement de leur vie, ils ont la douceur du ciel, la température de l'air, la bonté des eaux. Pour leur défense et logement, les matériaux y sont propres et commodes à bâtir maisons et fortifier places. . . . Si c'est un extrême sujet de contentement à vos peuples de se voir nés et élevés en la France, c'est-à-dire au plus beau, plus libre et plus heureux climat du monde, Votre gloire ne doit pas être moindre d'y tenir un empire que l'on peut avec raison appeler l'incomparable. Car la France seule se peut passer de tout ce qu'elle a de terres voisines, et toutes les terres voisines nullement d'elle. Elle a des richesses infinies, connues et à connaître. Qui la considérera bien,[2] c'est le plus complet corps du royaume que le soleil puisse voir depuis son lever jusques à son coucher, dont les membres sont plus divers, et toutefois mieux se rapportants selon la symétrie requise à un bel état. En chacune de ses provinces sont ou se peuvent établir toutes sortes d'artifices [3] beaux et utiles. Lui seul se peut être tout le monde. . . . La moindre des provinces de la France fournit à Vos Majestés ses blés, ses vins, son sel, ses toiles, ses laines, son fer, son huile, son pastel,[4] la rendant plus riche que tous les Pérous du monde. C'est cela qui les transporte tous chez elle. Mais de ces grandes richesses la plus grande, c'est l'inépuisable abondance de ses

[1] Situation.
[2] i.e. 'si on la considère bien'.
[3] 'arts, industries.'
[4] Woad (for dyeing).

hommes, qui les saurait ménager[1]; car ce sont gentils esprits, actifs et pleins d'intelligence, de qualité de feu, composés par une ingénieuse, artificielle[2] nature, capable d'inventer et de faire. (Montchrestien, *Traité de l'économie politique*, pp. 23-4.)

It was thanks to her large population and her wealth that in the second half of the seventeenth century France succeeded Spain as the dominant power in Europe. Even when a few decades later Louis XIV's ambitions had been thwarted by England and the coalition which she headed, France remained the leading power on the Continent right through the eighteenth century down to the period of the Revolutionary Wars and the emergence of Napoleon. Only in the nineteenth century, when her population increased more and more slowly in comparison with that of other countries, was France left behind by England and Germany, and so lost her commanding position in Europe.

Since 1700 the economic life of France has undergone many changes, and yet these have been on the whole less drastic than on this side of the Channel. In the seventeenth century and even in the eighteenth England was, like France, a predominantly agricultural society. In the second half of the eighteenth century began the revolution which transformed England into an industrial nation, so that today only about 2 per cent. of her active population is engaged in agriculture. France on the other hand never experienced an industrial revolution. She was not transformed in the space of a century or less from a predominantly agricultural country into a predominantly industrial one. In the last century and in this (down to the Second World War) there was a slow and very gradual drift from agriculture to trade, industry, transport and similar occupations; but it is only since 1945 that a really massive movement away from the countryside has occurred. Even in the 1930's the proportion of the active population engaged in agriculture was about 36 per cent., against only 5 per cent. in this country. With the dramatic speeding up of the industrialization of France since 1945, it has fallen sharply to

[1] 'si on savait les ménager' (i.e. make good use of them).
[2] Skilful.

some 18 per cent., only half what it was in the 1930's. Yet with an area more than twice that of the United Kingdom and roughly the same population, France is much nearer being self-supporting in food. If it is no longer possible to speak of the French as 'a nation of peasants', even today agriculture occupies a much more important place in the French economy than it does in ours.

Three centuries ago France was, like England, essentially an agricultural country. Towns were small: Paris had perhaps 500,000 inhabitants, and of provincial towns only Lyons had a population of over 100,000. Probably as many as 90 per cent. of the population lived in small market towns, villages and hamlets or scattered over the countryside. The economy of the country and the outlook of its inhabitants were thus dominated by agriculture and the land.

To understand how French people lived in the seventeenth century, it is not enough to compare how they lived at that period with their way of life today. One must also make a comparison with their position in mediaeval times. In some respects seventeenth century France was still close to the Middle Ages—closer on the whole than seventeenth century England. Indeed right down to the Revolution of 1789 France was to remain a semi-feudal state.

Feudalism arose in Western Europe out of the chaos of the Dark Ages after the collapse of the Roman Empire. Under this form of social organization which, in France at least, may be said to have reached its height about A.D. 1000, wealth consisted almost exclusively of land, and the land was owned almost exclusively by the two dominant classes of society, the nobility and clergy, although it was worked by peasants, most of whom were serfs. In this period money wealth (capital) was almost non-existent, since trade had virtually dried up and each community had to be economically self-sufficient, that is to say, had to satisfy by its own efforts all its economic needs, to produce its own food, drink, clothing, furniture, household goods and the like. Travel was difficult and dangerous and each community lived in almost complete isolation from the rest.

Thus, at least at its height, feudalism implied two ruling classes—the nobility and clergy—exalted above the mass of the peasants, who were mainly serfs, and no trade, no towns of any size and consequently no middle class. Yet in the course of the Middle Ages great changes took place in France. Slowly and gradually trade revived. New towns sprang up and older ones expanded. Artisans and merchants formed a new class—the middle class or *bourgeoisie* in between the ruling classes and the peasantry.

The position of the peasants also improved, as they began to be 'emancipated', that is, ceased to be serfs and became more or less free men, owning their own land, even if they still owed feudal dues and services to their lord.

Thus by the beginning of the seventeenth century decisive changes had taken place in France since feudal times. If these changes had taken place more slowly than in England, France had progressed further away from feudalism than many countries on the Continent. The purely local economy of feudal times, when each community had been compelled to be self-sufficient, had been broken down by the revival of trade. Goods were now produced not merely for use on the spot, but for a national market; indeed, with the growth of overseas trade, especially since the Age of Discoveries, even for a world-market. Land was no longer the sole source of wealth, since the progress of trade and industry had given rise to a new form of riches—money, capital. And this was in the hands of the middle classes who owed their increasing power to the development of trade and industry.

Yet, judged by modern standards, even by 1600 economic change had not gone very far; seventeenth century France was still in the transition stage from Feudalism to the Modern Age. As in most other parts of the Continent and even in England, trade and industry were still only of relatively minor importance in the economic life of the country. Scarcely any signs of the coming of the modern industrial age were as yet visible. For all its mighty strides in the age of Galileo and Newton, science had still scarcely begun to be applied to transforming industrial processes. There were as yet practically no machines to do the work of men for them, and thus no large factories gathering together hundreds or even thousands of workers under one roof. Banking and credit, on which modern industrialism rests, were still in their infancy, and, judged by modern standards, the volume of trade both inside France itself and overseas was minute. Three hundred years ago agriculture was the occupation of the overwhelming majority of the inhabitants of the country. Socially France still remained, even more than seventeenth century England, a semi-feudal state. The nobility and clergy were still privileged orders, divided off socially and legally from their inferiors—the middle classes, artisans and peasantry. There were in France 'two nations'—*nobles* and *roturiers*—and despite the economic progress and social changes of the seventeenth and eighteenth centuries, the country was to continue thus divided until the Revolution.

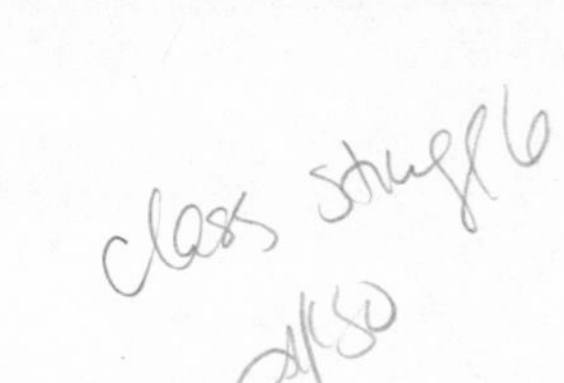

CHAPTER I

THE PEASANTRY

To understand the position of the classes who owned and cultivated the soil of seventeenth century France, one must first examine for a moment their position in feudal times. Feudal society was a vast hierarchy, consisting of overlords, then of their vassals, lay or ecclesiastical, who held land in return for military service, and, finally, at the base of the pyramid came the great mass of peasants who cultivated their own holdings as well as those of their lord. Each lord of the manor (*seigneur*) had part of his estate (his *domaine*) cultivated by his peasants, who shared the rest of the land on the manor among themselves. Most of the peasants were serfs, and were looked upon as so many pieces of property; they were part and parcel of the manor on which they lived, and could be bought and sold with it.

It is true that the peasant was no slave. He could bequeath his house and holding of land to his children and could own other land besides: he could go to law. Yet he was far from being a free man. In taxation he was at the mercy of his lord: he was *taillable à merci*. He might be subject to *mainmorte*, that is, if he had no children living with him at the time of his death, his lord inherited all his belongings. He could not marry anyone from outside the manor without his lord's permission, and even then only after paying a fee in return for the privilege. Above all, he was bound for life to the manor of his birth: if he left it without his lord's permission, he could be pursued and brought back.

Even in feudal times serfdom varied greatly in severity in different parts of France. There was, too, a fairly numerous class of freemen (*vilains*) who could not be arbitrarily taxed by their lord and whose holdings were in practice their own property. Moreover, particularly from the twelfth century onwards, the serfs began to gain their freedom. This movement of emancipation had two main causes. So great was the attraction of the new towns which were springing up that the lord found it difficult to keep the peasants on his manor unless he improved their lot. Above all, the lord often badly needed money, and the peasants, who now found a market for their produce in the towns, were willing to pay for their freedom. By the seventeenth century serfdom persisted only in one or two backward provinces of France, and then in a much mitigated form. The vast majority of French peasants were no longer bound to the land, or subject to the other limitations on personal freedom which serfdom involved. They were thus in a much better position than the peasants of many other European countries where serfdom lingered on until much closer to our own times.

Moreover, considerable changes had taken place in the ownership of land in France since feudalism had been at its height. Right down to the Revolution of 1789, it is true, the peasant continued to have to pay feudal dues and services to his lord in return for his holding, but this holding tended more and more to become his own property which he could sell, exchange or bequeath as he wished. Again, need for money drove the lord to let out parts of his *domaine* to peasants, and while they often had to pay a heavy rent and even perform certain services, these tenant-farmers were far removed in status from the mediaeval serf. Finally, especially in the sixteenth century, the nobles were often compelled by their debts to sell their estates, sometimes to peasants, but more often to well-to-do *bourgeois* from the neighbouring towns.

Only the landed property of the Church remained intact. Yet modern estimates of the amount of land owned by the Church before the Revolution are much more modest than those which were once put forward. Six per cent. is now suggested as a very approximate estimate of the average over the whole of France. In reality the Church's wealth derived less from the ownership of land, though some of its urban property was very valuable, than from tithes.

It is thus, broadly speaking, true to say that by the seventeenth century the nobility and clergy had lost the predominant economic position which they had held in feudal society as the two classes which owned the greater part of the land of France. Nominally, of course, they continued, by virtue of their feudal privileges, to exercise a right of property over nearly all the land of France, and to levy feudal dues accordingly. But their real property, in the modern sense of the word, was limited to their *domaine*, and this was generally let out to tenant-farmers, as they rarely cultivated it themselves.

The amount of land in the hands of the nobles varied greatly from province to province. The proportion was generally higher in the west than in the east of France, though the average amount was probably smaller than has often been supposed. In Artois and Picardy, in the north-east, it has been estimated at about 30 per cent., in Burgundy at 35 per cent., but in Dauphiné at only 12 per cent. In the neighbourhood of the towns the wealthy bourgeois had made considerable inroads into the land of both peasants and nobles.

Finally, a considerable proportion of land, varying from about one-fifth in Normandy and Brittany to over 50 per cent. in Languedoc, was in the hands of the peasants. On this land the peasants were still, as we have seen, compelled to pay feudal dues to their lord, whether noble or ecclesiastical. Again, the fact that the peasants were by far the largest group of landowners meant that their individual holdings were mostly very small.

Thus, in the centuries which had passed since feudalism was at its height, the lot of the French peasants had greatly improved. They were no longer serfs, and had gradually come to own their own holdings; even though they still had to pay feudal dues on them, they were free to sell, exchange or bequeath their land. However miserable their lot may often have been in the seventeenth century, they were on the whole better off than their forefathers in earlier ages or their contemporaries in many other European countries where serfdom was still long to persist.

Since the peasantry formed by far the largest section of the population of seventeenth century France, we are naturally interested in knowing what were their conditions of life. One generally first encounters this extremely complex problem in one of the rare mentions of the peasant in the literature of the Classical Age—the famous paragraph in which La Bruyère paints a terrible picture of brutish toil, sweat and hunger:

> L'on voit certains animaux farouches, des mâles et des femelles, répandus par la campagne, noirs, livides et tout brûlés du soleil, attachés à la terre qu'ils fouillent et qu'ils remuent avec une opiniâtreté invincible; ils ont comme une voix articulée, et, quand ils se lèvent sur leurs pieds, ils montrent une face humaine; et en effet ils sont des hommes. Ils se retirent la nuit dans des tanières, où ils vivent de pain noir, d'eau et de racines; ils épargnent aux autres hommes la peine de semer, de labourer et de recueillir [1] pour vivre, et méritent ainsi de ne pas manquer de ce pain qu'ils ont semé. (*Les Caractères*, xi. 128.)

To decide how far this sombre picture corresponded to reality is by no means as simple as might be imagined. The plain fact—and it is one on which the experts are for once agreed—is that, until the question has been systematically studied region by region and decade by decade, our knowledge of the subject is so small that we can merely hazard a few generalizations.

It must be borne in mind that the term *peasant* is somewhat misleading, since it lumps together under one heading the relatively prosperous, the less well-off and the miserably poor. For our purpose (bearing in mind that this classification is rough and ready and that there was no sharp line of demarcation between these groups) it is possible to divide the peasantry of seventeenth century France into five main groups.

The wealthiest group, the *laboureurs*,[2] who might be said to form a kind of peasant-aristocracy, owned enough land to make a good living from it. They were, of course, the exception, as the majority of peasants were not in this happy position. Those that could afford to do so, rented land, generally from their lord; the whole of their rent was some-

[1] Harvest.

[2] Distinguish between French *laboureur* (=*husbandman*) and English *labourer* (=French *journalier*).

times paid in money, as is customary today, but often part was paid in kind, sometimes even in services. More numerous than this class of tenant-farmers (*fermiers*) were the 'share-croppers' (*métayers*),[1] peasants who were too poor either to pay a money-rent or to stock a farm. They received from their landlord not only the use of the land, but also the necessary stock, seed and implements, and in return paid in rent a share of the produce, generally one-half. Sometimes they might have to pay, in addition, a small money-rent. *Métayers* were much commoner in seventeenth century France than tenant-farmers, particularly in the centre, west and south. The poorer the region, the more common was the system of *métayage*; indeed, the situation of this class of peasants was often wretched.

Other peasants, whose holding of land was not large enough to provide them with a living, would take up some other calling to supplement their income. They might be artisans (cobblers, masons, etc.) or millers, inn-keepers or dealers. Their condition again varied considerably; some of those who traded in grain and fodder, or who acted as collectors of feudal dues or tithes, might be fairly comfortably off.

At the bottom of the scale came those whose holding of land was extremely small (even non-existent) so that they had to earn their living as day-labourers (*journaliers*). In the seventeenth century this class was not very large, as most farms were small, and could well be run by the peasant and his usually large family. There were nevertheless a few regions with a fairly large number of landless or almost landless peasants; their standard of living was generally very low, as their earnings, even when they could secure regular employment, were very small.

Whatever might be the status of the different classes of peasants, all those who owned land were in one respect in the same position: they had to pay feudal dues to their lord. It must be remembered that feudal dues were something quite distinct from the rent of land. The peasant had to continue to pay them, even though by the seventeenth century his holding was virtually his own property, to the extent that he could sell,

[1] Derived from the same word as *moitié*.

exchange or bequeath it. Nor should it be forgotten that feudal dues had long since lost their original justification: the help and protection which the lord of the manor gave in return for these dues. The maintenance of law and order was now no longer the concern of the nobles, who had gradually in the course of time lost all such political and administrative powers. It was now the affair of the central government, to the upkeep of which the peasant had to contribute in the form of heavy taxes. Yet he still had to continue to pay feudal dues, and got nothing in return from his lord.

The peasant's obligations towards his lord naturally varied from province to province, even from manor to manor, and it is therefore impossible to give an accurate account of the feudal régime as it affected all French peasants in the seventeenth century. But for practical purposes the situation may be summarized under the following headings:

1. *L'aveu.* Every time a piece of land changed hands, the new holder was obliged to present to his lord a document describing his holding and all the dues to be paid on it. Besides this, every ten, twenty or thirty years, as the case might be, all the subjects of the lord had simultaneously to produce a similar document. The drawing up of these documents was naturally both a vexatious and costly business.

2. *Le cens.* This was an annual sum of money due from the peasant to his lord, in proportion to the amount of land which he held in the manor. Since the amount of the *cens* had generally been fixed many centuries before, the subsequent fall in the value of money had reduced it to an almost insignificant amount. In fact, the chief reason for insisting on its payment was that the *cens* involved other more important obligations. Its collection had, however, one very objectionable feature from the peasant's point of view: if anyone failed to pay his quota, all the other peasants were compelled to make up the amount due.

3. *La corvée,* the obligation to work for so many days a year on the lord's domain, had gradually been modified since the Middle Ages. Generally in the seventeenth century the peasant was obliged to give his labour free on only a few days

in the year, and sometimes he merely made a small money payment in lieu of this labour. This *corvée* must be distinguished from the *corvée royale*, which consisted of the obligation to help in the construction or maintenance of the roads; although not unknown under Louis XIV, the *corvée royale* did not become universal until the next reign.

4. *Les redevances en nature* (payments in kind) still remained a heavy burden on the peasant, since their amount had not been altered by the fall in the value of money. One of the most common payments of this type was the *champart*, a tax closely resembling the tithe, and levied particularly on grain-crops. It varied according to district from one-sixteenth to one-sixth of the crop: one estimate of the average amount levied is 12 per cent., a considerable proportion of the crop, especially when the tithe was added to it.

5. *Le rachat: les lods et ventes.* These dues still remained an important source of income for the lord of the manor, as they were levied on the value of property when it changed hands. If a piece of property was bequeathed to a person who was not a relative in the direct line of succession, he had to pay the *droit de rachat*, which amounted generally to a year's income from the piece of land. The *droit des lods et ventes*, which was still more profitable to the lord and was the heaviest of all feudal dues paid in money, was levied on any piece of land which changed hands by sale or its equivalent, and amounted on an average to some 8 to 10 per cent. of the purchase price.

6. *Les banalités du moulin, du four et du pressoir.* In many places the peasants were compelled to bring their grain to the lord's mill to be ground, to take their flour to be baked in his oven, and their grapes to be pressed in his wine-press. This monopoly, particularly that of milling all grain, was extremely unpopular. The mill was generally let out to a miller who was nominally entitled to one-sixteenth of the flour, but who had the reputation of giving short weight and inferior flour. Since mediaeval times, in all countries, the miller was an unpopular figure: witness Chaucer's miller in the prologue to the *Canterbury Tales*, 'Wel coude he stelen corn, and tollen thryce.'

A contemporary offers a vivid description of the frauds which they were in the habit of perpetrating:

> Je parlerais ici des meuniers, si chacun ne savait combien leur conscience est large et ne découvrait tous les jours les divers larcins qu'ils commettent en leurs moulins et ne s'en font que rire, sous ombre, disent-ils, qu'ils ne prennent que ce qu'on leur porte. C'est pourtant bien mal fait à eux de changer un blé pour l'autre, d'acheter le son pour le remettre avec la bonne farine, afin que le poids de ce qu'ils ôtent sur les sacs, se retrouve. (Montchrestien, *Traité de l'économie politique*, p. 263.)

Besides, the whole arrangement was extremely inconvenient, especially when the mill happened to be miles away from the village.

7. *Les péages.* Tolls were levied by the lord for the use of roads, ferries, bridges and rivers on his estates. Throughout the *ancien régime* the Crown struggled in vain to make the owners keep these roads and bridges in good repair, and to reduce the number of illegal tolls. The *péages* were a great hindrance to trade in general, for tolls might have to be paid every few miles on a consignment of goods and they made it more difficult for the peasant to dispose of his produce.

8. *Le droit de chasse.* The lord of the manor possessed the sole right to kill game on his estates. Strangely enough, the *droit de chasse* was not of mediaeval origin, but a comparatively recent innovation. It was, however, none the less rigidly enforced. Up to 1669 the third infringement of this monopoly was punished by death. An edict of that year abolished the death penalty, but renewed the ban on hunting by all *roturiers*. It must be remembered that the peasant was not allowed to hunt *even on his own land*; the ban was complete:

> Faisons défense aux marchands, artisans, bourgeois et habitants des villes, bourgs, paroisses, villages et hameaux, paysans et roturiers de quelque état et qualité qu'ils soient . . ., de chasser en quelque lieu, sorte et manière, sur quelque gibier de poil ou de plume que ce puisse être.

The result of this prohibition was that the peasant was unable to guard against the destruction of his crops by game. He was not allowed to cut his hay before midsummer or even to enclose a piece of land with a stone wall without permission, because that would have interfered with hunting. It is true that the edict of 1669 also forbade hunting over land when the corn was in stalk, and in vineyards from May 1st to the harvest; but like so many edicts of the *ancien régime*, it remained a dead letter. The result of all these obvious injustices was that the *droit de chasse* was the most hated of all the privileges of the aristocracy.

9. *La justice seigneuriale* (the judicial rights of the lord of the manor). Since the Middle Ages it had been the constant endeavour of the French monarchy to reduce the judicial powers of the nobility on their estates, and by the seventeenth century a great part of these powers had been taken away from them; but what remained was still very vexatious to the peasants. In general, the royal courts had replaced the manorial courts in most criminal cases, but the right to try such cases had on the whole been gladly abandoned by the lord, as it brought in no revenue, and might even prove costly, since he had to pay the expense of sending prisoners before higher courts when an appeal was made, and even had to bear the cost of executions.

But the manorial courts still dealt with a large number of civil cases, often to the great disadvantage of the peasant. First, there were so many degrees of jurisdiction that, starting from the manorial court, the litigant might have to appear before five or six courts before a case could be finally settled. The complications, delays and final denial of justice so frequent in seventeenth century France are vividly summed up by a jurist of the time, especially in so far as they concerned the peasant:

> . . . Cette multiplication de degrés de jurisdiction rend les procès immortels, et à vrai dire ce grand nombre de justices ôte le moyen au peuple d'avoir justice. . . .
>
> Car qui est le pauvre paysan qui, plaidant . . . de ses brebis et de ses vaches, n'aime mieux les abandonner à celui qui les retient injustement qu'être contraint de passer par cinq ou six

justices avant qu'avoir arrêt; et s'il se résout à plaider jusques au bout, y a-t-il brebis ni vache qui puisse tant vivre, même que le maître mourra avant que son procès soit jugé en dernier ressort. (Charles Loyseau, *Discours de l'Abus des Justices de Village*, in *Œuvres*, p. 10.)

Perhaps an even greater injustice to the peasant was that by the seventeenth century the manorial courts were chiefly limited to the trying of cases concerned with the rights and privileges of the lord of the manor. Consequently, the peasant who had a dispute with his lord over the payment of feudal dues, or the *droit de chasse* or some other monopoly, had as his judge his lord or at least his lord's agent.

A glance through this list shows that though the lot of the peasant had undoubtedly improved since the Middle Ages, what remained of feudalism in seventeenth century France was still oppressive. Such institutions as the *droit de chasse* and the lord's monopoly of the mill, wine-press and so forth, were both vexatious and costly to the peasant. The survival, even in a limited form, of *la justice seigneuriale*, made justice always slow and often impossible to obtain. It is true that money dues such as *le cens*, the amount of which had been fixed many centuries before, were no longer a heavy burden; nor was the *corvée* generally very onerous. But the dues payable when property changed hands (*lods et ventes*) were still profitable sources of income for the lord, and a very heavy drag on the peasant who, even if he happened to be fairly comfortably off, rarely possessed much capital. Again, the levying of payments in kind both by his lord and the Church took away a considerable portion of his crops. Moreover, both feudal dues and tithes [1] lacked their former justification; no longer did the lord give his peasants help and protection, while tithes were seldom used for their original purpose, the maintenance of a priest and parish church and the relief of the poor.

Besides, when the peasant had paid his feudal dues to his lord and his tithes to the Church, he was not free to sit back and enjoy what remained of the fruits of his labours. The

[1] See below, pp. 89-90.

tax-collector would be waiting outside to see him. In seventeenth century France the system of direct taxation, while no doubt admirable from the point of view of the privileged classes, the clergy and nobility, who paid scarcely anything, bore hardly on the non-privileged, the *roturiers*, on whom the main weight fell. And it was the peasants who suffered most from the system, for the middle classes in their turn succeeded in putting part of their burden on to the peasants' shoulders.

The most important form of direct taxation was the *taille*, a tax which dated from the later Middle Ages. As the clergy and the nobility were completely exempt from it, and as the middle classes had frequently succeeded in obtaining exemption, the tax fell mainly on the peasants. In the words of an official report written towards the end of the century:

> Il n'y a pas la moitié des biens [1] du royaume qui payent la taille; les nobles, qui en possèdent la plus grande partie, n'en payent point; les bourgeois de plusieurs villes du royaume, et qui possèdent une partie des biens de la campagne, en sont exempts par le droit de bourgeoisie [2]; d'autres s'en exemptent par les offices,[3] et d'autres par faveur; il n'y a que le misérable qui la paie. (*Mémoires des Intendants*, ed. Boislisle, i. 766.)

In seventeenth century France the *taille* took two different forms. In the majority of provinces it was *personnelle*, that is, levied according to the estimated means of the individual taxpayer; in others it was *réelle*, or levied on the amount of land which he owned. The *taille personnelle* was generally considered to be the worse of the two methods, because it was inevitably very arbitrary, while the *taille réelle* was on the whole preferred by the peasants as it was considered to be less unjust to base the amount of tax on the value of land than on an individual's estimated ability to pay. Moreover, under the latter system, once a piece of land was held liable to the *taille*, it could not cease to be so taxed, even if it came to be acquired by a nobleman; whereas, under the system of the *taille personnelle*, every time an inhabitant of a parish acquired noble rank and

[1] Land.
[2] The privileges granted to the citizens of a town.
[3] Official posts (see Chaper II).

therefore exemption from the *taille*, the other inhabitants had to pay more.

The already heavy burden which the *taille* imposed upon the peasants was further increased by the way in which it was assessed and levied. Every year the Royal Council would fix the quota to be furnished by each province; statistics show that some provinces were treated much more leniently than others. Then the quota to be paid by each district of the province was fixed until finally in each parish the collectors were informed of the total amount which they had to gather in. The collectors in the parishes were not, as one might expect, civil servants; they were elected every year by a meeting of the inhabitants of the parish. The post was not an eagerly sought for honour; in fact, it is said that the wealthiest inhabitants would take refuge in the towns rather than face the task. Not only did the post keep a man from his work for two years and make him thoroughly unpopular in the parish; it might well mean financial ruin, since the collectors were responsible for the payment of the taxes of defaulters. 'Il n'y a qui que ce soit', declared a contemporary, 'jusqu'au plus misérable, qui ne vende sa chemise pour être exempt de cette servitude.' (Boisguilbert, *Factum de la France*, p. 322.)

If they lived in a province in which the *taille* was *personnelle*, the first task of the collectors was to assess the capacity to pay of all the inhabitants of the parish. Even the most conscientious collectors would not find it easy to do strict justice, for who could estimate exactly the financial position of his neighbours, particularly as, in order to avoid paying any more taxes than they could help, they did their best to appear poverty stricken? In practice, the collectors had to do their best to reconcile two conflicting points of view. It was obviously wisest to avoid offending their richer and more powerful neighbours, and therefore the best thing to do was to make the poor and defenceless pay as much as possible. On the other hand, since they were responsible for the collection of the parish's quota, it was useless to assess people quite beyond their capacity to pay. In practice, it generally happened that their solution to this difficult problem was to tax most heavily those people who, though moderately well off, were not in a position, for one reason or another, to intimidate the tax-collector.

The work of assessment completed, the collectors had then to begin the slow and arduous task of getting in the money. As the peasants were afraid that, if they paid promptly, they might be thought rich and thus have their next year's assessment raised, they were never in a hurry to oblige the collectors. On the contrary, as a contemporary put it, they would only 'payer sou à sou, après mille contraintes et mille exécutions,[1] soit pour se venger des collecteurs de les avoir imposés à une somme trop forte, . . . ou pour rebuter ceux de l'année suivante de les mettre en une pareille somme, par les difficultés des paiements. Ainsi il faut que toute l'année tous les collecteurs soient chaque jour sur pied; et tel les fait venir cent fois en sa maison pour avoir le paiement de sa taille, qui a de l'argent caché.' (Boisguilbert, *Détail de la France*, p. 186.) Inability to produce the money or sheer obstinacy merely increased the amount which the peasant had finally to pay; the legal expenses, which were added to the original bill, provided a living for an army of bailiffs and their hangers-on.

A most vivid picture of the abuses connected with the assessment and collection of the *taille* is to be found in the writings of its greatest contemporary critic, Marshal Vauban, the great engineer of the wars of Louis XIV. Writing at the end of the century, he declared that in the last thirty or forty years the value of land had dropped by a third, especially in the provinces where the *taille personnelle* held sway.

Pour peu qu'on ait de connaissance de ce qui se passe à la campagne, on comprend aisément que les tailles sont une des causes de ce mal, non qu'elles soient toujours et en tout temps trop grosses; mais parce qu'elle sont assises[2] sans proportion, non seulement en gros de paroisse à paroisse, mais encore de particulier à particulier; en un mot, elles sont devenues arbitraires, n'y ayant point de proportion du bien[3] du particulier à la taille dont on le charge. Elles sont de plus exigées avec une

[1] Distraint on goods (for non-payment of the tax due).
[2] Apportioned. [3] Wealth.

extrême rigueur et de si grands frais, qu'il est certain qu'ils vont au moins à un quart du montant de la taille. Il est même assez ordinaire de pousser les exécutions jusqu'à dépendre les portes des maisons, après avoir vendu ce qui était dedans, et on en a vu démolir, pour en tirer les poutres, les solives et les planches qui ont été vendues cinq ou six fois moins qu'elles ne valaient, en déduction de la taille.

L'autorité des personnes puissantes et accréditées fait souvent modérer l'imposition d'une ou de plusieurs paroisses, à des taxes bien au-dessous de leur juste portée, dont la décharge doit conséquemment tomber sur d'autres voisines qui en sont surchargées; et c'est un mal invétéré auquel il n'est pas facile de remédier. Ces personnes puissantes sont payées de leur protection dans la suite, par la plus-value de leurs fermes ou de celles de leurs parents et amis, causée par l'exemption de leur fermiers et de ceux qu'ils protègent, qui ne sont imposés à la taille que pour la forme seulement; car il est très ordinaire de voir qu'une ferme de trois à quatre mille livres de revenu ne sera cotisée qu'à quarante ou cinquante livres de taille, tandis qu'une autre de quatre à cinq cents livres en payera cent, et souvent plus; ce qui fait que les terres n'ont pas ordinairement la moitié de la culture dont elles ont besoin.

Il en est de même de laboureur à laboureur, ou de paysan à paysan; le plus fort accable toujours le plus faible; et les choses sont réduites à un tel état que celui qui pourrait se servir du talent qu'il a de savoir faire quelque art ou quelque trafic, qui le mettrait, lui et sa famille, en état de pouvoir vivre un peu plus à son aise, aime mieux demeurer sans rien faire; et que celui qui pourrait avoir une ou deux vaches, et quelques moutons ou brebis, plus ou moins, avec quoi il pourrait améliorer sa ferme ou sa terre, est obligé de s'en priver, pour n'être pas accablé de taille l'année suivante, comme il ne manquerait pas l'être s'il gagnait quelque chose, et qu'on vît sa récolte un peu plus abondante qu'à l'ordinaire. C'est par cette raison qu'il vit non seulement très pauvrement, lui et sa famille, et qu'il va presque tout nu, c'est-à-dire, qu'il ne fait que très peu de consommation; mais encore, qu'il laisse dépérir le peu de terre qu'il a, en ne la travaillant qu'à demi, de peur que si elle rendait ce qu'elle pourrait rendre, étant bien fumée et cultivée, on n'en prît occasion de l'imposer doublement à la taille. Il est donc manifeste que la première cause de la diminution des biens de la campagne est le défaut de culture, et que ce défaut provient de la manière d'imposer les tailles, et de les lever. (*Dîme royale*, pp. 27-9.)

To the *taille* two new direct taxes were added in the last twenty years of the reign of Louis XIV—the *capitation* and the *dixième*. The former, introduced in 1695, in the midst of the War of the League of Augsburg, was to be paid by every class of the population from the Dauphin downwards; only the very poor were to be exempted. On paper at least, the privileged classes were thus at last to contribute some share of direct taxation. Indeed, they were even to pay in proportion to their wealth: the amount varied from 2000 *livres* (about £150) for the wealthiest class down to 1 *livre* for the poorest sections of the community, soldiers and labourers. Such at least were the conditions laid down in the edict announcing the tax. The reality proved very different. The nobles paid something, it is true, but they were assessed so lightly that it is estimated that they actually paid only one per cent. of their income. The clergy secured exemption from the new tax by paying a comparatively trifling sum. As usual, the main burden fell on the peasant; for him the *capitation* was merely an addition to the *taille*. The *dixième*, introduced in 1710, towards the end of the War of the Spanish Succession, was in theory a 10 per cent. tax on the incomes of the whole population of France. In practice, the privileged classes once more managed to evade most of the new tax, so that the peasant found that there was yet another addition to his *taille*.

The peasant's troubles were not over when he had finished paying his direct taxes. There were besides heavy taxes on articles of everyday consumption, such as the *aides* levied on wines and spirits. The most unpopular of these indirect taxes was the salt-tax (*la gabelle*), which varied considerably from region to region. It was heaviest in the provinces known as *les pays de grande gabelle*, which stretched from Normandy and Picardy southwards to Touraine and Burgundy. There salt was a government monopoly; not only was it sold at a very high price, quite out of proportion to its real value, but it was compulsory to purchase a fixed quantity, which was very large.

Moreover, this salt could only be used at table and for cooking. When salt was needed for preserving—and it was extensively used for this purpose in the seventeenth century—a special kind had to be bought over and above the regulation quantity. The effect of the *gabelle* on the peasant household is well brought out in the words of a contemporary:

> La cherté du sel le rend si rare qu'elle cause une espèce de famine dans le royaume, très sensible au menu peuple, qui ne peut faire aucune salaison de viande pour son usage, faute de sel. Il n'y a point de ménage qui ne puisse nourrir un cochon, ce qu'il ne fait pas, parce qu'il n'a pas de quoi avoir pour le saler. (Vauban, *Dîme royale*, p. 83 note.)

In other provinces of France salt was less heavily taxed; in others again it was not taxed at all, so that there the price of salt was only 1/25th of what it was in the *pays de grande gabelle*. There was an obvious temptation to try to smuggle salt from regions where it was cheap to those where it was absurdly dear; and despite ferocious punishments, the government never succeeded in checking the practice. Some of the abuses in the collection of the *gabelle* are summed up very vividly in the following contemporary criticism of it:

> Le roi reçoit beaucoup d'argent des gabelles, mais le peuple en paie excessivement au delà de ce qui en entre dans ses coffres. Le nombre infini d'officiers de grenier à sel,[1] les commis,[2] les archers, les frais, les voitures,[3] les droits des officiers auxquels on en fait des présents, absorbent des sommes immenses que le roi ne touche pas et que le peuple porte; car il n'y a pas un petit gabelleur [4] qui ne subsiste très commodément de son emploi, pas un commis qui ne fasse sa fortune et qui ne s'y enrichisse, en faisant grande chère et grande dépense. C'est à quoi il est très important de remédier; et en effet on ne saurait comprendre les vexations que souffrent les sujets du roi sous prétexte de la gabelle. Les archers entrent dans les maisons pour voir, disent-ils, s'il n'y a point de sel caché. On leur ouvre avec obéissance. Cependant ils en coulent [5] eux-mêmes quelques sacs, et là-dessus font leurs procès-verbaux, sur lesquels le maître est condamné à

[1] A court which tried cases arising out of the *gabelle*.
[2] High officials.
[3] Transport.
[4] 'Garde, archer de la gabelle.'
[5] Introduce surreptitiously.

de grosses amendes, et enfin ne sortent point qu'après avoir pillé tout ce qu'ils ont pu prendre. . . . (Paul Hay du Châtelet, *Traité de la politique de France*, p. 182.)

Another burden which fell on the peasant if he lived in a frontier district or in a region through which armies happened to pass, was the billeting of troops. Not until the following century were barracks constructed on the main routes to the frontier. It was chiefly the peasants who had to bear the insults and exactions of a horde of undisciplined ruffians. 'Il n'y a pas un cavalier en Champagne qui n'ait mérité la corde' is a typical description of the soldiery of the period; it comes from an official document. We have the word of Mazarin for the fact that to have troops billeted on one for three days was worse than a year's *taille*. Such evidence helps one to understand the place of the word *soldats* in the list of the sufferings endured by the peasant of La Fontaine's fable, *La mort et le bûcheron*:

> 'Quel plaisir a-t-il eu depuis qu'il est au monde?
> En est-il un plus pauvre en la machine ronde? [1]
> Point de pain quelquefois, et jamais de repos.'
> Sa femme, ses enfants, *les soldats*, les impôts,
> Le créancier, et la corvée
> Lui font d'un malheureux la peinture achevée.

All the burdens which the peasant had to bear in the seventeenth century, especially feudal dues, tithes, and direct and indirect taxes, quite apart from the injustice and oppression frequently involved in their collection, must have diminished his already meagre income. For the income of the mass of the peasants was undoubtedly small. The great majority owned, or farmed as *métayers*, only small holdings, from which it was even more difficult to make a living than it is today, as farming methods were still very primitive. If peasants are generally slow to adopt new methods, inevitably they were even slower in seventeenth century France, for the vast majority lacked the capital with which to carry out improvements on their land.

In most regions of France the proportion of land which still remained uncultivated in the seventeenth century was very

[1] The world.

high; this was partly because the lack of good pasture-land made it necessary to have waste-land on which to graze cattle. Farm buildings were wretchedly poor; barns were often non-existent; cowsheds were small and dirty. Horses were little used on farms; and even oxen were only used for ploughing on large holdings. The plough itself was still of a most primitive type.

Intensive cultivation was unknown. Nearly everywhere land was left fallow for at least one year in three, and sometimes even every other year. The system of rotation of crops which allows land to be almost continuously productive had not yet been introduced. Methods of cultivation were often extremely defective: the land was often not ploughed deeply enough, or sufficiently weeded. Above all, the scarcity of cattle made farmyard manure so difficult to obtain that along the coasts it had to be replaced by seaweed, and inland by leaves, ferns and broom. Inevitably the yield of crops was very low. In our period cattle- and sheep-breeding played only a minor part in French agriculture; and here again the methods employed were very primitive and unproductive. Vineyards, on the other hand, would appear to have been relatively prosperous; although once more the lack of good transport facilities and the backwardness of agricultural methods are demonstrated by the fact that vineyards were still to be found in the North of France, where the unfavourable climate allowed only a very low yield. In the seventeenth century specialization was still almost unknown; each district tried to supply all its needs in food, since bad communications made it difficult, if not impossible, to import agricultural products from other parts of the country.

The burden of feudal dues, tithes and taxes was, of course, in part responsible for the backwardness of French agriculture in the seventeenth century. The peasant had not the means to improve his land and increase its productivity. And since it was with the scanty products of a primitive agriculture that he had to meet all these demands on his income, the money which was left over could not in general provide him and his family with a high standard of living.

J. Lagniet, Le noble est 'araignée et le paysan la mouche

2. *N. Guérard*, L'homme du village. Né pour la peine

3. *A. Bosse,* Le mariage à la campagne: les présents

4. *A. Bosse,* Le mariage à la campagne: la danse villageoise

Generalizations on this subject are naturally difficult. We have already seen that the term *peasant* includes people of very different economic status. Again, conditions of life varied in different regions of France, according to the degree of fertility of the soil. It is true that the better-off peasants possessed adequate if primitive furniture, such as beds and wardrobes, a good supply of household utensils and linen, some crockery and glassware, and a fair supply of clothes. But the poorer peasants would have only one or two chests, a rough table, a kneading-trough, a bench and some miserable bedding. Most peasants' houses were built of mud and thatched. The only rooms would be very low, without proper floorboards, and windows devoid of glass. Working-clothes were of coarse cloth. Taxes on leather made leather boots too expensive for the majority of peasants; wooden clogs took their place. In fact, many peasants went barefoot.

Although the diet of the mass of the rural population might be considered by modern dieticians to contain many healthy ingredients, it was meagre and monotonous. The fact that rye, not wheat, was the commonest cereal-crop is very significant for the general standard of living of the peasant. Wheat was often cultivated only in order to pay feudal dues or rent, or else for export to other regions. Rye was the staple food of the peasant; bread, soup, milk foods and butter were the basis of his diet. In the poorest regions of France the peasant lived chiefly on *galettes* or gruel made of buckwheat (now chiefly used as food for horses and poultry), or even on chestnuts or maize. Meat was rarely to be seen on his table, though bacon was rather more frequent. Unless he happened to live in a wine-producing area, he drank only water. A meagre diet at the best of times. . . .

Village life was not, of course, all gloom and endless toil. There were numerous saints' days scattered throughout the year at which young and old disported themselves at the traditional amusements of the country. Dancing was one of the main pastimes of the peasants under the *ancien régime*. On Easter Monday 1676 the English philosopher Locke noted as he passed into Provence the antics of the inhabitants of a small town on the way: 'At St Gilles a congregation of men and wenches danced heartily to the beating of a drum for want of better music; nay, their natural inclinations wrought so effectually that it helped them to dance even when the dubbing of the drum failed them' (*Travels in France*, p. 68). A few months later he recorded his impressions of some village sports held near Montpellier:

> Men ran at Celleneuve about twelve score yards or something more over ploughed land, very stoney, barefoot, and maidens the same, about half so far. There were also races of boys together and girls in other courses. He that won among the men had a hat, among the maidens a ribbon, and less fry smaller matters, all which were given at this annual Olympiad by the Cardinal who is the *seigneur* of the place, and was all tied to the end of a pole which was held up at the end of the race. The whole prize thus exposed was a hat, several ribbons and tagged laces, two or three purses and a few pennies. Jumping also was another exercise, and after all what never fails, dancing to oboe and tabor. (*Ibid.*, p. 109.)

But times were not always good. In different periods of the seventeenth century parts of Eastern France were exposed to all the ravages of war. Whole villages would be depopulated, and a great deal of land go out of cultivation. Nor should the dire effects of the Fronde, the long civil war in the middle of the century, be forgotten. More widespread in their effects were the frequent food-shortages which occurred when bad harvests reduced even further the meagre yield of a still primitive agriculture; famine caused terrible sufferings, especially among the labourers and poorer sections of the peasants. It seems clear that, generally speaking, the lot of the peasants grew worse instead of better towards the end of the century. From about 1670 onwards there set in a heavy fall in the prices of agricultural products which lasted, except in famine years, well into the eighteenth century. Thus the almost incessant wars in which Louis XIV involved France led to increases in existing taxation and the introduction of new taxes, at the very moment when the peasants were even less able to bear them. The result was undoubtedly great distress among at least some sections of the peasantry.

Perhaps we should do well not to take too literally the picture of the brutish state of the peasantry in the *Caractères* of La Bruyère or even the evidence provided by other documents of the period. To see them in their true perspective, one must bear in mind that there was not one but several classes of peasants; that conditions inevitably varied from district to district, and from harvest to harvest.

Yet from the opening years of the personal reign of Louis XIV down to its very close document after document depicts the sufferings of the peasants in a way which cannot be ignored by the historian. In 1662 a doctor at Blois wrote:

> Depuis trente-deux ans que je fais la médecine en cette province, je n'ai rien vu qui approche de la désolation qui y est, non seulement à Blois où il y a quatre mille pauvres par le reflux des paroisses voisines et par la propre misère du lieu, mais dans toute la campagne. La disette y est si grande que les paysans manquent de pain et se jettent sur les charognes. Aussitôt qu'il meurt un cheval ou quelque autre animal, ils le mangent, et c'est une vérité que dans la paroisse de Cheverny on a trouvé un homme, sa femme et son enfant morts, sans être malades, et ce ne peut être que de faim. Les fièvres malignes commencent à s'allumer, et lorsque la chaleur donnera sur tant d'humidité et de pourriture, tous ces misérables qui manquent déjà de force, mourront bien vite et, si Dieu ne nous assiste extraordinairement, on ne doit attendre qu'une grande mortalité. (This quotation by P. M. Bondois, *La Misère sous Louis XIV, La Disette de 1662*, p. 74 is reprinted from *Revue d'Histoire Économique et Sociale* by permission of the Editor.)

In 1687 an official report gives a vivid picture of the sufferings of the peasants of Le Maine and l'Orléanais. The writers speak first of the disappearance of the well-to-do peasants (*laboureurs*) who had formerly been numerous in the province:

> Il n'y a presque plus de laboureurs aisés. Autrefois ils étaient montés [1] et fournis de tout ce qui était nécessaire pour l'exploitation des fermes; ils avaient des bestiaux pour le labour et pour l'engrais, ils avaient nombre de valets,[2] ils pouvaient garder le blé qu'ils recueillaient, et le vendaient dans la saison.

[1] Equipped.

[2] 'Valets de ferme' (farm-labourers)

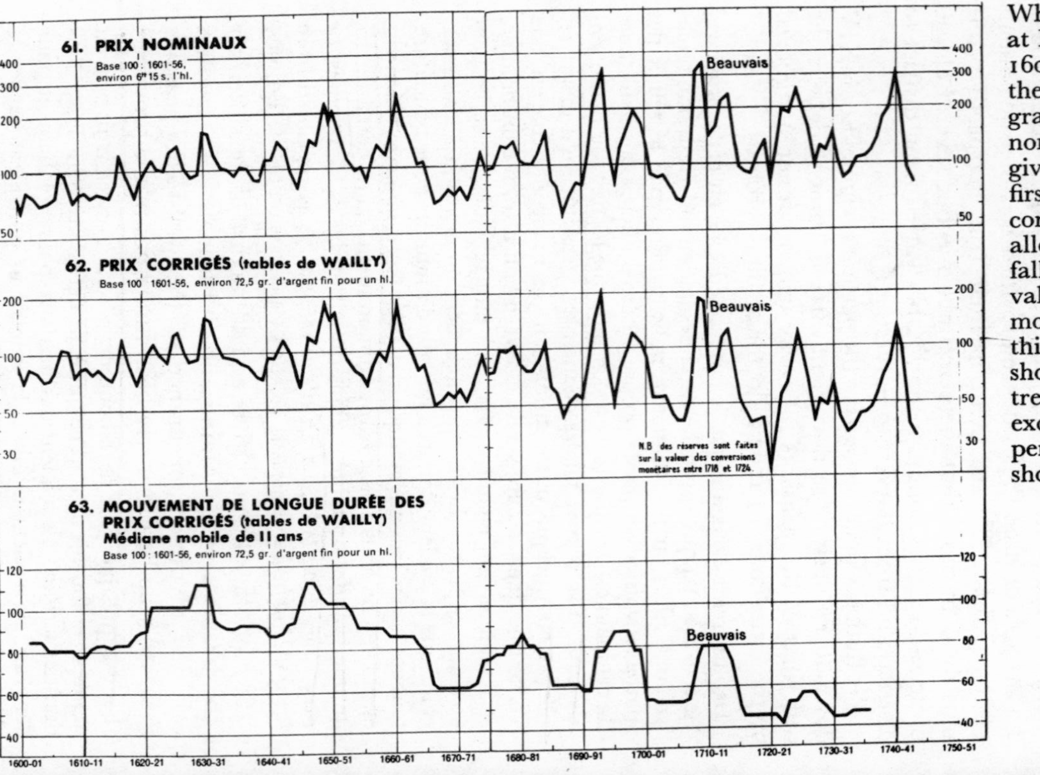

Wheat prices at Beauvais, 1600-1715. In the second graph the nominal prices given in the first graph are corrected to allow for the fall in the value of money. The third graph shows the trend of prices, except in periods of shortage.

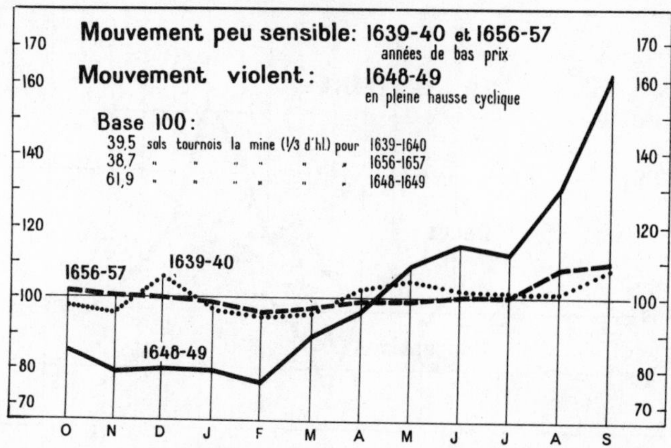

Seasonal fluctuations in wheat prices at Beauvais.

By 1687 these well-to-do *laboureurs* had been replaced by poverty-stricken *métayers*:

> Aujourd'hui il n'y a plus que de pauvres métayers qui n'ont rien; il faut que les maîtres leur fournissent les bestiaux, qu'ils leur avancent de quoi se nourrir, qu'ils payent leurs tailles, et qu'ils prennent en paiement toute leur portion de la récolte, laquelle même, quelquefois, ne suffit pas. Ainsi les métayers ne gagnent jamais rien, ils sortent aussi gueux des métairies qu'ils y sont entrés. A peine peuvent-ils entretenir un valet. Les terres, n'étant pas si bien cultivées, ne rapportent pas tant; une maladie, une grêle et mille autres accidents qui arrivent à ces pauvres gens, les mettent à l'aumône.

Then follows a description of the wretched diet, clothing and housing of the peasants of this region:

> . . . Les paysans vivent de pain fait avec du blé noir[1]; d'autres, qui n'ont pas même du blé noir, vivent de racines de fougère bouillies avec de la farine d'orge ou d'avoine et du sel . . . Mais où l'on connaît mieux que partout ailleurs la misère des paysans, c'est dans leurs maisons, où l'on voit une misère extrême. On les trouve couchés sur la paille; point d'habits que ceux qu'ils portent, qui sont fort méchants; point de meubles, point de provisions pour la vie; enfin, tout y marque la nécessité. (*Mémoires des Intendants*, i. 782-3.)

[1] Buckwheat.

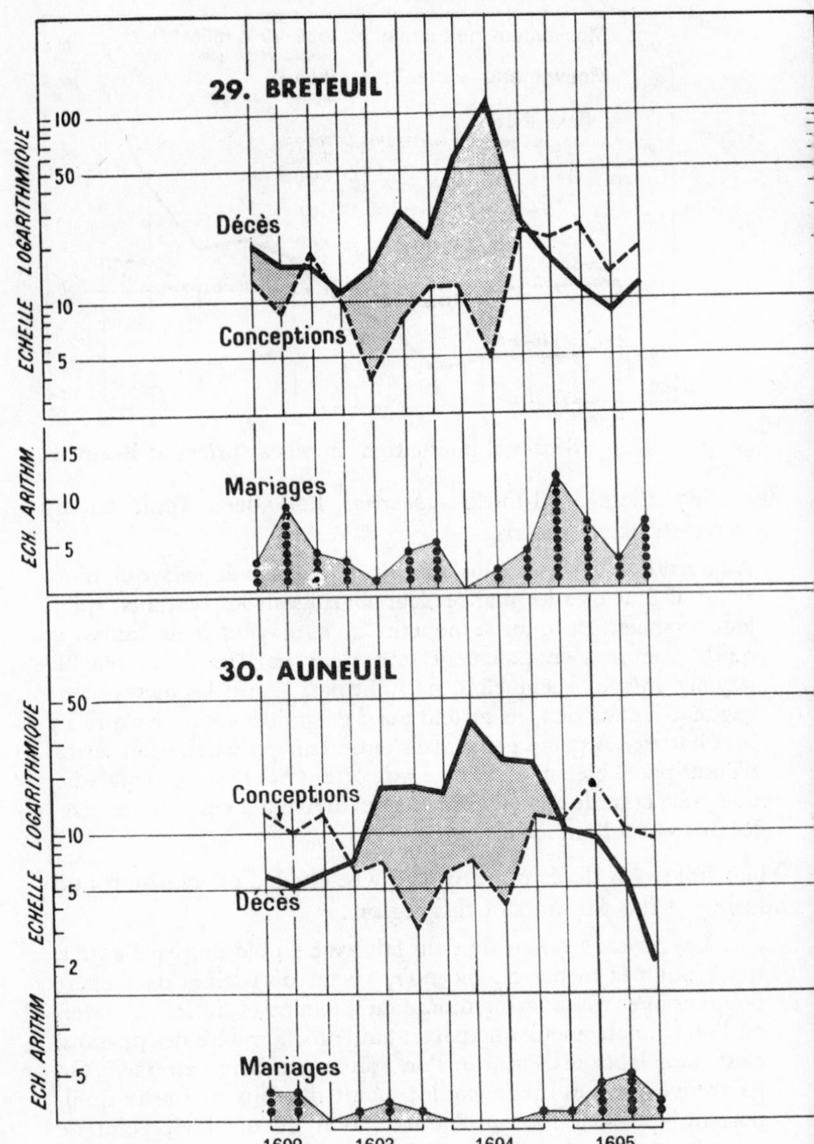

The effects of the famine of 1693-1694 on the population of two villages in the Beauvais region.

Many of the details contained in this report are confirmed in an account, written nine years later by Vauban, of the neighbouring district of Vézelay:

> . . . Tout ce qui s'appelle bas peuple, ne vit que de pain d'orge et d'avoine mêlés, dont ils n'ôtent pas même le son. . . . Ils se nourrissent encore de mauvais fruits, la plupart sauvages, et de quelque peu d'herbes potagères de leurs jardins, cuites à l'eau, avec un peu d'huile de noix, ou de navette, le plus souvent sans, ou avec très peu de sel. Il n'y a que les plus aisés qui mangent du pain de seigle mêlé d'orge et de froment.
>
> Les vins y sont médiocres et ont presque tous un goût de terroir qui les rend désagréables. Le commun du peuple en boit rarement, ne mange pas trois fois de la viande en un an et use peu de sel. . . . Il ne faut donc pas s'étonner, si des peuples si mal nourris ont si peu de force. A quoi il faut ajouter que ce qu'ils souffrent de la nudité y contribue beaucoup, les trois quarts n'étant vêtus, hiver et été, que de toile à demi pourrie, et déchirée, et chaussés de sabots, dans lesquels ils sont le pied nu toute l'année. (*Description géographique de l'élection de Vézelay*, in Coornaert ed. of *Dîme royale*, p. 279.)

Vauban goes on to give a very similar account of the predominance of poverty-stricken *métayers*:

> Il faut que le maître qui veut avoir un nouveau métayer, commence par le dégager [1] et payer ses dettes, garnir sa métairie de bestiaux, et le nourrir, lui et sa famille, une année d'avance, à ses dépens; et comme ce métayer n'a pour l'ordinaire pas de bien [2] qui puisse répondre de sa conduite, il fait ce qu'il lui plaît et se met souvent peu en peine de qui payera ses dettes. (*Ibid.*, p. 280.)

In his *Projet d'une dîme royale*, which was finally published in 1707, Vauban gives a very gloomy picture of this same district, though it should be noted that he admits the soil is exceptionally poor:

> . . . Cette taille, à laquelle se rapportent toutes les autres impositions, selon l'usage qui se pratique, désole cette élection,[3] et réduit les trois quarts de ses habitants au pain d'orge et d'avoine, et à n'avoir pas pour un écu d'habits sur le corps. D'où s'ensuit

[1] Free him from his debts. [2] Property.
[3] An administrative district (part of a province).

> la désertion des plus courageux, la mort et la mendicité d'une partie des autres, et une très notable diminution de peuples, qui est le plus grand mal qui puisse arriver dans un état. Il y a six ou sept ans que cette remarque a été faite; et depuis ce temps-là le mal s'est fort augmenté, sans compter que la septième partie des maisons sont à bas, la sixième partie des terres en friche, et les autres mal cultivées; que beaucoup plus de moitié de la superficie de cette élection est couverte de bois, de haies et de broussailles; que la cinquième partie des vignes est en friche, et les autres très mal faites. (*Dîme royale*, pp. 134-5.)

In the same work Vauban offers an interesting family-budget of an agricultural labourer. Assuming he found work on 180 days in the year, at 9 *sous* a day, his total money-income would be about 90 *livres* a year. If he paid, under Vauban's scheme for a more equitable system of direct taxation, the relatively moderate sum of 6 *livres*, and purchased enough salt for four persons at a cost of 8 *livres*, he would be left with a tax-free income of just over 75 *livres*. When he had bought the amount of grain (half wheat, half rye) necessary for feeding himself, his wife and two children, he would be left with just over 15 *livres* in cash:

> . . . Sur quoi il faut que ce manouvrier paie le louage [1] ou les réparations de sa maison, l'achat de quelques meubles, quand ce ne serait que de quelques écuelles de terre; des habits et du linge; et qu'il fournisse à tous les besoins de sa famille pendant une année.
>
> Mais ces quinze livres quatre sols ne le mèneront pas fort loin, à moins que son industrie, ou quelque commerce particulier ne remplisse les vides du temps qu'il ne travaillera pas, et que sa femme ne contribue de quelque chose à la dépense, par le travail de sa quenouille, par la couture, par le tricotage de quelque paire de bas, ou par la façon [2] d'un peu de dentelle, selon le pays; par la culture aussi d'un petit jardin; par la nourriture de quelques volailles, et peut-être d'une vache, d'un cochon ou d'une chèvre pour les plus accommodés,[3] qui donneront un peu de lait; au moyen de quoi il puisse acheter quelque morceau de lard, et un peu de beurre ou d'huile pour se faire du potage. Et si on n'y ajoute la culture de quelque petite pièce de terre,

[1] Hire (i.e. rent). [2] Making. [3] 'Those who are best off.'

il sera difficile qu'il puisse subsister, ou du moins il sera réduit, lui et sa famille, à faire une très misérable chère. (*Ibid.*, pp. 80-1.)

When one reads this vivid account of the small income of the poorest class of rural inhabitants, it does not require a great effort of imagination to see what havoc could be created by unemployment or bad harvests and high prices or increased taxation.

It is interesting to compare with this passage one written some thirty years earlier by a foreign traveller, the English philosopher John Locke, who relates in his Journal a conversation with a peasant woman, the wife of an agricultural labourer of the wine-producing region of Graves, near Bordeaux:

> Talking in this country with a poor peasant's wife, she told us she had 3 children; that her husband got usually 7s. per diem, finding himself, which was to maintain their family, 5 in number. She indeed got 3 or 3½s. per diem when she could get work, which was but seldom. Other times she span hemp, which was for their clothes and yielded no money. Out of this 7s. per diem they 5 were to be maintained, and house rent paid and their *taille*, and Sundays and holy days provided for.
>
> For their house, which, God wot, was a poor one room and one storey open to the tiles, without window, and a little vineyard which was as bad as nothing (for though they made out of it 4 or 5 tierce of wine—3 tierce make 2 hogheads—yet the labour and cost about the vineyard, making the wine and cask to to put it in, being cast up, the profit of it was very little) they paid 12 *écus* per annum rent and for *taille* 4 *livres* for which, not long since, the collector had taken their frying pan and dishes, money not being ready.
>
> Their ordinary food rye bread and water. Flesh is a thing seldom seasons their pots, and, as she said, they make no distinction between flesh and fasting days; but when their money reaches to a more costly meal, they buy the inwards of some beast in the market and then they feast themselves. And yet they say that in Saintonge and several other parts of France the peasants are much more miserable than these, for these they count the flourishing peasants which live in Graves. (*Travels in France*, pp. 236-7.)

It is also interesting to see how the authors of the report on Le Maine and l'Orléanais account for the impoverished state of the peasants of that area. The provinces, they declare, are drained of all their wealth by taxes, feudal dues and tithes, for most of this money finds its way to Paris, to the Treasury, the nobles and the higher clergy, and fails to find its way back again:

One could go on quoting endless passages on this theme without being able to arrive at any definite conclusion, since all of them are subject to the qualifications enumerated above. Nevertheless, the evidence which they contain cannot be lightly dismissed. When we think of the pomp and magnificence of the French court in the seventeenth century, offering to all Europe a model of luxury, refinement and culture, we must not forget the mass of the population which made possible that magnificence. The splendour of the court of Louis XIV was built upon the toil, and often the sufferings, of the peasantry, of whose existence the courtiers of Versailles remained contemptuously oblivious. It was from the peasants that the State, the Church and the aristocracy derived the major part of their incomes. It was the peasant who bore the greatest share of the burdens of seventeenth century French society; in the words of an eminent French historian: 'Le paysan est la bête de somme de cette société.'

Illiterate and isolated, the peasants could merely do their best to put up with their lot. They could have no thought of a better organization of society and of the state. Only if their sufferings became unbearable did they offer any resistance to their oppressors. The history of France in the seventeenth century is strewn with peasants' revolts; but they were sporadic outbursts, generally local in character, without any clear aims, without hope. All of them were easily and savagely repressed. It was not until 1789 that the peasants were capable of concerted action to win more land for themselves and to sweep away feudal dues and tithes. Then the grievances borne through centuries of oppression boiled over.

CHAPTER II

THE TOWNS. TRADE AND INDUSTRY

JUDGED by present-day standards, the development of trade and especially of industry in France down to the seventeenth century appears almost insignificant.

Everything depends, however, on one's point of view. To see what degree of commercial and industrial development had been attained by seventeenth century France, it is not sufficient to make comparisons with modern times; it is more important, perhaps, to see first what changes had taken place during the centuries which had elapsed since feudalism was at its height. In the ninth and tenth centuries trade had almost entirely disappeared; it was an age of economic self-sufficiency when each community, almost each family, was compelled to supply as far as possible its own needs. Gradually, however, trade began to revive, and new towns were founded or old settlements expanded with the rebirth of trade. The growth of the towns meant the rise of a new class, in between the nobility and the peasantry of feudal times: the middle class, or *bourgeoisie*.[1] Each century saw a steady progress in its economic power, despite the obstacles presented by the frequent wars of mediaeval times. By the end of the Middle Ages it had already attained a position of some prominence in the life of the country, and the sixteenth century, an age of rapid economic expansion, was to increase its importance at the expense of the nobility. In the seventeenth century it did not yet occupy the position which it was to hold in the eighteenth, and still more in the nineteenth century; nor did the Age of Louis XIV represent such a period of rapid economic and social change as the period of the Renaissance and Reformation. Nevertheless, in the course of the seventeenth century, despite various setbacks, the middle class continued to acquire an ever increasing importance in the life of the country.

[1] The first recorded use of the word *bourgeois* (literally, inhabitant of a *bourg* or town) is about 1100.

Any signs of the coming Industrial Revolution which was to make slow beginnings in France on the eve of 1789, and develop more fully in the nineteenth century, were as yet scarcely perceptible. While seventeenth century science was in many ways concerned with contemporary technical problems, it had not yet paved the way for a revolution in industry, which, with few exceptions, was still conducted on the traditional, small-scale lines. It was for the most part organized on the mediaeval system of a master working in his shop with the aid of journeymen (*compagnons*) and apprentices (*apprentis*), whose numbers varied according to the trade and the economic status of their master.

Apprenticeship was the first stage in the career of those who aspired to become masters in their turn. A boy would be bound apprentice to a master for a certain number of years on such conditions as are contained in the following specimen of contemporary indentures:

> Pierre Gribolly, maître menuisier, loue et afferme, pour lui et les siens, à Jean Joly, maître imprimeur, Abraham Gribolly, son fils, ici présent et volontaire,[1] pour servir ledit Joly en l'art de la composition de l'imprimerie pour le terme et temps de sept ans consécutifs. . . . Pendant lequel temps ledit Joly promet bien et dûment apprendre, et, en outre, le bien et dûment nourrir de dépens de bouche, coucher et chauffer honnêtement.[2] L'apprenti promet de le servir en toute fidélité et prud'homie. P. Gribolly promet entretenir son fils de chausses et habillement, et en outre s'engage à donner à la femme dudit Joly, à chaque fête de Pâques, un dernier et devantier [3] de serge, comme il convient. (Baudrier, *Bibliographie Lyonnaise*, i. 200-1.)

The journeyman stood next in the hierarchy, although actually it was not legally necessary to pass through this stage. He was generally engaged by means of a verbal contract, and very often he was liable to dismissal at short notice, but in other respects the following document gives a fair idea of his obligations and those of his master:

> Denys Cotterel, compagnon imprimeur, s'afferme,[4] lui et ses

[1] 'Acting of his own free will.'
[2] Adequately.
[3] Dress.
[4] 'Hires himself out.'

services, à Pierre Michel, maître imprimeur, pour un an, à partir du 1er mars prochain, pour le prix de 12 écus d'or, payable par quart de trois en trois mois; promet servir bien et loyalement en toutes choses licites et honnêtes. Pierre Michel promet le nourrir des dépens de bouche, lui fournir couche et logis, comme il est de coutume; promet aussi ledit Cotterel, de non absenter, ni servir à autre, s'il n'y a cause légitime. (*Ibid.*, i. 106.)

The masters in each trade were organized together in a guild (*corporation* or *jurande*). They elected a certain number of *jurés* to see that the regulations of the guild were carried out. These regulations laid down such matters as the number of apprentices that each master might employ; the age at which they might be admitted and the length of their apprenticeship; the type of 'masterpiece' (*chef-d'œuvre*) which each candidate had to execute before he could be admitted to the guild; and the methods to be employed in the manufacture of the products of the guild. The object of this supervision by the guild of its members was, in part, to maintain certain standards in their products, but its chief aim was to establish a monopoly by eliminating all competition, whether from members or outsiders. Thus the number of apprentices was strictly limited so that no master should possess an unfair advantage over another; while the fixing of the length of apprenticeship and the imposition of the 'masterpiece' were intended to make it impossible for outsiders to set up in competition with the members of the guild.

In most large towns the different trades were organized in guilds, though, despite the efforts of the government to increase their number because they were a very profitable source of taxation, they were by no means universal. In practice, the difference between a trade which was organized in a guild and one which was not, was probably not very great. In the latter, it is true, anyone could set up shop without interference; nominally he could have as many apprentices as he pleased, but in practice their number was restricted; and if he was not liable to inspection by the officials of a guild, the local authority exercised supervision over him, and did not leave him to do as he pleased.

The small scale on which the greater part of the industry of the country was conducted is, of course, easily explained by the fact that the technique of most trades had scarcely changed since the Middle Ages. Even such an industry as printing, which had arisen out of a fairly recent mechanical invention, was generally conducted on quite a small scale; a printer with two presses would employ only seven or eight journeymen and apprentices. In most cases the master would have only a small house which he used both as dwelling-place and business-premises; above the door was a painted sign for advertisement, and on the ground floor the front of the house would open on to the street so that business could be conducted from outside. The degree of comfort inside the house depended largely on the kind of trade pursued by the master.

Among the Paris guilds there was actually a legal hierarchy; at the top came the *Six Corps*—drapers, grocers, haberdashers, furriers, hosiers and goldsmiths. In general, the wealthiest guilds were those whose members were not concerned with the production of goods, but with selling the products of others, such as the haberdashers and drapers. Other wealthy guilds were those connected with the food-trades, such as grocers and butchers; with the medical profession (doctors, surgeons and apothecaries); and, to a less degree, printers and booksellers. At the other end of the scale came the poorer artisans—tailors, carpenters, masons, shoemakers and especially cobblers. Many of these had a hard struggle to make a living, as competition was generally very fierce, since the number of artisans was quite out of proportion to the population of the towns.

As for the journeyman, his lot had on the whole grown worse in the course of the centuries. It is true that in those trades which were not regulated by guilds he was free to set up on his own account if he chose; but in the other trades it was becoming more and more difficult for him to become a master. The 'masterpiece' was often an onerous obligation because of the length of time which was required for its execution; and a new master had to pay a heavy fee to the *jurés*, to the guild and to the Treasury before he could be admitted, whereas the son or son-in-law of a master had no 'masterpiece' to execute and only insignificant fees to pay. As the number of new members admitted in any one year was very small, the guilds tended to become the monopoly of a few families; the great body of journeymen were excluded and compelled to remain wage-earners all their lives.

There thus arose in the towns the nucleus of an industrial proletariat, still insignificant in numbers but historically important in view of the role it was one day to play. The workman who was compelled to remain a journeyman all his life was condemned to a miserable existence. If he lived in, he generally inhabited a garret; wages were low, so that if he fell ill, or hard times came, he had no savings to fall back on. Hours of work were inordinately long: from sunrise to sunset in summer, and often far into the evening in winter. A twelve-hour day was by no means rare, and even fourteen or sixteen hours were worked. It is true that his task was much less exacting than modern factory-work, and that, besides Sundays and other modern holidays, work would stop on an extraordinary number of saints' days (*fêtes*). These were, no doubt, very welcome to the journeymen, though they greatly annoyed La Fontaine's cobbler in the fable of *Le savetier et le financier*, as he was, of course, working on his own account:

Eh bien, que gagnez-vous, dites-moi, par journée?
—Tantôt plus, tantôt moins; le mal est que toujours
(Et sans cela nos gains seraient assez honnêtes),
Le mal est que dans l'an s'entremêlent des jours
  Qu'il faut chômer; on nous ruine en fêtes;
L'une fait tort à l'autre; et monsieur le curé
De quelque nouveau saint charge toujours son prône.

The long hours, poor wages and wretched living conditions of many seventeenth century journeymen no doubt aroused in them feelings of resentment against their masters. Yet it would be a mistake to attribute to them the outlook and feelings of the workers of more modern times. It must be remembered that the journeyman was not working in a large factory owned by some impersonal combine. In most cases he followed his trade in a small workshop alongside his master on terms, if not of equality, at least of something approaching it. Moreover, if by the seventeenth century it was difficult for the ordinary journeyman to become a master, he could always cherish the hope that one day his turn might come. Yet if the journeymen were forced to accept what terms their masters dictated to them, it was not always without a struggle. The journeymen had their associations, the *Compagnonnages*, which were the forerunners of modern trade unions. Little is known of their history, and such fragments as have come down to us must not be given an exaggerated importance. Yet we do know that in some industries the journeymen were strongly organized, and that the Age of Louis XIV had its strikes and even revolts, though they were rare and sporadic, and always savagely repressed by the authorities.

The changes in the guild system in the seventeenth century through the exclusion of a growing number of journeymen were paralleled by the growing importance of big merchants who stood outside, and above, the guilds. Despite all the obstacles in the way of its expansion, trade was acquiring an ever increasing importance in the life of the nation. It is clear from the literature of the age that the wealthier classes of society were able to lead more luxurious lives than ever before. The moralist naturally tends to see in the contrast between the simplicity and frugality of earlier generations and the luxury of his contemporaries proofs of moral degeneration rather than of an increase in trade and wealth. La Bruyère is no exception to the rule in the following denunciation of the luxury of the wealthier classes of his time; but the historical interest of the passage is none the less obvious.

> Les empereurs n'ont jamais triomphé [1] à Rome si mollement, si commodément, ni si sûrement même, contre le vent, la pluie, la poudre [2] et le soleil, que le bourgeois sait à Paris se faire mener par toute la ville; quelle distance de cet usage à la mule de leurs ancêtres! Ils ne savaient point encore se priver du nécessaire pour avoir le superflu, ni préférer le faste aux choses utiles. On ne les voyait point s'éclairer avec des bougies,[3] et se chauffer

1 'Made a triumphal entry. 2 Dust.
3 Wax candles (much more expensive than those made of tallow).

5. *Louis Le Nain,* La charrette

6. *Louis Le Nain*, Paysans dans la campagne

7. *Louis Le Nain*, Paysans devant leur maison

à un petit feu: la cire était pour l'autel et le Louvre. Ils ne sortaient point d'un mauvais dîner pour monter dans leur carrosse; ils se persuadaient que l'homme avait des jambes pour marcher, et ils marchaient. . . . On n'avait pas encore imaginé d'atteler deux hommes à une litière [1]; il y avait même plusieurs [2] magistrats qui allaient à pied à la chambre ou aux enquêtes [3] d'aussi bonne grâce qu'Auguste allait de son pied au Capitole. L'étain, dans ce temps, brillait sur les tables et sur les buffets, comme le fer et le cuivre dans les foyers; l'argent et l'or étaient dans les coffres. Les femmes se faisaient servir par des femmes; on mettait celles-ci jusqu'à la cuisine. Les beaux noms de gouverneurs et de gouvernantes n'étaient pas inconnus à nos pères; ils savaient à qui l'on confiait les enfants des rois et des plus grands princes; mais ils partageaient le service de leurs domestiques avec leurs enfants, contents de veiller eux-mêmes immédiatement à leur éducation. Ils comptaient en toutes choses avec eux-mêmes: leur dépense était proportionnée à leur recette; leurs livrées, leurs équipages, leurs meubles, leur table, leur maison de la ville et de la campagne, tout était mesuré sur leurs rentes et sur leur condition. Il y avait entre eux des distinctions extérieures qui empêchaient qu'on ne prît la femme du practicien [4] pour celle du magistrat, et le roturier ou le simple valet pour le gentilhomme. . . . (*Les Caractères*, vii. 22.)

A dozen similar passages could be quoted to show the growth of luxury brought about by the development of trade.

It is true that there were a great many obstacles to the commercial expansion of France in the seventeenth century. First of these was the still backward state of communications. Even the main roads remained in poor condition despite the efforts of various ministers to improve them. A vivid picture of a journey in seventeenth century France is given in one of the letters of Mme de Sévigné in which she describes to her daughter the tribulations she went through in Brittany on the way from Rennes to her estate at Les Rochers:

Nous partîmes à dix heures, et tout le monde me disant que j'avais trop de temps, que les chemins étaient comme dans cette chambre, car c'en est toujours la comparaison; ils étaient si

[1] A sedan chair.
[2] Many (not 'several').
[3] Different sections of the *Parlement* (see p. 45).
[4] *Avocat* or *procureur*.

> bien comme dans cette chambre, que nous n'arrivâmes ici qu'après douze heures du soir toujours dans l'eau, et de Vitré ici, où j'ai été mille fois, nous ne les reconnaissions pas: tous les pavés sont devenus impraticables, les bourbiers sont enfoncés, les hauts et bas, plus haut et bas qu'ils n'étaient; enfin, voyant que nous ne voyions plus rien, et qu'il fallait tâter le chemin, nous envoyâmes demander du secours à Pilois; il vient avec une douzaine de gars; les uns nous tenaient, les autres nous éclairaient avec plusieurs bouchons de paille, et nous parlaient extrêmement breton, que nous pâmions de rire. Enfin, avec cette illumination, nous arrivâmes ici, nos cheveux rebutés, nos gens tout trempés, mon carrosse rompu, et nous assez fatigués . . . (31 May 1680.)

In the course of the century an attempt was made to improve water transport: the navigation of such rivers as the Seine, Loire and Rhône was improved; several canals, such as the famous Canal du Midi, were constructed. It is also true that the postal service was improved during our period: regular mail-services were set up, postage charges were reduced, and the amount of mail greatly increased. Nevertheless, transport still remained primitive. Coaches took two days to go from Paris to Orleans; ten or eleven to Lyons; eleven to Strasbourg, and so on. Mme de Sévigné's letters to her daughter when the latter was engaged on her journey to Provence make interesting reading in this connection. Her daughter set out from Paris on a Thursday, and her mother wrote to her four days later, following her in her imagination on every mile of her slow and, at times, dangerous journey:

> Rien ne me donne de distraction; je suis toujours avec vous; je vois ce carrosse qui avance toujours, et qui n'approchera jamais de moi; je suis toujours dans les grands chemins; il me semble même que j'ai quelquefois peur qu'il ne verse; les pluies qu'il fait depuis trois jours me mettent au désespoir; le Rhône me fait une peur étrange.[1] J'ai une carte devant les yeux; je sais tous les lieux où vous couchez; vous êtes ce soir à Nevers, et *vous serez dimanche à Lyon*, où vous recevrez cette lettre. (9 February 1671.)

[1] Mme de Sévigné's fears about the Rhône were justified. Mme de Grignan was met at Avignon by her husband, and being in a hurry to cross the Rhône, they set out in the midst of a storm, with the result that their boat was driven violently against one of the arches of the ruined bridge.

If it took Mme de Grignan ten days to proceed as far as Lyons, it can be imagined that commercial transport was a very slow business. For example, it took goods four days to cover the 75 miles from Paris to Orleans.

Another handicap to trade, particularly in the closing years of the reign of Louis XIV, was manipulations of the coinage, a proceeding which did not help the Treasury in its distress, but merely hampered trade. Even more serious obstacles, however, were to be found in the dues which goods had to pay in transit across France. First, the users of many roads and rivers had to pay tolls (*péages*) to the lord on whose territory they were situated, a system which gave rise to many abuses, eloquently described by a merchant of Nantes in the following passage:

> Les péages particuliers qui sont sur les rivières sont encore une des principales choses qui perdent le commerce. Il y en a si grand nombre qu'on en compte sur la Loire plus de trente, depuis Roanne jusqu'à Nantes, qui composent autant de bureaux auxquels ils sont obligés de s'arrêter. On y exige tellement qu'on a souvent vérifié qu'une balle de marchandise descendant de Roanne à Nantes, qui naturellement n'aurait dû en tout que 10 écus de droits, en payait, par tous ces bureaux, 30 ou 40. D'ailleurs, les pauvres malheureux matelots sont obligés de donner des présents à chaque péageur; sans quoi ils les retardent à plaisir et mettent par ces exactions les voituriers en obligation de voler le marchand pour se tirer d'affaire. Il en est de même sur les autres rivières. (Boislisle, *Correspondance des Contrôleurs généraux*, ii. 486.)

Even more extraordinary in modern eyes was the system of internal customs-barriers; *inside France itself* goods passing from one group of provinces to another had to pay customs duties, known as *traites*. The whole system was extremely complicated; it was, in fact, not the result of rational organization, but of the gradual growth of the kingdom of France. One group of provinces, comprising Normandy, Picardy, Ile de France, Champagne, Burgundy, Bourbonnais, Nivernais, Berry, Orléanais, Touraine, Poitou, Aunis, Anjou, and Le Maine, traded freely with one another, and had at their boundaries uniform duties on all goods leaving or entering the group. The second group of provinces—Artois, Flanders, Brittany, Guyenne, Saintonge, Languedoc, Provence, Dauphiné, Lyonnais, all situated on the fringe of the first group—had to pay duties on

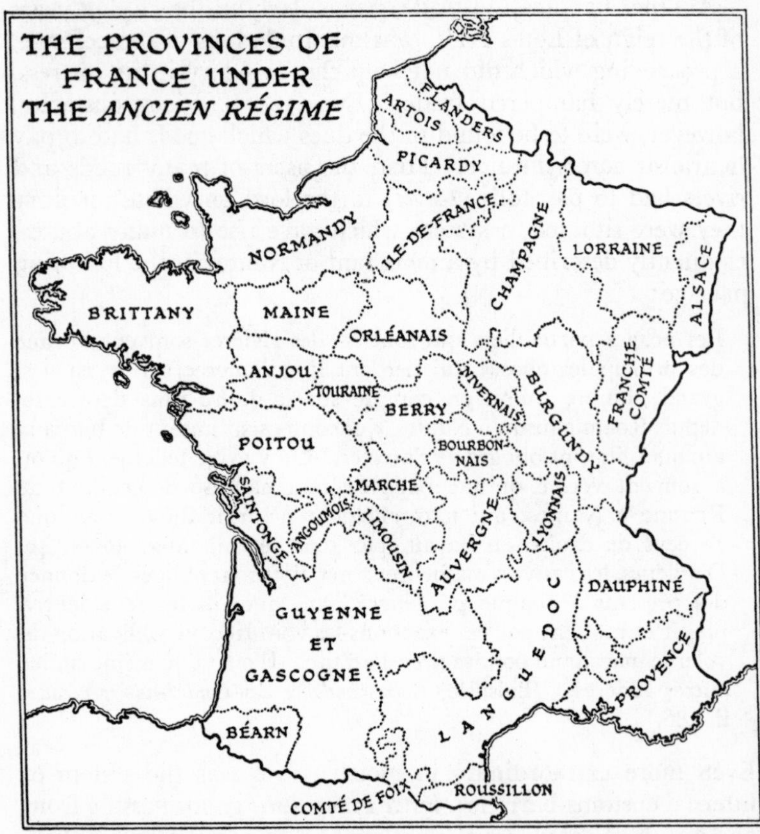

the export or import of goods passing from one of these provinces to the other; or from one of them to one of the provinces in the first group; or to the most recently acquired provinces, Alsace, Lorraine, and Franche-Comté. These last-named provinces enjoyed free trade with foreign countries, but were cut off by customs-barriers from the rest of France. Despite many protests, both *péages* and *traites* remained in force until 1789; the effect of such obstacles on the development of trade can well be imagined. Vauban complained bitterly of their serious consequences for agriculture and for trade in general.

> On a trouvé tant d'inventions pour surprendre[1] les gens et pouvoir confisquer les marchandises, que le propriétaire et le paysan aiment mieux laisser périr leurs denrées chez eux que de les transporter avec tant de risques et si peu de profit. De sorte qu'il y a des denrées, soit vins, cidres, huiles et autres choses semblables, qui sont à très grand marché sur les lieux, et qui se vendraient chèrement et se débiteraient très bien à dix, vingt et trente lieues de là, où elles sont nécessaires, qu'on laisse perdre, parce qu'on n'ose hasarder de les transporter. (*Dîme royale*, pp. 29-30.)

Boisguilbert gives a concrete example of the mischief caused by these internal customs-barriers:

> . . . La Provence a des denrées que l'on ne prend pas presque la peine de ramasser de terre sur le lieu, lesquelles sont vendues un très grand prix à Paris, en Normandie et autres contrées éloignées. Cependant, on n'en fait venir que pour l'extrême nécessité, et la raison est évidente. C'est que dans ce trajet, qui est de 200 lieues, il faut passer par une infinité de villes et lieux fermés, où, les voituriers étant obligés de faire les stations marquées ci-devant aux articles des douanes et des aides, cela emporte tant de temps, et met les choses sur un pied tel qu'il faut trois mois et demi pour faire ce voyage, qui ne demanderait pas plus d'un mois ou cinq semaines sans ces obstacles; ce qui ne pouvant être porté par la marchandise, à cause des frais qui accompagnent une si longue voiture,[2] en fait abandonner le commerce, et par conséquent celui du retour. La Normandie a semblablement des denrées, comme des toiles, très rares et très chères en Provence, que la certitude d'un pareil sort empêche de se mettre en chemin. (*Détail de la France*, pp. 233-4.)

Nevertheless, despite all these obstacles, it is a fact that the volume of French trade increased considerably in the course of the century. The greatest increase was in overseas trade, since bad transport and the *péages* and *traites* weighed heavily

[1] Cheat.

[2] Distance to be transported.

on the progress of trade at home. Yet even inside France itself the expansion of trade led to the creation of a new class of wealthy wholesale merchants, especially haberdashers and drapers; these big merchants stood above the organization of the guilds, and next to the aristocracy. Indeed, an edict of 1627 conferred noble rank on wholesale merchants.

Nevertheless, overseas trade played a greater role in the economic life of seventeenth century France than trade at home. In the course of the century commercial relations with other European countries, with the French colonies in the West Indies, Madagascar and Canada, and with the East, were greatly extended. In the second half of the century such Atlantic ports as Nantes, La Rochelle and Bordeaux experienced a great increase in trade, and their merchants and shipowners often acquired large fortunes. It may be noted that trade with the West Indies consisted for a good part in the exchange for sugar and tobacco of 'les nègres que l'on va acheter en Afrique sur la côte de Guinée. Ce commerce est d'autant plus avantageux qu'on ne peut se passer de nègres dans les dites îles pour travailler aux sucres, pétuns [1] et autres ouvrages.' It should be added that the author of this passage —Jacques Savary in his *Le Parfaict Négociant* (1675)—goes out of his way to defend the slave-trade, which proves incidentally that it had its critics even at this period: 'Ce commerce paraît inhumain à ceux qui ne savent pas que ces pauvres gens sont idolâtres ou mahométans, et que les marchands chrétiens, en les achetant à leurs ennemis, les tirent d'un cruel esclavage, leur font trouver non seulement une servitude plus douce, mais même la connaissance du vrai Dieu et la voie du salut.' (i. 139-40.)

This expansion of trade, both by increasing the capital of the nation and by demanding, in order to supply the needs of new markets, more highly developed methods of manufacture than those of the guilds, influenced in its turn the progress of industry. Industrial development was fostered by the deliberate policy of most French governments and ministers, especially Colbert. The State itself set up its own industrial

[1] Tobacco.

undertakings, such as arsenals for military and naval supplies, and the famous tapestry-works of Les Gobelins and Beauvais. More important than these were the new undertakings which bore the somewhat misleading title of *manufactures royales* because of the privileges conferred upon them by the Crown. These privileges might consist of interest-free loans or else the owners might be given free premises, or a grant towards the cost of their machinery. Again, an individual might be given a monopoly of the manufacture of a certain product, or else a direct subsidy on the goods which he produced.

The new industries established in France in the seventeenth century produced chiefly luxury goods, such as Venetian lace, velvet, silver and gold cloth, taffeta, silk stockings, mirrors, glassware and porcelain. In addition, the manufacture of hosiery and woollens was encouraged and greatly developed in the course of the period, and a number of foundries and ironworks were established. It would, however, be a mistake to imagine that these new industries were carried on under anything resembling modern factory conditions. One or two establishments, it is true, grouped together in a single factory a considerable number of workers; but this was altogether exceptional.

For the most part the manufacturers let out the work to a number of small producers, who thus became dependent on them for their livelihood. The finished product might have passed through the hands of half a dozen different workers before it was finally ready for sale by the manufacturers. The organization of the guilds was profoundly affected in certain trades by the appearance on the scene of this new type of merchant-manufacturer. In Lyons, for instance, there emerged in the silk industry, above the master-artisans who were concerned with the actual production, a number of master-merchants, who really controlled the whole industry and reduced the master-artisans to the position of journeymen. Having a considerable capital at their disposal, they were able to sell in distant markets; and they thus formed a new class, far above the artisans whom they supplied with patterns and raw materials and paid at piece-rates. Many of the new 'manufactures' were carried on, not in the towns but in the country—once again outside the framework of the guilds. This domestic industry, as it is called, was carried on in their own homes, either by full-time specialist workmen or by agricultural labourers and their families in the slack season on the land. In many cases the necessary raw materials were supplied by the manufacturers, who thus had the workers under their control. These developments in industry are summed up in *Le Parfait Négociant* of Jacques Savary:

> Dans les lieux où il y a des manufactures considérables, comme à Paris, Lyon, Saint-Chaumond, Tours, Sedan, Amiens, Châlons, Reims, Rouen, Laval et autres villes du royaume, il y a plusieurs négociants associés [1] qui font le commerce des matières qui y sont nécessaires, qu'ils vendent aux ouvriers et qui achètent d'eux des marchandises qu'ils ont manufacturées pour les vendre ensuite à ceux des autres villes qui les vont acheter sur les lieux, ou qui leur en donnent la commission. (ii. 10.)

It is thus clear that these new industries set up or expanded in France in the course of the century were very different from the large-scale undertakings of modern times. It must also be added that many of the new industries established by Colbert during the reign of Louis XIV did not have a lasting success, as they were unable to survive the expulsion of the Huguenots and the crushing taxation of the second half of the reign. Yet, when all allowances have been made, it remains true to say that in the course of the seventeenth century there was a considerable development of industry, which was to bear fruit in the following period.

Nevertheless, we must not neglect an important factor in French social history which greatly retarded the expansion of trade and industry. In Holland and England at that period, the merchant or trader who had made a fortune was driven on by ambition to launch out still further in the pursuit of wealth. His sons would continue his work, and with their inherited wealth strive to increase still further the family fortune. In France tradition and circumstance led to a very

[1] 'In partnership together.'

different state of affairs. Because trade and industry were less developed there than in Holland and England, and therefore played a less important part in the national life, the commercial class did not occupy such a high place in society. The merchant was despised by the nobleman; and, what is more, he in his turn showed an equal contempt for his own class; his one desire was to rise out of it into the aristocracy. This state of affairs is well summed up in a passage in an official report on French trade, drawn up in 1701:

> On sait que le mépris qui règne en France pour le commerce et les commerçants les engage presque tous, depuis longtemps, à se retirer d'abord [1] qu'ils ont gagné du bien [2] assez pour prendre un état [3] dans lequel ils trouvent plus de douceur et d'agrément, plus de relief [4] et plus de distinction. Ils établissent leurs enfants, ils mettent leur argent en terres ou en charges et contrats. De là vient que les étrangers ont tant d'avantages sur nous dans le commerce, parce que le négoce et les habitudes [5] ne se perpétuent pas dans nos familles, que toutes sortes de gens avides s'y jettent, qu'on voit peu de bonne foi, beaucoup de banqueroutes, peu de négociants assez riches et assez entendus [6] pour aller négocier en concurrence avec les étrangers, que nous sommes presque réduits au détail, et à prendre des Hollandais et Anglais, à prix d'argent et à notre grand dommage, les marchandises nécessaires à notre consommation. (Boislisle, *Correspondance des Contrôleurs Généraux*, ii. 484.)

No doubt, Monsieur Jourdain in Molière's *Bourgeois Gentilhomme* is a caricature; and yet his yearning to rise out of the bourgeoisie into the aristocracy is merely a social fact turned into comedy. 'Lorsque je hante la noblesse', he tells his protesting wife, 'je fais paraître mon jugement, et cela est plus beau que de hanter votre bourgeoisie.' There, in comic exaggeration, is the outlook of the seventeenth century French bourgeois who had made his pile or inherited a fortune from a successful father.

This desire to abandon trade and to rise in the social scale was encouraged by the Monarchy. As its power developed through the centuries, as its administrative machine and its

[1] 'As soon as.' [2] Wealth. [3] Social position.
[4] Eminence. [5] Connections. [6] Experienced.

court became more and more costly, as the carrying on of foreign wars demanded greater and greater funds, the Monarchy was compelled to turn to the trading classes for financial help. Knowing that the merchant despised his own calling, it offered him various means of investing his money in such a way as to rise in the social scale. Thus it came about that much of the capital created by the expansion of trade and industry was directed, not to the further expansion of trade and industry, but into other less productive channels, above all, that of the royal Treasury.

As soon as a merchant had acquired a modest fortune, he wished to lead a life of ease and comfort. A very simple method of doing so had been provided by the Crown in the first part of the sixteenth century. It began then to issue loans (*rentes*), at first on a very small scale, but later, as its financial needs grew, at an ever increasing rate. The merchant, anxious to leave behind his despised calling, could find in the *rentes* a relatively safe investment for his money. Moreover, by becoming a *rentier* he rose in the social scale. Instead of being a despised trader, to use the language of the time, *il vivait noblement*: in other words, and this is a delightful explanation of the role of the nobility under the *ancien régime*, he did not soil his hands with work!

Rentes were not, however, the only form of investment which the Monarchy offered the wealthy members of the middle class. Towards the end of the fifteenth century the growing financial needs of the Crown had forced it to begin to sell posts in the administration and judiciary. Hence arose the system known as *la vénalité des charges*. The opportunity for investment was one which appealed to all sections of the middle class who had saved money, and the purchase of a *charge* or *office* for themselves or their sons became the great ambition of the mass of the bourgeoisie. The rush to invest their money in this way could hardly be described in stronger terms than in those used by a writer of the first half of the century:

> On a beau ériger des offices. Sur le bruit d'une érection nouvelle ils sont retenus avant que l'édit en soit minuté.[1] Que le roi en

[1] Drawn up.

fasse tant qu'il voudra, il trouvera toujours à les débiter, car, comme dit le Sage,[1] 'Le nombre des fols est infini', et c'est maintenant un commun dire [2] parmi nous 'qu'il y a toujours plus de fols que d'états'.[3] S'il y a jamais un roi en France qui ait dessein de s'approprier tous les biens de ses sujets, comme fit ce roi d'Égypte en sa chère année, il ne faut que créer force offices. Chacun à l'envi portera sa bourse au roi. Qui n'aura argent, vendra sa terre. Qui n'aura assez de terre, se vendra soi-même, si on lui permet, et consentira d'être esclave pour devenir officier. (Charles Loyseau, *Œuvres*, pp. 152-3.)

The purchase of official posts was thus one more way in which capital acquired in trade and industry was diverted from further commercial and industrial expansion.

There was a great variety of posts to suit all purses; there were *offices* not merely for the upper middle class, but also for the comfortable *petits bourgeois*. In fact, from the time of Richelieu onwards the financial needs of the Crown were often so pressing that, instead of putting an end to the sale of posts as they had promised, various ministers were compelled to carry it to preposterous lengths, simply in order to fill an empty Treasury. New posts were set up, often with utterly ridiculous functions, merely to attract the money of the middle classes. Another ingenious idea, developed in the second half of the century, was to divide a post among two or even three holders, each of whom paid his purchase price and officiated every second or third year, as the case might be. Not surprisingly, the rush to acquire these posts slackened off somewhat towards the end of the century, and even this mine of wealth began to be worked out.

In general, the posts which could be purchased were those concerned with local or national government, the collection of direct taxes, and the administration of justice. This is not the place to attempt an analysis of the highly chaotic government and judicial machinery of seventeenth century France; it is enough for our purpose to notice that the very complexity of the machinery meant that thousands of posts, often little more than sinecures, were available for purchase by the well-to-do

[1] Solomon. [2] Saying. [3] '*Offices, charges.*'

bourgeois. These posts offered their holders many advantages: first, they were an investment for their capital, though not always, it must be said, a very remunerative investment, as the government did not scruple to cut salaries or to keep their officials waiting for payment. Again, an *office* was a form of property; it could be sold or mortgaged. Moreover, it became in the course of time—from the beginning of the seventeenth century—hereditary and could thus be handed down from father to son. Finally, the possession of an *office* conferred upon its holder not merely social distinction, and in the case of the highest posts, noble rank; it generally meant also exemption from the *taille* and most taxes.

It is naturally difficult to generalize about such a variety of posts as existed in the administrative machine of seventeenth century France. It goes without saying that the greater the cost of the *office*, the greater the advantages attached to it. Many of these posts were held by people with a legal training, for the collection of the various direct and indirect taxes gave rise to much civil and criminal litigation. It is noteworthy that many of the famous French writers of the seventeenth century were themselves members, or were connected through their fathers, with this comfortably-off section of the middle class, ensconced in *offices* which offered a reasonable living and social standing. Corneille's family had held for two generations before him official, legal posts in Normandy; he became an *avocat* in his turn, and acquired by purchase two legal posts at Rouen which offered a modest income and a reasonable amount of leisure, since they left him time both to write his plays and to come to Paris to arrange for them to be performed. Racine's father held posts in the local law-courts, and in the trying of cases arising out of the collection of the *gabelle*; these posts had been in the family for several generations. When the poet had made a name for himself, Louis XIV gave him the post of *trésorier de France*, a pure sinecure in the machinery of tax-collection, which conferred noble rank on his children. La Bruyère's father held a post in the administration of the *Rentes*; he himself bought a post of *trésorier de France* at Caen; not only did he never carry out any of his duties, but he appears to have been extremely annoyed at having to spend three whole weeks there in order to be admitted. La Fontaine's father held a post as *maître des eaux et forêts*; and after the poet had been admitted an *avocat*, his father handed it over to him. It cannot, of course, be claimed that La Fontaine was a great success as a civil servant! Molière was the son of a well-to-do upholsterer who had bought the post of *tapissier du roi*; he too studied law, and was admitted an *avocat*; but was seduced from a respectable, bourgeois career by the lure of the stage. Boileau, to quote one last example, was the descendant of a family associated for centuries with the law. His father held an important legal post in Paris. Boileau himself studied law and was admitted an *avocat*; but at his father's death he was left with an income large enough to lead a comfortably independent existence, unencumbered by any professional obligations.

Important as was this moderately well-to-do class of *officiers*, both for its numbers and for the great writers which it produced, it was overshadowed by a much wealthier and more influential social group—the members of the *Parlements*. We shall see later the role of the *Parlements* in the political and administrative sphere; for our present purpose it is sufficient to say that they were first and foremost concerned with the administration of justice, being the highest courts of France. The members of these courts were *officiers*: they acquired their posts either through purchase or inheritance, and could hand them on to their sons in return for the payment of an annual tax. In practice, hereditary succession was by far the most common procedure; posts in the *Parlements* rarely came on the market. They generally remained in the same family for generations, for with the establishment of the principle of heredity the *Parlements* tended more and more to become a closed caste.

The principle of heredity inevitably brought with it certain disadvantages, at least for the general public. It is true that a certain number of families in the *Parlements* were distinguished all through the seventeenth and eighteenth centuries for their independence and devotion to duty. Often, however, fathers were succeeded by very youthful sons, in defiance of all the regulations. The examinations for admission to the *Parlements*, the highest courts of justice in the country, were a farce; the most stupid and ignorant candidates were admitted, provided they had the necessary money, or, better still, a father to succeed. Tallemant gives a most amusing account of one candidate's admission:

> La Barroire . . . était fils d'un riche marchand de la Rochelle. Il épousa ici [1] la fille de M. l'Hoste, beau-frère de l'intendant Arnaut. Après il acheta un office de conseiller au Parlement qui lui coûta onze mille écus. Il se présenta pour être reçu, c'était une grosse bête; mais son beau-père avait du crédit; on le reçut à cause de lui. On disait: 'C'est M. l'Hoste, et non son gendre, qu'on reçoit.' Cumont fut examiné en même temps, et fit fort bien. 'Il les faut recevoir, dit-on, l'un portant l'autre.' [2] (Tallemant, *Historiettes*, vi. 348.)

The evils of the system of hereditary succession are well summed up in a sermon of Bourdaloue:

> Ce jeune homme est de telle famille où telle dignité est héréditaire; dès là son sort est décidé; il faut que le fils succède au père. Et de cette maxime, que s'ensuit-il? Vous en êtes tous les jours témoins; c'est qu'un enfant, à qui l'on n'aurait pas voulu confier la moins importante affaire d'une maison particulière, a toutefois dans ses mains les affaires de toute une province et les intérêts publics. Il peut prononcer comme il lui plaît, ordonner ce qu'il lui plaît, exécuter tout ce qu'il lui plaît. On en souffre, on en gémit; le bon droit est vendu, toute la justice renversée; c'est ce qui importe peu à un père, pourvu qu'il n'en ressente point de dommage, et que ce fils soit établi. (*Sermon sur le devoir des pères par rapport à la vocation de leurs enfants.*)

An interesting example of the youthful judges of the period is to be found in the letters of Madame de Sévigné; writing from Nantes to her daughter, she gives a vivid picture of the contrast between the imposing title of *Premier président* and the youth of the holder of so important a post:

> Il faut que je vous conte ce que c'est que ce premier président. . . . C'est un jeune homme de vingt-sept ans, neveu de M. d'Harouys;

[1] Paris. [2] 'Taking one with another.'

un petit de la Brunelaye fort joli, qui a été élevé avec le petit de la Silleraye, que j'ai vu mille fois sans jamais imaginer que ce pût être un magistrat; cependant il l'est devenu par son crédit,[1] et moyennant quarante mille francs il a acheté toute l'expérience nécessaire pour être à la tête d'une compagnie souveraine,[2] qui est la chambre des comptes de Nantes; il a de plus épousé une fille que je connais fort, que j'ai vue cinq semaines tous les jours aux états [3] de Vitré; de sorte que ce premier président et cette première présidente sont pour moi un jeune petit garçon que je ne puis respecter, et une jeune petite demoiselle que je ne puis honorer. (27 May 1680.)

Many of these young men were totally unfitted for the important judicial posts which they occupied, both because of their ignorance and their frivolous mode of life. In a famous passage La Bruyère ridicules the way in which some of them aped the vices of the court dandies (*petits-maîtres*):

Il y a un certain nombre de jeunes magistrats que les grands biens [4] et les plaisirs ont associés à quelques-uns de ceux qu'on nomme à la cour de *petits-maîtres*: ils les imitent, ils se tiennent fort au-dessus de la gravité de la robe, et se croient dispensés par leur âge et par leur fortune d'être sages et modérés. Ils prennent de la cour ce qu'elle a de pire: ils s'approprient la vanité, la mollesse, l'intempérance, le libertinage, comme si tous ces vices leur étaient dus et, affectant ainsi un caractère éloigné de celui qu'ils ont à soutenir, ils deviennent enfin, selon leurs souhaits, des copies fidèles de très méchants originaux. (*Les Caractères*, vii. 7.)

The *Parlementaires* were not only a closed caste, but at the same time an extremely wealthy oligarchy. A *charge* was an expensive investment, open only to men of wealth. It is true that the nominal income of these posts, even when it was paid regularly, which was rare, did not offer a very high return for the capital invested in them; but there were compensations. In civil cases the judges received certain fees, called *épices*, from the litigants in return for their services, and the income from this source was considerable. In addition, the *Parlementaires* enjoyed valuable privileges: their posts brought them hereditary nobility, exemption from most taxes, and consider-

[1] Influence.
[2] 'One of highest lawcourts of the country.'
[3] Provincial Estates.
[4] Wealth.

able social standing. Besides, like many other bourgeois they were enabled by their wealth to buy up the estates of impoverished noblemen, or the land of peasants who had fallen into debt. By the seventeenth century a great part of the land in the neighbourhood of those towns which possessed a *Parlement* had fallen into the hands of the *Parlementaires*.

Although they owed their rise in the social scale to the wealth which their fathers or grandfathers had accumulated in trade and industry, the *Parlementaires* were only too anxious to forget their plebeian origins. Beside the old feudal nobility, called the *noblesse d'épée* because they possessed their lands by virtue of their military service to their overlord, there arose a new aristocracy, the *noblesse de robe*, composed of wealthy judges who possessed hereditary nobility, backed by recently acquired landed property. This new aristocracy refused to be confused with the middle class from which it came. Forgetful of their bourgeois origins, conscious of their wealth and their importance in the life of the country, the *noblesse de robe* claimed equality with the old feudal aristocracy, maintaining that there was only one aristocracy in France, not an old and a new one. See the proud words of a *Président au Parlement* at the end of the reign of Louis XIV:

> Il n'y a qu'une sorte de noblesse; elle s'acquiert différemment par les emplois militaires et par ceux de la judicature, mais les droits et les prérogatives en sont les mêmes.
>
> La robe a ses illustrations comme l'épée; les chanceliers, les gardes des sceaux sont en parallèle avec les connétables et les maréchaux de France; les présidents à mortier avec les ducs et pairs, qui cèdent comme eux sans peine au chef de la justice[1]; mais si l'on en vient à l'examen des familles, nous ne craindrons point de dire qu'il y a un grand nombre de maisons[2] dans le Parlement qui sont fort au-dessus de la plupart des pairs. (Président de Novion, *Requête anonyme de Messieurs du Parlement à S.A.R.M. le Duc d'Orléans, Régent*, p. 107.)

This claim to equality was, of course, haughtily rejected by the *noblesse d'épée*: in a society in which the notion of a hierarchy was so rigid, it was only natural that such claims

[1] The Chancellor. [2] Noble families.

8. *Louis Le Nain,* Repas de paysans

9. *Louis Le Nain,* Le retour du baptême

10. Frontispiece of *Le Parfait Négociant* of Jacques Savary (1675)

should not be accepted. Yet in practice, in the course of the seventeenth and eighteenth centuries, the *noblesse d'épée* and the *noblesse de robe* tended more and more to coalesce, partly because the latter's sons frequently engaged in a career in the army, but chiefly through intermarriage, for the large dowries of the daughters of the *Parlementaires* soon overcame the pride in rank of the impoverished members of the *noblesse d'épée*.

Closely allied to the *noblesse de robe*, and yet forming a separate body, were the King's ministers and what one might call the upper civil servants—the members of the various Royal councils, and the representatives of the central government in the provinces, the *Intendants*. These men were also of middle-class origin, and generally had some sort of legal training; sometimes they had served in the *Parlements* before entering upon an administrative career. By their education and training they were far better suited to work an increasingly complicated administrative machine than nobles who despised any other profession but the army. Moreover, they were less likely than the once powerful great lords to abuse the authority which the King gave them, since they were entirely dependent on him for the continuance of his good graces. These bourgeois ministers and administrators came fully into their own in the second half of the century under Louis XIV, who was determined not to have any *grands seigneurs* in posts of responsibility, and therefore sought his ministers and upper civil servants among the members of the middle class. As he wrote in his instructions to the Dauphin:

> Il n'était pas de mon intérêt de prendre des sujets [1] d'une qualité plus éminente. . . . Il m'importait qu'ils ne conçussent pas eux-mêmes de plus hautes espérances que celles qu'il me plairait de leur donner; ce qui est difficile aux gens d'une grande naissance. (*Mémoires*, p. 30.)

Despite the jealous rage of the great noblemen, these new bourgeois ministers were loaded with favours by Louis XIV. They were allowed to nominate their sons as their successors,

[1] Persons.

and thus their posts became settled in the family. They saw their families ascend into the aristocracy: Le Tellier handed on his post to his son, the Marquis de Louvois; Colbert, the son of a merchant of Rheims, was succeeded by his son, the Marquis de Seignelay. Colbert and Louvois are both said to have left the enormous sum of ten million *livres* (something like £800,000 in the money of the time). Because of the wealth and power of their fathers, the daughters of these bourgeois ministers were quickly snapped up by great noblemen.

Yet, despite their wealth and power, these bourgeois ministers were still uncertain of themselves; they saw above them a higher class, the old *noblesse d'épée*, and their great desire was to cover up their bourgeois origins and to be assimilated into the aristocracy. Like Colbert, many bourgeois, instead of being content to acquire noble rank by the ordinary means of purchasing *lettres de noblesse*, would pretend that their families were originally aristocratic, and that their rank had only temporarily been lost through a member of the family engaging in trade. They would therefore appeal to the courts to be 'rehabilitated', that is, to have their noble rank 'restored'. This practice explains a sarcastic passage in La Bruyère:

> *Réhabilitations*, mot en usage dans les tribunaux, qui a fait vieillir et rendu gothique [1] celui de *lettres de noblesse*, autrefois si français et si usité. Se faire réhabiliter suppose qu'un homme, devenu riche, originairement est noble, qu'il est d'une nécessité plus que morale qu'il le soit; qu'à la vérité, son père a pu déroger [2] ou par la charrue, ou par la houe, ou par la malle,[3] ou par les livrées; mais qu'il ne s'agit pour lui que de rentrer dans les premiers [4] droits de ses ancêtres, et de continuer les armes de sa maison, les mêmes pourtant qu'il a fabriquées, et tout autres que celles de sa vaisselle d'étain [5]; qu'en un mot, les lettres de noblesse ne lui conviennent plus; qu'elles n'honorent que le roturier, c'est-à-dire celui qui cherche encore le secret de devenir riche. (*Les Caractères*, xiv. 3.)

[1] Archaic.
[2] 'Faire des actions indignes d'un homme noble.'
[3] The basket in which pedlars carried their wares.
[4] Original.
[5] Which he used when he was still poor.

The bourgeois ministers of Louis XIV were merely large-scale examples of the rise of the middle classes to wealth and high social position.

So far we have seen how the wealth accumulated by the middle classes through trade and industry was drained off into the acquisition of posts in the administration and judiciary. It remains to examine what other uses were made of the wealth which trade and industry put in their hands. The sale of *rentes* and *offices* was not the only way in which the wealth of the middle classes helped to satisfy the Crown's incessant need for money. This need, ever more pressing as the cost of the court, of the administration and of wars grew, was met in a more direct fashion by an army of tax-gatherers who battened on the Treasury and still more on the people of France. They helped to provide for the money-needs of the Crown, but at a heavy price to the community at whose expense they built up their vast fortunes.

The urgent necessity of raising money, and the general chaos in the system of tax-collection, provided opportunities for all kinds of men to make fortunes. Outwardly at least, these *financiers*, as they were called, formed two distinct groups. There were, first, those who held posts in the civil service: the various high officials of the Treasury, and the officials in the provinces to whom the *taille* was paid over on its way to its final destination in Paris. These men bought their posts and could hand them on to their sons like any other *officiers*. In the confusion which reigned in the finances of France during the seventeenth century it was easy for them to build up for themselves tremendous fortunes; in addition to the commission which they received on the money they handled, they made large profits by such devices as advancing money at high rates of interest to an impecunious Treasury. Tallemant des Réaux, himself the son of a wealthy *financier*, has left famous portraits of these wealthy tax-gatherers who, starting often from the most humble origins, succeeded in making enormous fortunes, in buying estates and titles, and marrying their daughters into the aristocracy—despite the sarcastic comments of the noblemen on their sudden rise to wealth.

For instance:

> Bordier, aujourd'hui intendant des Finances, est fils d'un chandelier de la place Maubert, qui le fit étudier. Il fut quelque temps avocat; puis, s'étant jeté dans les affaires,[1] il y fit fortune et fut secrétaire du Conseil. . . . Bordier maria en 1659 sa nièce Liebaud, fille de sa sœur, à Lamezan, lieutenant des gendarmes.[2] Mme Pilou, voyant qu'on mettait des armes et des couronnes au carrosse, dit chez Mme Margonne, bonne amie de Bordier: 'Ma foi, cela sera plaisant de voir ses armoiries. Qu'y mettront-ils? Trois chandelles?' (*Historiettes*, iv. 262-3.)

Another Treasury official who at his death left four million *livres*, has his rise to wealth sketched by Tallemant:

> Feu La Bazinière, trésorier de l'Épargne, se nommait Macé Bertrand; il était fils d'un paysan d'Anjou, et à son avènement à Paris, il fut laquais chez le président Gayan: c'était même un fort sot garçon, mais il fallait qu'il fût né aux finances. Après, il fut clerc chez un procureur, ensuite commis,[3] et insensiblement il parvint à être trésorier de l'Épargne. (*Ibid.*, iv. 297.)

Some of these *financiers* were, we see, of very humble origin; others came from the wealthier sections of the middle class. The greatest figure among the latter was Nicolas Fouquet, the embodiment of the rich and intelligent bourgeoisie of the time, unhampered by any scruples: his bold ambition was summed up in his motto, *Quo non ascendam?* The rise of his family illustrates the fortunes of the successful members of the middle classes of the time. Grandson of a merchant of Nantes, whose wealth enabled his son to purchase a post in the Paris *Parlement*, Nicolas Fouquet belonged both to the *noblesse de robe*, through his post of *Procureur général* in the Paris *Parlement*, and to the world of the *financiers*. He finally reached the post of *Surintendant des Finances*, and for a number of years, until Louis XIV had him arrested, he was all-powerful. The grandson of a merchant had the great lords and ladies of the court at his feet: he lent them money and gave them pensions, and could

[1] 'Les affaires du roi' (i.e. tax-collecting).
[2] Troops of the royal household.
[3] A high official.

therefore count on their support. His magnificent château and gardens at Vaux-le-Vicomte gave a foretaste of the splendours of Versailles, till at last his career was brought to a sudden end by his arrest and trial in 1661.

Besides the Treasury officials, there was an even larger group of *financiers* who derived a living from the money needs of the Crown. It is true that until they had succeeded in making their pile, the lot of many of these *financiers* was very wretched; and, of course, the brilliant schemes which they worked out did not always bring them the wealth for which they had hoped. The class which found it hardest to make their fortune was that of the *donneurs d'avis*, men who would rack their brains to think of some new way of taxing the people, or else to discover and reveal some method by which the Treasury was being defrauded. Once they had hit upon a scheme, they would proceed to lay it before the authorities. If they had the good fortune to have their idea accepted, they would be suitably rewarded, for half the annual revenue produced by their ingenuity went into their pockets. Naturally, the *donneurs d'avis* were not very popular with the taxpayer, witness La Bruyère's sarcastic portrait:

> Laissez faire *Ergaste*, et il exigera un droit de tous ceux qui boivent de l'eau de la rivière, ou qui marchent sur la terre ferme; il sait convertir en or jusques aux roseaux, aux joncs et à l'ortie. Il écoute tous les avis, et propose ceux qu'il a écoutés. Le prince ne donne aux autres qu'aux dépens d'Ergaste, et ne leur fait de grâces [1] que celles qui lui étaient dues. C'est une faim insatiable d'avoir et de posséder; il trafiquerait des arts et des sciences, et mettrait en parti [2] jusqu'à l'harmonie. Il faudrait, s'il en était cru, que le peuple, pour avoir le plaisir de le voir riche, de lui voir une meute et une écurie, pût perdre le souvenir de la musique d'*Orphée*, et se contenter de la sienne. (*Les Caractères*, vi. 28.)

In the nature of things, the career of the *donneur d'avis* was highly precarious, as everything depended on his schemes being accepted by the authorities. More important as a class,

1 'Confer favours upon them.'
2 'Lay a tax which would be farmed out.'

and even more unpopular, were the tax-farmers, to whom the King farmed out the collection of the indirect taxes, and even, at one period of the century, the *taille*. These tax-farmers were known by a variety of names: *partisans* or *traitants* (because they made a *parti* or *traité*, i.e. an agreement, with the King about their respective shares in the revenue which was to be collected), and finally *fermiers-généraux*. The reputation of the tax-farmers was at its very lowest in the seventeenth century. In a country in which social distinction still counted for so much, it seemed to most of their contemporaries an intolerable scandal that such low-born fellows should form the wealthiest section of society. Besides, it was notorious that their enormous wealth was often due to fraud and to remorseless squeezing of the taxpayer. The greater the distress of the country, the greater the profits of the tax-farmers, for in addition to collecting indirect taxes they advanced money to the government at high rates of interest; the greater the Treasury's need of money, the greater the profits to be made.

One could fill whole chapters with passages from well-known French authors of the seventeenth century dealing with the evil practices and scandalous wealth of the tax-farmers. First, the preacher who laments the change from the good old days when wealth was the reward of honest toil:

> S'enrichir par une longue épargne ou par un travail assidu, c'était l'ancienne route que l'on suivait dans la simplicité des premiers siècles; mais de nos jours on a découvert des chemins raccourcis et bien plus commodes. Une commission [1] qu'on exerce, un avis qu'on donne, un parti [2] où l'on entre, mille autres moyens que vous connaissez, voilà ce que l'empressement et l'impatience d'avoir a mis en usage. En effet, c'est par là qu'on fait des progrès surprenants; par là qu'on voit fructifier au centuple son talent et son industrie; par là qu'en peu d'années, qu'en peu de mois on se trouve comme transfiguré, et que, de la poussière où l'on rampait, on s'élève jusque sur le pinacle. (Bourdaloue, *Sermon sur les richesses*.)

[1] 'Un emploi qu'on exerce comme y ayant été commis pour un temps' (in the machinery of tax-collection).

[2] Company of tax-farmers.

Another famous picture of the outlook of the *financiers* of the period is to be found in one of Boileau's satires:

Veux-tu voir tous les grands à ta porte courir?
Dit un père à son fils dont le poil va fleurir.
Prends-moi le bon parti. Laisse-là tous les livres.
Cent francs au denier cinq,[1] combien font-ils?—Vingt livres.
—C'est bien dit. Va, tu sais tout ce qu'il faut savoir.
Que de biens,[2] que d'honneurs sur toi s'en vont pleuvoir!
Exerce-toi, mon fils, dans ces hautes sciences,
Prends, au lieu d'un Platon, le *Guidon des Finances*,[3]
Sache quelle province enrichit les traitants,[4]
Combien le sel au Roi peut fournir tous les ans.
Endurcis-toi le cœur. Sois arabe, corsaire,
Injuste, violent, sans foi, double, faussaire.
Ne va point sottement faire le généreux,
Engraisse-toi, mon fils, du suc des malheureux,
Et, trompant de Colbert la prudence importune,
Va par tes cruautés mériter la fortune . . .
Quiconque est riche est tout. Sans sagesse, il est sage,
Il a sans rien savoir la science en partage.
Il a l'esprit, le cœur, le mérite, le rang,
La vertu, la valeur, la dignité, le sang.
Il est aimé des grands, il est chéri des belles.
Jamais surintendant ne trouva de cruelles.[5]
L'or même à la laideur donne un teint de beauté,
Mais tout devient affreux avec la pauvreté.
C'est ainsi qu'à son fils un usurier habile
Trace vers la richesse une route facile:
Et souvent tel y vient qui sait pour tout secret:
Cinq et quatre font neuf, ôtez deux, reste sept.[6]

(Satire VIII.)

An unforgettable picture of the rise of these *financiers* to wealth, power and even social standing is to be found in the

[1] A *denier* was a twelfth of a *sou*. The expression 'au denier cinq' was an old way of stating interest-rates (1 *denier* interest for 5 *deniers* capital, i.e. 20 per cent.).

[2] Wealth.

[3] A manual on taxation.

[4] Tax-farmers.

[5] An allusion to Fouquet's success with the ladies.

[6] i.e. addition and subtraction.

chapter, 'Des biens de fortune', of La Bruyère's *Caractères.* First, the moralist's denunciation of their lust for wealth:

> Il y a des âmes sales, pétries de boue et d'ordure, éprises du gain et de l'intérêt, comme les belles âmes le sont de la gloire et de la vertu; capables d'une seule volupté, qui est celle d'acquérir ou de ne point perdre; curieuses et avides du denier dix,[1] uniquement occupées de leur débiteurs, toujours inquiètes sur le rabais ou le décri [2] des monnaies, enfoncées et comme abîmées dans les contrats, les titres et les parchemins. De telles gens ne sont ni parents, ni amis, ni citoyens, ni chrétiens, ni peut-être des hommes: ils ont de l'argent. (vi. 58.)

He draws the portrait of a lackey who rises to wealth by the most unscrupulous methods, and finishes up enjoying high social rank, and even respected as a churchwarden:

> *Sosie,* de la livrée, a passé, par une petite recette, à une sous-ferme [3]; et, par les concussions, la violence et l'abus qu'il fait de ses *pouvoirs,* il s'est enfin, sur les ruines de plusieurs familles, élevé à quelque grade.[4] Devenu noble par une charge, il ne lui manquait que d'être homme de bien: une place de marguillier a fait ce prodige. (vi. 15.)

Next, the famous portrait which contrasts the arrival at church of a poor woman, with her entry when her husband has made his pile:

> *Arfure* cheminait seule et à pied vers le grand portique de Saint***, entendait de loin le sermon d'un carme ou d'un docteur [5] qu'elle ne voyait qu'obliquement, et dont elle perdait bien des paroles. Sa vertu était obscure, et sa dévotion connue comme sa personne. Son mari est entré dans le *huitième denier* [6]: quelle monstrueuse fortune en moins de six années! Elle n'arrive à l'église que dans un char; on lui porte une lourde queue; l'orateur s'interrompt pendant qu'elle se place; elle le voit de front, n'en perd pas une seule parole ni le moindre geste; il y a une brigue entre les

[1] Interest at 10 per cent.
[2] Allusion to the reduction in value (*rabais*) or ban on the use (*décri*) of various coins, an expedient frequently used by the Treasury in the seventeenth century.
[3] Two stages in the machinery for collecting indirect taxes.
[4] Rank.
[5] 'Docteur en théologie.'
[6] An indirect tax which was farmed out.

prêtres pour la confesser; tous veulent l'absoudre, et le curé l'emporte. (vi. 16.)

The moralist, however, finds one consolation: these *financiers* may make money easily, but many of them lose it just as quickly. Their speculations may fail, or the government may make them disgorge their wealth:

> Les P.T.S.[1] nous font sentir toutes les passions l'une après l'autre: l'on commence par le mépris, à cause de leur obscurite[2]; on les envie ensuite, on les hait, on les craint, on les estime quelquefois, et on les respecte; l'on vit assez pour finir à leur égard par la compassion. (vi. 14.)

Despite the unhappy fate of individual members of their class, the tax-farmers and *financiers*, starting out from bourgeois or even more humble homes, formed the wealthiest section of society in seventeenth century France. Their rise, together with that of the other prosperous sections of the middle class, brought about a gradual transformation of French society. All these wealthy bourgeois despised their humble origins: in a society in which noble rank, with the social and material privileges which it conferred, seemed the highest prize, their one desire was to rise into the aristocracy. This their wealth enabled them to do, either in their own person or in that of their sons and daughters: *lettres de noblesse*, an official post or an estate could bring noble rank and a title to them or their sons; a marriage with an impecunious nobleman, whose aristocratic prejudices were forgotten in contemplation of a large dowry, would soon provide a title for a daughter. Like Monsieur Jourdain in the *Bourgeois Gentilhomme*, many a *nouveau riche* might say: 'J'ai du bien[3] assez pour ma fille, je n'ai besoin que d'honneur, et je la veux faire marquise.' (Act iii. Sc. 12.)

This new social phenomenon produced a corresponding change in the general outlook of society. Up till this time social rank had been determined largely by birth: high rank depended on possessing noble ancestors. Now that noble rank could be bought, all values seemed reversed. The importance

[1] *Partisans* (tax-farmers). [2] Humble origin. [3] Wealth.

of money in social relationships which now stood out clearly is a new phenomenon noted by all the moralists of the age. The growth of trade and industry, and the uses made of the capital thus accumulated, had profoundly modified the existing social hierarchy and the whole attitude towards it. The power of money in a society which was hitherto accustomed only to the power conferred by noble birth, is noted with an almost naïve astonishment by La Bruyère: 'Si l'on ne le voyait de ses yeux, pourrait-on jamais s'imaginer l'étrange[1] disproportion que le plus ou moins de pièces de monnaie met entre les hommes?' (*Les Caractères*, vi. 5.) The omnipotence of money is described by Boileau with an astonishment bordering on indignation:

> L'argent! l'argent! dit-on; sans lui tout est stérile;
> La vertu sans l'argent n'est qu'un meuble[2] inutile;
> L'argent en honnête homme érige un scélérat;
> L'argent seul au Palais peut faire un magistrat . . .
>
> (Épître V.)

Thus the coming predominance of wealth over birth is clearly visible in outline in France long before 1700. The old social hierarchy based on birth was already beginning to crumble, now that money enabled bourgeois *parvenus* to buy their way into the aristocracy. And yet the old hierarchy was not destroyed; it was merely modified by this influx of wealthy bourgeois. The wealthy section of the middle class had no thought of doing away with the aristocracy and its privileges. Gradually, in the next century, their outlook was to change; they would in time cast aside their feeling of inferiority in face of the aristocracy. In the seventeenth century, and for many years to come, their one aim was not to abolish the aristocracy but to raise themselves and their families up into this higher class. Directly or indirectly it was trade and industry that had brought them wealth, but such callings were a sign of inferiority. Monsieur Jourdain summed up their attitude in four words: 'Je veux être gentilhomme.' Thus the old social hierarchy, with its gulf between *noble* and *roturier*, still persisted as before.

[1] Extraordinary. [2] Encumbrance.

Only very gradually, as 1789 approached, did the wealthy middle class begin to wish to abolish the gulf, instead of leaping over it. In the seventeenth century wealth had already brought about great changes; but only another century of economic progress could produce the Revolution of 1789 and the abolition of the distinction between *noble* and *roturier*.

CHAPTER III

THE NOBILITY

In the last chapter we have already dealt with the newer sections of the French aristocracy in the seventeenth century: all those who obtained their noble rank by purchase or by the possession of an official post. It only remains to consider the oldest and most exalted section of the aristocracy, the *noblesse d'épée*. The seventeenth century descendant of the old feudal nobility was in many ways an anachronistic survival from an earlier age. To understand the position and problems of this class it is once again necessary to make a short excursion into the past. We have already seen the place occupied by the nobility in the hierarchy of feudalism. At the top of the pyramid came the suzerain or overlord—the King of France. Beneath him came vassals who, in return for homage and military service, received from their overlord a *fief*, or rights over so much territory. Beneath these vassals came a series of smaller noblemen, each of whom owed homage to his overlord and received in return a fief from him. Over this fief the vassal possessed not merely rights of property, but also of administration and justice. From the peasants on his fief the lord raised taxes, and exacted services (both agricultural and military) as well as various payments in money and in kind.

In feudal times, when land was almost the only source of wealth, and life was in general simple, not to say primitive, the nobleman could generally manage on the income, in money and in kind, which he derived from his manors; but the gradual development of trade meant that a new form of wealth was created—money, capital—in which the nobleman had no share, since it was impossible for him to engage in trade or industry, unless (as was unthinkable) he renounced his noble rank. At the same time, the general progress of civilization was making the nobleman desire a more luxurious standard of living—fine clothes, a new and more comfortable château and so forth. But in the sixteenth century, at the very moment when, with the Renaissance and the development of court-life, the nobleman needed more money, his income suddenly began to shrink. The arrival of large quantities of gold, and especially of silver, from the mines of the New World, produced a monetary revolution in France as in other European countries: prices rose very rapidly, sometimes by as much as 400 per cent. This fall in the purchasing-power of money meant that those with fixed incomes were badly hit. A considerable part of the income which the nobleman received from his estates was paid in cash; moreover, the amount had often been fixed several centuries before, when the value of money was much greater. The sudden rise in prices in the sixteenth century had catastrophic effects for most French noblemen. Many were forced to mortgage their estates to wealthy bourgeois, and then had to part with them to their creditors. Even those who were not completely ruined were generally very hard hit. The impoverishment of the nobility as a class is one of the most important factors in the social history of seventeenth century France, and one which, as we shall see, had in its turn a profound influence on the political developments of the period.

It would, of course, be a mistake to imagine that the nobility formed a homogeneous bloc. As in all the other classes of society, there existed very wide differences in status. The memoirs of the period are full of tedious accounts of disputes as to rank and precedence between the various grades of the hierarchy. Sometimes these quarrels ended in blows and other very unseemly incidents: a less dramatic, but none the less amusing incident of this type is related in a letter of Mme de Sévigné. The woman whom she was so pleased to see snubbed by her friend was a duchess, but happened to come from a family of the *noblesse de robe*:

> Je vis hier une chose chez Mademoiselle [1] qui me fit plaisir. La Gêvres arrive, belle, charmante et de bonne grâce; Mme d'Arpajon était au-dessus de moi. Je pense qu'elle s'attendait que je lui dusse offrir ma place; ma foi, je lui en devais de l'autre jour, je lui payai comptant, et ne branlai pas. Made-

[1] Daughter of Gaston d'Orléans and cousin of Louis XIV.

> moiselle était au lit[1]: elle fut donc contrainte de se mettre au bas de l'estrade; cela est fâcheux. On apporte à boire à Mademoiselle, il faut donner la serviette. Je vois Mme de Gêvres qui dégante sa main maigre; je pousse Mme d'Arpajon: elle m'entend et se dégante; et d'une très bonne grâce, elle avance un pas, coupe la Gêvres, et prend, et donne la serviette. La Gêvres en eut toute la honte, et est demeurée toute penaude. Elle était montée sur l'estrade, elle avait ôté ses gants, et tout cela pour voir donner la serviette de plus près par Mme d'Arpajon. Ma bonne, je suis méchante, cela m'a réjouie; c'est bien employé. A-t-on jamais vu accourir pour ôter à Mme d'Arpajon, qui est dans la ruelle,[2] un petit honneur qui lui vient tout naturellement? (13 March 1671.)

Innumerable other incidents of this type could be quoted to show the tremendous importance which the aristocracy of the time attached to keeping up the dignity of their rank, even in the most trifling details of everyday life.

Roughly speaking, the different sections of the *noblesse d'épée* can be placed in the following order. At the head of the aristocracy came the *princes du sang*, in other words all the relatives of the King, apart from his immediate family; amongst the *princes du sang* the most powerful family was that of the Condés. Next to them came the *princes légitimés*, the illegitimate children, or descendants of illegitimate children, of French Kings: their position was very clearly differentiated from that of the *princes du sang*, and in practice they stood little higher than any other great nobleman. Another strange category near the summit of the hierarchy was that of the *princes étrangers*, such as the Duc de Bouillon, who was an independent prince at Sedan, and at the same time, through holding a post in the French army, was a subject of the King of France. Beneath these again came the families who boasted the title of *prince*, but whose claim had never received official recognition, and for whom the title was merely an ornament.

Legally speaking, the rank which followed immediately upon the King and the royal family was that of *duc et pair*: the holders of this title were honoured with the appellation of

[1] The normal way for a lady to receive visitors in the seventeenth century.
[2] The space between the bed and the wall (see p. 222).

cousins du roi, their wives had the right to be seated on a *tabouret* in the Queen's presence, while they also had the privilege of driving into the courtyard of the Louvre in their carriages. Beneath the *princes du sang*, *princes étrangers* and *ducs et pairs* came the mass of the French aristocracy. For them it is quite impossible to establish a hierarchy based on titles, for many of these had been usurped by *nouveaux riches*, so that the titles of *comte*, *marquis* and *baron* were often quite meaningless terms by the seventeenth century. Titles were attached to an estate, and when an estate changed hands, the new proprietor acquired the title. Thus it came about that a title such as *marquis* might merely serve to cover up a fortune of very recent acquisition. That is why Mme de Sévigné speaks with such contempt of it in a letter to her cousin, the Comte de Bussy-Rabutin:

> Vous ne voulez plus qu'on vous appelle comte; et pourquoi, mon cher cousin? Ce n'est point mon avis. Je n'ai encore vu personne qui se soit trouvé déshonoré de ce titre. Les comtes de Saint-Aignan, de Sault, du Lude, de Grignan, de Fiesque, de Brancas et mille autres l'ont porté sans chagrin. Il n'a point été profané comme celui de marquis. Quand un homme veut usurper un titre, ce n'est point celui de comte, c'est celui de marquis, qui est tellement gâté qu'en vérité je pardonne à ceux qui l'ont abandonné. (20 December 1675.)

In discussing the position of the French nobility of the seventeenth century, one broad distinction can be made. There was a great gap between those nobles who frequented the court (*noblesse de cour*) and those who remained on their estates in the provinces (*noblesse de province*). The latter might sometimes be comparatively well off: their income from their estates and from feudal dues could provide them with a comfortable, if undistinguished existence among their peasants, looking after their estates and seeing to the collection of their rents and feudal dues. An amusing and somewhat ironical account of the life of a nobleman and his wife on their estates is given in a poem chiding M. and Mme de Sévigné for their long absence in Brittany: it must be remembered that to their

friends in Paris exile in the provinces, even if self-imposed, appeared horribly dull:

Salut à vous, gens de campagne,
A vous, immeubles [1] de Bretagne,
Attachés à votre maison
Au delà de toute raison:
Salut à tous deux, quoique indignes
De nos saluts et de ces lignes;
Mais un vieux reste d'amitié
Nous fait avoir de vous pitié,
Voyant le plus beau de votre âge
Se passer en votre village,
Et que vous perdez aux Rochers [2]
Des moments à tous autres chers.
Peut-être que vos cœurs tranquilles,
Censurant l'embarras des villes,
Goûtent aux champs en liberté
Le repos et l'oisiveté.
Peut-être aussi que le ménage [3]
Que vous faites dans le village
Fait aller votre revenu
Où jamais il ne fût venu:
Ce sont raisons fort pertinentes,
D'être aux champs pour doubler ses rentes,
D'entendre là parler de soi,
Conjointement avec le Roi,
Soit aux jours, ou bien à l'église,
Où le prêtre dit à sa guise:
'Nous prierons tous notre grand Dieu
Pour le Roi, et Monsieur du lieu;
Nous prierons aussi pour Madame,
Qu'elle accouche sans sage-femme,
Prions pour les nobles enfants
Qu'ils auront d'ici à cent ans.
Si quelqu'un veut prendre la ferme,
Monseigneur dit qu'elle est à terme,
Et que l'on s'assemble à midi.

[1] Literally 'real estate'; here used jokingly for people who will not budge from their estates.
[2] Les Rochers was the name of their estate.
[3] Economical life which you lead.

11. *A. Bosse,* Le mariage à la ville: le contrat

12. *A. Bosse,* Le mariage à la ville: la visite à l'accouchée

13. *Philippe de Champaigne,* Le prévôt des marchands et les échevins de Paris

14. *A. Bosse,* Le savetier

Or disons tous *De profundi*
Pour tous messeigneurs ses ancêtres',
Quoiqu'ils soient en enfer peut-être.
Certes ce sont là des honneurs
Que l'on ne reçoit point ailleurs:
Sans compter l'octroi de la fête,
De lever tant sur chaque bête,
De donner des permissions,
D'être chef aux processions,
De commander que l'on s'amasse
Ou pour la pêche, ou pour la chasse;
Rouer de coups qui ne fait pas
Corvée de charrue ou de bras. . . .

(*Lettres de Mme de Sévigné* . . ., i. 348-9.)

In these lines we see the nobleman enjoying amidst his peasants the privileges attached to his rank; we also see him looking after the letting of one of his farms, compelling his peasants to carry out their *corvées*, or to act as beaters when he went hunting. Indeed, one of the chief occupations of a nobleman who lived in the provinces was to exercise to the full his exclusive privilege of hunting over his estate.

No doubt many a seventeenth century nobleman led a pleasant, if somewhat monotonous existence in the provinces; but it would be wholly false to imagine that the lot of the great majority of the *noblesse de province* was always commensurate with the exalted position which the nobleman enjoyed among his peasants. The sudden rise in prices which took place in the sixteenth century bore most hardly on the minor nobility, who, of course, formed the great majority of the French aristocracy. Since the Middle Ages the value of feudal dues and rents paid in money had steadily declined along with the purchasing-power of money; by now only those feudal dues and rents which were paid in kind were really valuable. Burdened with debts and mortgages, the lesser nobles were often compelled to dispose of their land to peasants, or more often to wealthy bourgeois. Lack of money made it impossible to provide dowries for their daughters, or to purchase a commission in the army for their sons. Often the only thing which distinguished them from the peasants around them was their noble rank.

The *hobereau*, the small provincial nobleman, was heartily despised in Paris and at the court: Molière's *Georges Dandin* is only one of several comedies of the period which makes fun of members of this class. Too poor to bring up his family properly or to afford a career in the army, he languished on his diminutive estate, living on what he could wring out of the peasants in feudal dues, and because of his very poverty, clinging tenaciously to his only possession, his noble rank. La Bruyère sums up the contempt in which he was generally held in the following lines:

> Le noble de province, inutile à sa patrie, à sa famille et à lui-même, souvent sans toit, sans habit et sans aucun mérite, répète dix fois le jour qu'il est gentilhomme, traite les fourrures [1] et les mortiers [2] de bourgeoisie, occupé toute sa vie de ses parchemins et de ses titres qu'il ne changerait pas contre les masses [3] d'un chancelier. (*Les Caractères*, xi. 130.)

The contrast between the position of the well-to-do and the impoverished sections of the country gentry is well brought out in a contemporary account of a journey which included first a halt at a most primitive and dilapidated château:

> Nous arrivâmes à une heure de nuit par la neige. On nous reçut dans une salle plus basse que la cour, où je suis assurée que les murailles étaient humides durant la canicule; elle était décarrelée en beaucoup d'endroits, en sorte qu'on n'y pouvait aller qu'à courbettes.[4] Pendant qu'on était allé abattre les arbres dont on devait nous chauffer, on nous fit asseoir dans de grandes chaises qui n'étaient pas garnies, devant une cheminée où il n'y avait point de feu. . . . Un quart d'heure après nous vîmes deux paysans rapporter sur leur cou une voiture de bois couvert de neige qu'ils mirent sur les chenets; une servante de peine vint ensuite avec une botte de paille si mouillée qu'elle ne la put jamais allumer; et cela faillit à nous faire étouffer de fumée.

[1] Graduates of a University, from the fur on their gowns.
[2] The judges of the *Parlements*, from the *mortiers* worn by *présidents*.
[3] The maces borne before the Chancellor.
[4] 'Except by leaping (like a horse).'

> Enfin elle fut contrainte de recourir aux paillasses des lits, et tout ce que cela put faire après que nous eûmes longtemps attendu, ce fut de faire fondre la neige qui était sur le bois, et de faire une espèce de mare qui, nous gagnant les pieds, nous fit reculer jusques au milieu de la salle. . . .
>
> Le souper fut aussi méchant que le feu: les potages n'étaient que de l'eau bouillie; de toute la viande qu'on servit, il n'y avait rien qui ne fût vivant quand nous étions arrivés; le pain était frais et n'était pas cuit, le vin était aigre et trouble, le linge n'était pas seulement humide, il était mouillé; et la chaleur des potages faisait fumer la nappe. Ce nuage épais acheva de nous ôter le peu de lumière que rendait une petite chandelle de vingt-quatre à la livre. Un autre désagrément de ce repas, c'était que les cuillers (qui véritablement étaient d'argent) étaient de l'épaisseur de l'oripeau[1]; pour moi, qui ne suis pas heureux, il m'en tomba une entre les mains qui était à moitié rompue, de sorte qu'en la retirant de ma bouche, elle s'accrocha à ma lèvre de dessus et faillit à me la déchirer. . . .

What a contrast between this decayed and inhospitable château and that in which the travellers arrived the following evening, with its air of prosperity and comfort:

> On nous faisait la plus grande chère du monde avec le plus de magnificence et de propreté.[2] Il y avait dans cette maison une quantité de vaisselle d'argent qu'on ne trouvait pas dans une autre maison de province; le linge était d'une finesse incomparable, les meubles y étaient à l'antique, mais si conservés d'ailleurs qu'on ne reconnaissait l'ancienneté qu'à la richesse des étoffes, dont on ne faisait plus de pareilles. Enfin cette maison et celle dont nous étions partis pour y arriver étaient les deux extrémités. (Bussy-Rabutin, *Mémoires*, i. 70-6.)

For the French *hobereau* and the younger sons of a moderately well-to-do nobleman there was no escape from a life of poverty. In England, at the same period, the younger sons of noblemen would often try a career in trade or industry, and finally succeed in making a fortune, especially overseas. In France the prejudice against trade among the nobility was too strong; the efforts of such French statesmen as Richelieu and Colbert to encourage a similar movement were a failure. If

[1] Tinsel.

[2] Elegance.

the *hobereau* or younger son could not manage to afford a commission in the army or to obtain a comfortable post in the Church, he preferred either to vegetate on his tiny estate, or to enter the service of some great nobleman.

Hand in hand with the nobility's decline in economic status since the Middle Ages had gone the loss of its political and administrative powers. In feudal times the lord of the manor had possessed almost complete judicial and administrative powers on his estates, and the great barons had played an important political role in the life of the country. Since that period the Crown had gradually, step by step, taken away these prerogatives. In seventeenth century England the members of the aristocracy played their part in the government of the country through the House of Lords, while the country squires were entrenched in the House of Commons; from the time of Elizabeth down to the nineteenth century local government remained largely in the hands of the justices of the peace, drawn from the ranks of the gentry. In France things were very different. Just as the nobility was deprived of any role in the central government, so all influence in local affairs was taken from it by the *Intendant*, the agent of the central government in the province. The only vestige of its former powers which remained to the nobility in the seventeenth century was its judicial rights. Yet here again the monarchy had so encroached on them in the course of the centuries that what remained of them, while still vexatious to the peasant, was of no great advantage to the nobleman. It was only in backward provinces like Auvergne that the nobleman still retained something of his feudal privileges: there he was free to rob, torture and murder with impunity until in the second half of the century the royal power came to restore order and bring security to the inhabitants of the province. Here is an account of how one nobleman tyrannized over the inhabitants on his estates:

> Pour exécuter ses desseins plus facilement et pour empêcher les murmures, il entretenait dans des tours douze scélérats dévoués à toute sorte de crimes, qu'il appelait ses douze apôtres, qui catéchisaient avec l'épée ou avec le bâton ceux qui étaient

> rebelles à sa loi, et faisaient de terribles violences lorsqu'ils avaient reçu la cruelle mission de leur maître. Il leur avait donné des noms fort apostoliques, appelant l'un Sans-Fiance, l'autre Brise-Tout, et ainsi du reste. . . . Sur la terreur que donnaient ces noms effroyables, il imposait des sommes assez considérables sur les viandes [1] qu'on mange ordinairement, et comme on pratiquait un peu trop d'abstinence, il tournait l'imposition sur ceux qui n'en mangeaient pas. Le plus grand revenu qu'il avait, était celui de la justice: il faisait pour la moindre chose emprisonner et juger des misérables, et les obligeait de racheter leurs peines par argent. Il eût voulu que tous ses justiciables eussent été de son humeur, et les engageait souvent à de méchantes actions, pour les tous faire payer après, avec beaucoup de rigueur. Enfin personne n'a jamais tant fait et n'a jamais tant souhaité, et n'a jamais tant profité des crimes que lui. Non seulement il faisait payer les mauvaises actions qu'on avait faites, il fallait encore acheter la liberté d'en faire, et lorsqu'on avait de l'argent à lui donner, on pouvait être criminel ou le devenir. (Fléchier, *Mémoires sur les grands jours d'Auvergne en 1665*, pp. 261-2.)

Besides the exercise of fraud, blackmail and physical violence, another favourite occupation of the wilder nobles in the provinces was turning out counterfeit money. In Anjou, for instance, a certain count was notorious for this and other crimes:

> Le comte de Monsoreau était un homme fort violent, un grand faux-monnayeur et grand violent. Il avait vingt satellites qui rançonnaient tout le voisinage. . . . Il se rencontra une fois chez un hôtelier à qui un sergent vint apporter un exploit.[2] 'Comment! coquin', lui dit-il, 'apporter un exploit à un homme chez qui je loge!' Il le prend, dit qu'il le fallait condamner à être pendu, fait des juges de ses coupe-jarrets: on le condamne. 'Il faut', dit-il, 'le confesser, et, pour le communier, lui faire avaler son exploit.' . . . Effectivement ils lui firent avaler son exploit en petits morceaux, et puis le laissèrent aller. (Tallemant, *Historiettes*, vi. 338.)

Finally the count came into conflict with justice when his coining activities and other crimes came to light; he fled to England, where he died in exile after being executed in effigy.

[1] Foods. [2] Writ.

Such violence, reminiscent of the disorder of feudal times, was gradually suppressed in the course of the seventeenth century as the royal power reached even into the remotest provinces. Another feudal survival, the duel, tended in the course of the century to fall more and more into discredit. In the first half of our period, despite the death penalty imposed by laws issued under Henry IV, despite the execution of the famous duellist, Bouteville, in 1627 by order of Richelieu, the practice was still extremely common. Duels took place after the most futile quarrels; often several people were engaged on each side, with the result that casualties were apt to be heavy. A good idea of what a duel was like is to be found in the memoirs of Bussy-Rabutin. The events which he here relates took place in 1638:

> Un jour, au sortir de la comédie [1] de l'hôtel de Bourgogne avec quatre de mes amis, un jeune gentilhomme gascon, appelé Busc, dont le père était capitaine au régiment de Navarre, me tira à part pour me demander s'il était vrai que le comte de Thianges, cousin germain de mon père, eût dit qu'il était un ivrogne, et son cadet un fou. Je lui répondis que je voyais si peu le comte de Thianges que je ne savais pas ce qu'il disait. Il me répliqua qu'il était mon oncle, et que, ne pouvant pas avoir cet éclaircissement avec lui à cause qu'il ne bougeait de la province, il s'adressait à moi.
>
> 'Ah, puisque vous voulez, lui dis-je, que je réponde pour lui, je vous dirai que quiconque le fait parler de la sorte a menti.'—'C'est mon frère, me dit-il, qui est un enfant.' 'Il lui faut donner le fouet, lui repartis-je; mais il a menti comme un grand homme.' Et en disant cela, nous mîmes l'épée à la main tous deux en même temps. Il n'avait qu'un de ses amis avec lui, et moi, j'en avais quatre, auxquels il s'en joignit encore d'autres, m'entendant nommer, lesquels mirent tous l'épée à la main et vinrent se ranger auprès de moi.

We see here the usual absurd quarrel, the ready acceptance of the challenge, and the haste with which all the friends rush to join in the fray. The arrangements for the duel were here

[1] Theatre.

somewhat complicated by the fact that, to prevent their duel being stopped by the authorities, the two protagonists moved into hiding, with the result that for two days they had some difficulty in making contact with one another:

> Enfin le troisième [jour], un gentilhomme que je ne connaissais point, et du nom duquel il ne me souvient plus, me vint trouver pour me dire qu'ayant appris que j'avais querelle avec Busc et que je le cherchais, il me venait offrir de m'apprendre où il était, pourvu que je me voulusse servir de lui, et que ne connaissant ni l'un ni l'autre que de réputation, il avait eu inclination de me servir. Je lui rendis mille grâces des marques de son amitié; je le priai de considérer que j'avais déjà quatre de mes amis auprès de moi, que ce serait une bataille si je recevais l'honneur qu'il me voulait faire; mais que je lui étais autant obligé que s'il l'avait fait. Il me témoigna être content de mes raisons; 'et puisque, me dit-il, monsieur, je ne puis être des vôtres, vous ne trouverez pas mauvais que j'aille offrir mes services à M. de Busc, et que je lui dise que vous êtes ici'. J'estimai le procédé de ce gentilhomme; nous nous embrassâmes, et je ne fus pas longtemps après cela sans voir Busc passer en carrosse devant mon logis avec quatre hommes, entre lesquels était mon aventurier.
>
> Je les suivis à cheval avec mes amis jusques auprès du Bourg-la-Reine, où, choisissant tous ensemble un endroit pour nous battre, nous vîmes venir à toute bride un cavalier qui criait de si loin qu'il se put faire entendre, 'Tout beau, messieurs, tout beau!' C'était l'Aigues qui, ayant eu avis de cette querelle, venait pour servir Busc.

The arrival of this latecomer meant that one nobleman had five supporters, while the other had four—a striking example of the readiness of the contemporary nobles to seize upon the slightest pretext for a duel. To avoid an unequal combat the two protagonists finally decided to escape from their friends, and to fight the matter out between them: the result of this futile quarrel was that the challenger received wounds from which he died six months later. (Bussy-Rabutin, *Mémoires*, i. 21-5.)

The passion for duelling gradually diminished in the course of the century, not so much because of the severity of the laws, but because it was increasingly condemned by public opinion.

Nevertheless, the *noblesse d'épée* did not lose the quality of which duelling was merely an offshoot, their military valour. Cut off from any share in the government of the country, despising a career in the Church as fit only for weaklings and younger sons, holding trade and industry beneath contempt, the French nobility continued in the only profession which custom and the government permitted it to follow.

It is true that for the nobleman military service was a moral obligation, not a legal duty; a certain proportion did not serve in the army, either because they found the career distasteful, or because they were too poor to purchase a commission. The great majority, however, were brought up from earliest childhood in preparation for a career in the army. After a few years at school or under a private tutor, they passed on to an *Académie* where the chief accomplishments acquired were fencing, riding, dancing and a smattering of mathematics, which was all the education required for an officer and a gentleman. At fifteen or sixteen their career in the army would begin. If he were poor, a nobleman would start in the ranks; if he had the necessary money, he would begin as a volunteer and finally purchase a commission. A career in the French army in the seventeenth century was in most cases productive of glory rather than of wealth. It is true that the higher officers who distinguished themselves could win the King's favour and lucrative pensions, but the vast majority of officers were brought to the verge of ruin by the expenses in which their career involved them.

This was true both of the great noblemen and of the 'gentilshommes indigents' whose names figure in the Treasury accounts as receiving grants of fifteen or twenty *livres* to keep body and soul together. The fault lay partly with the nobles themselves, for despite their impoverished state, despite debts and mortgages, it was a matter of honour to plunge still further into debt in order to equip oneself for each campaign. In the spring of 1672, when preparations were being made for the opening of the war against Holland, Mme de Sévigné wrote to her cousin:

On est au désespoir, on n'a pas un sou, on ne trouve rien à

emprunter, les fermiers ne payent point, on n'ose faire de la fausse monnaie, on ne voudrait pas se donner au diable, et cependant tout le monde s'en va à l'armée avec un équipage. De vous dire comment cela se fait, il n'est pas aisé. Le miracle des cinq pains n'est pas plus incompréhensible. (24 April 1672.)

The *équipage* which the courtiers managed, despite their debts, to get together, might include, according to the rank of the officer, large numbers of servants, a carriage, silver plate, quite apart from more practical things such as clothes and weapons. Two young Dutchmen who came to Paris in 1657 were told by one of their acquaintances of the enormous cost:

Il nous dit qu'il était fort difficile de pouvoir s'imaginer combien coûtait l'équipage d'un jeune gentilhomme, et qu'il l'avait expérimenté en celui de son fils qui allait faire sa première campagne en qualité de cornette de M. de la Ferté. Il lui avait donné 20 chevaux, un maître d'hôtel, quelques gentilshommes, pages, laquais et tout ce qui lui était nécessaire; mais dès qu'il a été au quartier, il a acheté cinq bidets pour y aller au fourrage et à la provision, car on ferait autrement souvent mauvaise chère. (De Villiers, *Journal*, pp. 178-9.)

Yet, if the financial embarrassment of the nobles was due in part to living beyond their means, it was also caused by the irregularity with which salaries and pensions were paid, and the ruinous expenses entailed by many high posts. A captain or colonel of a regiment had to pay his soldiers out of his own pocket when the Treasury failed to provide the necessary money. The governor of a fortress might have to find the funds to keep it in a good state of repair. Once their money had been spent in the King's service, only after endless negotiations and intrigues could they succeed in getting it back again from the Treasury. Even patience and influence were not always sufficient to regain the money which they had laid out. Thus the only career open to the nobility was not one which led to wealth, or even financial security; indeed, only the more fortunate ones could hope to avoid the ruin which a career in the army so frequently brought with it.

The income of the nobility from landed property, from both

rents and feudal dues, had fallen, as we have seen, very considerably. Moreover, their incomes had shrunk at the very moment when, with the development of the court and of social life in Paris, luxury, not to say extravagance, had developed to an extraordinary degree. The wealthier sections of the aristocracy, the *grands seigneurs*, were obliged to assume crushing burdens in order to keep up the state which was expected of them. A great nobleman's household was organized on the model of a small court. The hosts of servants were organized in a vast hierarchy; as wages were low and often irregularly paid, most of the servants helped themselves, and took what they could in kind. A realistic picture of their depredations is given in the following remarks of a wealthy nobleman of the period:

> Mon sommelier [1] dit que le vin lui appartient dès qu'il est à la barre,[2] et n'a point d'autre raison à m'alléguer sinon qu'on en use ainsi chez M. le Cardinal; le piqueur prétend que le lard est à lui dès qu'il en a levé deux tranches; le cuisinier n'est pas plus homme de bien qu'eux, ni l'écuyer, ni les cochers; sans parler du maître d'hôtel, qui est le voleur *major*; mais ce qui me chicane le plus, c'est que mes valets de chambre me disent: 'Monsieur, vous portez trop longtemps cet habit, il nous appartient.' (Tallemant, *Historiettes*, viii. 58.)

A great lord might have half a dozen noblemen in attendance upon him, half a dozen secretaries and as many valets, not to mention all the other servants necessary for the running of the household, and the twenty or thirty lackeys which his mansion housed. In addition, he would often have a military bodyguard, composed of noblemen, who accompanied him on foot or on horseback. Like the innumerable pages who were trained in the mansion of a *grand seigneur*, these were either younger sons of noble families or provincial *hobereaux*, who, too poor to branch out on their own, became, in a phrase with none of the modern associations of the word, 'les *domestiques* d'un grand seigneur'. Every great nobleman, especially in the first half of the century, possessed a band of these retainers

[1] Wine-butler.

[2] Piece of wood attached to the staves of a barrel to support the bottom.

who lived in his mansion at his expense, sought his help in obtaining minor posts in the army or at court, and were at his service in the case of quarrels with other great noblemen or even in rebellions against the King. The relationship between these minor nobles and their patron is summed up in another picturesque phrase of the time, reminiscent of the feudal age: 'Ils étaient à lui.' Also numbered among the *domestiques* of great noblemen were a large number of the writers of the age, for, as we shall see, fashion demanded that a man of high rank should interest himself in literature and men of letters. To complete our picture of the household of a great nobleman, we must not forget the retainers, servants and hangers-on attached to his wife and his children. The expense involved in keeping up such an establishment is not easily imagined today.

Moreover, the nobleman had to keep several large and costly carriages, drawn by six horses. He also had to entertain on a lavish scale, for food and wine were consumed in quantities which in these days of rationing appear quite monstrous. Again, now that the court was more or less permanently fixed in Paris, it was an absolute necessity for the great nobleman to have a mansion there, even though the cost of living was much higher than in the provinces. The new mansions which were built from the beginning of the century onwards as the court became fixed in Paris (the Hôtel de Rambouillet was only one of these) were extremely costly, because of the new taste for more spacious rooms and luxurious furnishings. The greater refinement of the age was likewise reflected in the dress of both sexes; the wave of extravagance in clothes gave rise to various royal edicts which attempted, in vain, to check 'la passion effrénée de nos sujets à consommer leurs biens en luxe'. Expensive tastes in jewellery was another vice shared by men equally with women.

Finally, gaming provided yet another drain on the nobleman's purse. It is true that some impecunious noblemen managed to make a fortune out of gaming, but in the nature of things this was only possible for a minority. Playing for high stakes, both in Paris and at the court itself, was one more burden which social convention imposed upon the nobleman.

As usual, La Bruyère offers a moralist's view of this vice of his contemporaries:

> Mille gens se ruinent au jeu et vous disent froidement qu'ils ne sauraient se passer de jouer: quelle excuse! Y a-t-il une passion, quelque violente ou honteuse qu'elle soit, qui ne pût tenir ce même langage? Serait-on reçu à dire qu'on ne peut se passer de voler, d'assassiner, de se précipiter?[1] Un jeu effroyable, continuel, sans retenue, sans bornes, où l'on n'a en vue que la ruine totale de son adversaire, où l'on est transporté du désir du gain, désespéré sur la perte, consumé par l'avarice, où l'on expose sur une carte ou à la fortune du dé la sienne propre, celle de sa femme et de ses enfants, est-ce une chose qui soit permise ou dont l'on doive se passer? Ne faut-il pas quelquefois se faire une plus grande violence, lorsque, poussé par le jeu jusques à une déroute universelle, il faut même que l'on se passe d'habits et de nourriture, et de les fournir à sa famille? (*Les Caractères*, vi. 75.)

A less sombre picture of gaming at court is provided by Mme de Sévigné, though her account of the large winnings of Dangeau, who owed his success at court to his prowess at the card-table, allows one to infer that what he gained came from the pockets of the other courtiers. Mme de Sévigné is describing the scene at Versailles in the afternoon when the court assembled to amuse itself:

> Mille louis sont répandus sur le tapis, il n'y a point d'autres jetons. Je voyais jouer Dangeau; et j'admirais combien nous sommes sots auprès de lui. Il ne songe qu'à son affaire, et gagne où les autres perdent; il ne néglige rien, il profite de tout, il n'est point distrait; en un mot, sa bonne conduite[2] défie la fortune; aussi les deux cent mille francs en dix jours, les cent mille écus en un mois, tout cela se met sur le livre de sa recette. (29 July 1676.)

Financial need often drove noblemen to strange compromises with their conscience in a century which, seen from a distance, would seem to have attached overwhelming importance to questions of honour. Witness this contemporary story:

> Un cavalier de ma connaissance raisonnait un jour assez plaisamment avec un moine, auquel il avouait qu'il savait mettre quatre

[1] Into all manner of vices (?). [2] Skill.

as, ou quatre rois, dans le talon[1] au piquet[2], quand il était dernier, et que cette adresse lui avait souvent réussi. Le bon père lui dit qu'il était obligé à restituer l'argent gagné de la sorte. Le joueur lui soutint que non, en disant pour raison qu'il n'était pas plus défendu de bien mêler les cartes que de les bien jouer, et que le but de celui qui mêle, étant de se donner beau jeu, et de rompre celui de sa partie, il ne croyait pas qu'il y allât de sa conscience de se donner quatorze d'as[3] à point nommé. (J. de Callières, *La Fortune des gens de qualité*, pp. 329-30.)

All these different factors, which necessitated a higher expenditure at the very moment when the income of the aristocracy had fallen considerably, contributed to one of the outstanding features of the social history of seventeenth century France: the impoverishment of the nobility as a class. Nothing stands out more clearly in the letters and memoirs of the age than the simple fact that the French aristocracy, right down the hierarchy from the *prince du sang* to the provincial *hobereau*, were in dire financial straits. Nowhere does the sorry state of the finances of the nobility come out more clearly than in the memoirs of one of the financial wizards of the age, who had to come to the assistance of various great noblemen and try to put their affairs in order. Monsieur le Duc de La Rochefoucauld, the author of the *Maximes*, had to have recourse to this bourgeois expert in order to straighten out his affairs in 1661. The *financier's* account of the matter gives us an interesting glimpse of the economic troubles which so often underlay the pomp and splendour of the *Grand Siècle*:

M. de La Rochefoucauld, n'étant pas trop bien dans ses affaires, ayant de la peine à subsister, me demanda de vouloir bien lui faire recevoir les revenus de ses terres, et de lui faire donner tous les mois quarante pistoles pour ses habits et ses menus plaisirs, ce qui a duré jusqu'à sa mort. Non seulement je faisais payer les arrérages,[4] mais encore éteindre beaucoup de petites dettes dues pour sa maison, tant à Paris qu'en Angoumois; ce qui lui faisait un plaisir si sensible qu'il en parlait souvent à bien des gens pour l'exprimer. M. le prince de Marsillac[5] voulant aller à l'armée,

[1] The undealt cards.
[2] A popular card-game.
[3] The four aces, which counted fourteen points.
[4] Back-interest.
[5] The Duke's heir.

n'ayant ni argent ni équipage, et désirant avoir un service de vaisselle d'argent, sa famille jugea qu'il lui fallait jusqu'à soixante mille livres. Je les prêtai. (Gourville, *Mémoires*, i. 178.)

The last touch is typical: despite all its debts, the family had to keep up appearances, a future Duke must be provided with a luxurious *équipage* with which to go to the wars. And so more money was borrowed before the old debts could be paid off.

The same gentleman was called in a few years later to straighten out the finances of the *premier prince du sang*, the great general, Condé. Since his return to France after the years when he had fought on the side of Spain against his own country, he had spent a good part of his time dodging his creditors:

L'état des dettes, comme elles paraissaient alors, montait à plus de huit millions. Il était dû à une partie des domestiques [1] de Monsieur le Prince des cinq ou six années d'appointements . . .; et M. de Saint-Mard [2] avait été neuf ans sans rien recevoir. Monsieur le Prince était accablé d'un grand nombre de créanciers, qui se trouvaient souvent dans son antichambre quand il voulait sortir. Ordinairement il s'appuyait sur deux personnes, ne pouvant marcher; et, passant aussi vite qu'il lui était possible, il leur disait qu'il donnerait ordre qu'on les satisfît. Il m'a fait l'honneur de me dire depuis que ç'avait été une des choses du monde qui lui avait le plus fait de plaisir, lorsqu'il s'aperçut, quelque temps après que je fusse entré dans ses affaires, qu'il ne voyait plus de créanciers. (*Ibid.*, ii. 35-6.)

Such was the state of humiliation from which the victor of Rocroi had to be rescued by a plebeian *financier*.

Innumerable passages could be quoted to show the financial difficulties with which the aristocracy, high and low, had to struggle in the seventeenth century. It should be added that the poverty of the mass of peasants in the latter part of the century added to the financial troubles of the nobleman, for rents and feudal dues were paid only after long delays. Witness a letter to Bussy-Rabutin, written in 1687 by Mme de Sévigné about one of her estates in Burgundy:

Je ne sais comment vous vous trouvez de vos terres. Pour moi,

[1] Members of his household. [2] His Chamberlain.

mon cousin, ma terre de Bourbilly est quasi devenue à rien par le rabais [1] et par le peu de débit des blés et autres grains. Il n'y a que d'y vivre qui pût nous tirer de la misère; mais quand on est engagé ailleurs, il est comme impossible de transporter nos revenus. (May 31 1687.)

Yet even when it was possible to go down to one's estates from Paris, the result was not always very encouraging, as a letter of Mme de Sévigné to her daughter, written from her estates in Brittany, shows:

J'ai donné,[2] depuis que je suis arrivée, d'assez grosses sommes: un matin, huit cents francs, l'autre mille francs, l'autre cinq: un autre jour, trois cents écus. . . . Je trouve des métayers et des meuniers qui me doivent toutes ces sommes, et qui n'ont pas un unique sou pour les payer: que fait-on? il faut bien leur donner.

She adds that these losses were partly compensated by the product of the *lods et ventes*, and then follows an amusing account of further attempts at debt-collecting:

Il me vint voir l'autre jour une belle petite fermière de Bodégat, avec de beaux yeux brillants, une belle taille, une robe de drap de Hollande découpé sur du tabis, les manches tailladées: ah, Seigneur! quand je la vis, je m'en crus bien ruinée: elle me doit huit mille francs. Tout cela s'accomodera. . . . Ce matin, il est entré un paysan avec des sacs de tous côtés; il en avait sous ses bras, dans ses poches, dans ses chausses. . . . Le bon abbé [3] qui va droit au fait, crut que nous étions riches à jamais: 'Hélas! mon ami, vous voilà bien chargé: combien apportez-vous?' . . . 'Monsieur, dit-il, en respirant à peine, je crois qu'il y a bien ici trente francs.' C'étaient, ma bonne, tous les doubles [4] de France, qui se sont réfugiés dans cette province, avec les chapeaux pointus, et qui abusent ici de notre patience. (15 June 1680.)

The amusing tone of the letter cannot hide the bitterness of the disappointment felt by Mme de Sévigné when her hopes were raised only to be thus dashed.

One way out of an embarrassed financial position was for the nobleman to marry a wealthy heiress who would one day inherit the fortune of her *nouveau riche* father, and whose dowry

[1] Fall in prices. [2] Remitted. [3] Her uncle who looked after her affairs. [4] Half a *denier* (roughly 'a farthing').

might pay off the more pressing debts of the family. The literature of the age is full of accounts of such *mésalliances*. In a famous passage La Bruyère contrasts the great nobleman whose upbringing has made him unfit not only to take any part in the government of his country but even to manage his own affairs, with bourgeois ministers like Colbert, who through hard work have risen to high places in the state, and who, yesterday despised by the great nobles, are today sought after as fathers-in-law:

> Pendant que les grands négligent de rien connaître, je ne dis pas seulement aux intérêts des princes et aux affaires publiques, mais à leurs propres affaires; qu'ils ignorent l'économie [1] et la science d'un père de famille, et qu'ils se louent eux-mêmes de cette ignorance; qu'ils se laissent appauvrir et maîtriser par des intendants,[2] qu'ils se contentent d'être gourmets ou *coteaux*,[3] d'aller chez *Thaïs* ou *Phryné*, de parler de la meute et de la vieille meute, de dire combien il y a de postes de Paris à Besancon ou à Philisbourg, des citoyens s'instruisent du dedans et du dehors d'un royaume, étudient le gouvernement, deviennent fins et politiques, savent le fort et le faible de tout un état, songent à se mieux placer, se placent, s'élèvent, deviennent puissants, soulagent le prince d'une partie des soins publics. Les grands, qui les dédaignaient, les révèrent: heureux s'ils deviennent leurs gendres. (*Les Caractères*, ix. 24.)

The three daughters of Colbert, the son of a merchant of Rheims, all found husbands among the great noblemen at court; they married the Duc de Chevreuse, the Duc de Mortemart and the Duc de Beauvilliers respectively. Despite the difference in rank between these bourgeois girls and their husbands, these marriages, owing to the high position and power of Colbert, seem less surprising than some of those entered upon by impecunious noblemen who managed to 'redorer leur blason' by marrying the daughters of tax-farmers who had made scandalous fortunes almost overnight. La Bruyère summed up this social phenomenon in one trenchant sentence: 'Si le financier manque son coup, les courtisans disent de lui: "C'est un bourgeois, un homme de rien, un

[1] How to run their affairs. [2] Major-domo of a household.
[3] Connoisseurs of wine.

15. *Sébastien Bourdon*,
Nicolas Fouquet

16. *P. Drevet*,
Samuel Bernard
famous financier
the end of the
gn of Louis XIV)

malotru"; s'il réussit, ils lui demandent sa fille.' (*Les Caractères*, vi., 7.)

Saint-Simon, whose only thought in life was the maintenance of the dignities and prerogatives of his rank as *duc et pair*, has to admit in his memoirs that his mother-in-law was the daughter of one of the big *financiers* of the age. When his father-in-law received his marshal's baton, his only income was the totally inadequate pay attached to the post. In order to carry on his career in the army and to buy an estate to which he could attach his title of duke, he was compelled to swallow his aristocratic pride and contract a *mésalliance*. It is amusing to see the terms in which Saint-Simon speaks of the relationship between the husband who brought to the marriage only his rank and his reputation as a soldier, and the wife who owed her new-found social position to her father's money-bags:

> Il y rencontra une épouse qui n'eut des yeux que pour lui, malgré la différence d'âge, *qui sentit toujours avec un extrême respect l'honneur que lui faisait la naissance et la vertu de son époux. . . . Lui aussi oublia toute différence de ses parents aux siens*, et donna toute sa vie le plus grand exemple du plus honnête homme du monde avec elle, et avec toute sa famille, dont il se fit adorer. (*Mémoires*, x. 338.)

The solid material reasons which drove the worthy Marshal to such a *mésalliance* are given only passing mention; what is stressed is the condescending kindness with which he treated his wife and her bourgeois family.

It is almost impossible to pick up a volume of letters or memoirs of the period without coming across an example of a nobleman trying to solve his financial problems by this means. Bussy-Rabutin, Mme de Sévigné's cousin, finding that money was necessary if he was to get on in the army, and seeing that the only way to get money was to marry a wealthy *bourgeoise*, made an unsuccessful attempt to abduct a wealthy young widow of eighteen, who was the daughter of a *financier*. In the letters of Mme de Sévigné we read how she attempted to carry out her maternal duty of finding a wife for her son Charles. Naturally, the main thing was to find someone with a large dowry, and on one occasion she wrote to her daughter, thinking that she had found what she wanted · 'Je lui mande de venir ici, je voudrais le marier à une petite fille qui est un peu juive de son estoc,[1] mais les millions nous paraissent de bonne maison.'[2] (13 Oct. 1675.)

This marriage did not take place, but a typical example of a *mésalliance* is to be found in the marriage of Mme de Sévigné's grandson, the Marquis de Grignan, with a wealthy heiress. Year after year we follow in Mme. de Sévigné's letters to her daughter the progressive ruin of the Grignan family. Neither maternal advice nor liberal assistance from her own purse could stop the extravagance of her daughter and son-in-law, or check their mounting debts. In 1689 the Grignans were on the verge of complete ruin; Mme de Sévigné penned a despairing letter to her daughter:

> Je ne réponds rien à ces comptes et à ces calculs que vous avez faits, à ces avances horribles, à cette dépense sans mesure: cent vingt mille livres! Il n'y a plus de bornes; deux dissipateurs ensemble, l'un voulant tout, l'autre l'approuvant, c'est pour abîmer le monde. Et n'était-ce pas le monde que la grandeur et la puissance de votre maison? Je n'ai point de paroles pour vous dire ce que je pense, mon cœur est trop plein. Mais qu'allez-vous faire? Je ne le comprends point du tout. Sur quoi vivre? Sur quoi fonder le présent et l'avenir? Que fait-on, quand on est à un certain point? Nous comptions l'autre jour vos revenus; ils sont grands; il fallait vivre de la charge et laisser vos terres pour payer les arrérages.[3] . . . Enfin, cela fait mourir, d'autant plus qu'il n'y a point de remède. (1 April 1689.)

To her grief at the plight of her daughter and son-in-law was added the additional misfortune of her own financial troubles, and her consequent inability to assist them:

> Mon Dieu, que votre état est violent! qu'il est pressant! et que j'y entre tout entière avec une véritable douleur! Mais, ma fille, que les souhaits sont faibles et fades dans de pareilles occasions! et qu'il est inutile de vous dire que si j'avais encore, comme j'ai eu, quelque somme portative[4] qui dépendît de moi, elle serait bientôt à vous! Je me trouve en petit volume accablée et menacée de mes petits créanciers, et je ne sais même si je

[1] Stock, lineage.
[2] Noble family.
[3] Back-interest.
[4] In ready cash.

pourrai les contenter, comme je l'espérais; car je me trouve suffoquée par l'obligation de payer tout à l'heure cinq mille francs de lods et ventes des terres de Mme d'Acigné que j'ai achetées, pour n'en pas payer dix si j'attendais encore deux ans. Ainsi me voilà, mais ce n'est que pour vous dire la douleur que me donne mon extrême impossibilité.

To this letter her son Charles added a few lines, describing his own inability to come to the rescue because of the impossibility of getting any money out of his peasants:

Voici l'oncle maternel, ma chère petite sœur, qui vous écrit lui-même, et qui vous assure avec toute sorte de sincérité que s'il avait le bien [1] qu'il devrait avoir, c'est-à-dire, si les terres étaient du bien, et n'étaient pas purement des chansons, des illusions, etc., vous verriez par des marques essentielles combien je m'intéresse à ce qui vous touche; mais, ma très belle, je ne suis entouré que de gens que je puis faire mettre en prison, qui m'en prient tous les jours, qui sont logés dans les lieux qui m'appartiennent, qui prient Dieu pour moi, à ce qu'ils disent, et qui m'assurent en même temps que pour de l'argent, je n'y dois pas songer; voilà mon état. (22 Jan. 1690.)

When the time came to find a wife for the young Marquis de Grignan, the choice lay between a girl of noble birth, equal in rank to the Marquis, and the daughter of a wealthy *financier*: the first meant financial ruin, for no nobleman could offer a dowry which would help the Grignans out of their difficulties, and the second, financial salvation. Despite their terrible plight, the haughty Grignans could only with difficulty bring themselves to consent to such a humiliating marriage. 'Je ne crois pas qu'il y ait à balancer', wrote Mme de Sévigné, 'entre ce qui soutient votre fils et votre maison, et ce qui achèvera de vous accabler.' But the Grignans did hesitate; they were afraid of the sneers of their aristocratic friends. In the end, however, the urgent necessity of solving their financial problems triumphed over pride of birth. Perhaps they were won over by a letter from a friend of the family, who wrote with a charming blend of good sense and cynicism:

Faites, faites votre mariage; vous avez raison, et le public a tort, très grand tort. . . . Voulez-vous mettre le public dans son tort?

[1] Wealth.

Faites-vous donner une si bonne et grosse somme en argent comptant que vous vous mettiez à votre aise. Un gros mariage justifiera votre procédé. Tirez, comme je vous le dis, le plus d'argent comptant que vous pourrez; car voilà la précaution qu'il faut prendre en pareil cas. . . . Consolez-vous d'une mésalliance, et par le doux repos de n'avoir plus de créanciers dans le séjour de beaux, grands et magnifiques châteaux qui ne doivent rien à personne, et par la satisfaction de donner quelquefois dans le superflu, qui me paraît le plus grand bonheur de la vie. . . . Aujourd'hui, comme vous dites fort bien, on parle d'une chose, et demain on n'en parle plus; et quand vous présenterez au public une jolie marquise de Grignan et qu'il sera persuadé que vous en avez beaucoup de bien, il ne vous fera pas plus votre procès qu'à tous les gens de la première qualité [1] qui vous ont montré ce chemin, et qui ne croient pas à l'heure qu'il est en avoir la jambe moins bien tournée. (Mme de Sévigné, *Lettres*, x. 164.)

Certainly, as the friend points out, the Grignans were by no means the first family of noble birth to stoop to a *mésalliance*. Financially they did well enough out of the marriage. The tax-farmer gave his daughter a large dowry in ready money, half of which was to go to pay the debts of the Grignan family; and his generosity did not stop there, as Mme de Sévigné explains in a letter in which she announces the forthcoming marriage to one of her friends, and which also illustrates in passing how in seventeenth century France a marriage was much less an arrangement between two individuals than an affair settled between two families:

Il y a près d'un an que l'on parle d'un mariage pour le marquis de Grignan: c'est la fille d'un fermier-général nommé Saint-Amant. Vous ne doutez pas qu'il ne soit fort riche: il avait une commission à Marseille pour les vivres.[2] Sa fille aînée a dix-huit ans, jolie, aimable, sage, bien élevée, raisonnable au dernier point. Il donne quatre cent mille francs comptant à cette personne, beaucoup plus dans l'avenir; il n'a qu'une autre fille. On a cru qu'un tel parti serait bon pour soutenir les grandeurs de la

[1] 'Of the very highest rank.'
[2] i.e. he had made his money by supplying food to the armed forces.

> maison,[1] qui n'est pas sans dettes. . . . Le père et le contrat sont ici: sa femme et sa fille s'y sont rendues de Montpellier; et enfin, madame, après avoir vu et admiré pour cinquante mille francs de linge, d'habits, de dentelles et de pierreries, qu'il donne encore fort honnêtement, après huit ou dix jours de séjour ici pour faire connaissance, le marquis et cette fille seront mariés dimanche, 2e jour de l'année 95. (December 1694.)

Despite the somewhat brief introduction, the marriage proved happy, except that at the beginning Mme de Grignan, if we are to believe Saint-Simon, caused trouble by her haughty attitude in public towards the daughter-in-law who had brought financial salvation to a ruined family. At first her pride of birth made it difficult for her to swallow such a humiliation, with the result that her relations with her son's bourgeois father-in-law became rather strained because of the way she introduced his daughter to her acquaintances:

> Mme de Grignan, en la présentant au monde, en faisait des excuses, et, avec ses minauderies, en radoucissant ses petits yeux, disait qu'il fallait bien de temps en temps du fumier sur les meilleures terres. Elle se savait un gré infini de ce bon mot, qu'avec raison chacun trouva impertinent,[2] quand on a fait un mariage, et le dire entre bas et haut devant sa belle-fille. Saint-Amant, son père, qui se prêtait à tout pour leurs dettes, l'apprit enfin, et s'en trouva si offensé qu'il ferma le robinet. (*Mémoires*, xii. 288-9.)

The story of the marriage of the Marquis de Grignan has been recounted at some length because it illustrates so vividly the financial straits to which the aristocracy were reduced in seventeenth century France, and shows how, despite their pride of birth, aristocratic families were forced to marry off their sons to wealthy bourgeois heiresses. One of the most vivid descriptions of this aspect of French social history in our period is to be found in the satires of Boileau. He describes the extravagant tastes of the nobles, the ensuing debts, their eternal lawsuits and struggles with creditors, and finally the way out of all these troubles—a *mésalliance*. Noble birth, an illustrious name, are useless alone; now it is money which is

[1] Family. [2] Out of place.

all-powerful. In the following lines the high priest of French Classicism sums up in satirical style the fate of the seventeenth century nobleman:

> Alors, pour soutenir son rang et sa naissance,
> Il fallut étaler le luxe et la dépense;
> Il fallut habiter un superbe palais,
> Faire par des couleurs [1] distinguer ses valets;
> Et traînant en tous lieux de pompeux équipages,
> Le duc et le marquis se reconnut aux pages.
> Bientôt, pour subsister, la noblesse sans bien [2]
> Trouva l'art d'emprunter et de ne rendre rien;
> Et bravant des sergents [3] la timide cohorte,
> Laissa le créancier se morfondre à sa porte.
> Mais, pour comble, à la fin, le marquis en prison
> Sous le faix des procès vit tomber sa maison.[4]
> Alors, le noble altier, pressé de l'indigence,
> Humblement du faquin rechercha l'alliance [5];
> Avec lui trafiquant d'un nom si précieux,
> Par un lâche contrat vendit tous ses aïeux,
> Et corrigeant ainsi la fortune ennemie,
> Rétablit son honneur à force d'infamie.
>
> (Satire V.)

It is this impoverishment of all sections of the French aristocracy in the seventeenth century, revealed in innumerable documents of the period, which accounts in a large measure for the failure of the last efforts of the great noblemen under Richelieu and Mazarin to put the clock back and to regain some of the power which the gradual development of the Monarchy towards absolutism had taken from them. Living from hand to mouth, crushed by their debts and by an extravagant mode of living, compelled very often to swallow their pride and save their family from ruin by a *mésalliance* with a wealthy bourgeois heiress, the great noblemen were in no position to offer effective resistance to the growth of the royal power. When they revolted, it was less in order to regain political power than to wring money out of a weak

[1] Of their livery. [2] Impoverished. [3] Tipstaffs.
[4] Noble family. [5] 'Sought to marry into the family of a lowborn fellow.'

administration. When the government was in firm hands, as it was under Richelieu, and stili more under Louis XIV, only obedience to the Crown could allow them to keep up the costly mode of life to which they were accustomed. Only assiduous presence at court could bring to them and their families the pensions, gifts and other favours which their master had it in his power to bestow. In the last resort it is economic reasons which explain how in the course of the seventeenth century the turbulent great noblemen, still close in outlook to their ancestors of feudal times, were gradually transformed into the lackeys and flatterers whose presence added to the splendour of the court of Louis XIV.

CHAPTER IV

THE CLERGY

In seventeenth century France the Catholic Church presented remarkable contrasts of piety and indifference, of simplicity and ostentation, of other-worldliness and crude self-interest. On the one hand we think of the seventeenth century as the age of Saint Vincent de Paul, of Pascal, of Bossuet and Fénelon. We think too of the Counter-Reformation which brought about an extraordinary revival in the Catholic Church after the fierce struggle with Protestantism in the Wars of Religion. The religious fervour of the first thirty or forty years of the century brought about the foundation or the introduction into France of a succession of monastic orders, both of men and women, which were concerned with contemplation or, more often, with work in the outside world, particularly with charity and education. Controversy within the Church over such doctrines as Jansenism and, later, Quietism was a sign of the passionate seriousness with which Frenchmen of this age treated their religion.

Yet this is only one side of the medal. In our account of the organization of the Church and of the place which the clergy occupied in the society of the time, we shall come across circumstances which form a startling contrast with the piety and devotion displayed by these men and women. A work of this size and scope cannot concern itself with the religious outlook of the age; the task of resolving these contradictions is one which we leave to others. Our object is merely to show what place was occupied by the French clergy in the society of the time. As the first order in the state, their position was one of considerable importance; moreover, we shall see that the composition and outlook of the different sections of the clergy reflected to a high degree the structure and divisions of secular society.

Because of its landed property, the Church in the Middle

Ages inevitably became involved in feudal institutions. Bishops or abbots and priors could hold fiefs from an overlord or receive homage from vassals. Similarly, religious establishments stood in exactly the same relationship as the nobility to the peasants on their manors. To begin with, most of their peasants were serfs, and were treated in precisely the same way, whether their lord was a layman or churchman. The clergy levied feudal dues from the peasants on their estates, and exercised the same judicial and administrative rights as laymen. Since the Middle Ages most of their serfs had been emancipated, although right down to 1789 serfs continued to be found on Church lands. In general, however, the peasant on Church land, as elsewhere, had become in fact the owner of his holding, even though he still was obliged to pay feudal dues on it.

In contrast to the decline in the position of the nobility as landowners, the Church retained most of the land which it had possessed in the Middle Ages, and even tended to increase its property because of fresh bequests. Nevertheless, past estimates of the amount of land owned by the clergy under the *ancien régime* have often been wildly exaggerated. The main source of its income was not its agricultural land. It derived considerable wealth from the property which it owned in the towns; but its income from tithes was probably greater than that from all its feudal dues and rents.

Tithe (*la dîme*) was an ecclesiastical tax levied on the land of every parish, in order to provide for the maintenance of a priest and church and the assistance of the poor. It was levied on all land, irrespective of the rank of the owner. Despite its name, tithe was rarely exactly one-tenth of the crops. The actual amount varied enormously from place to place. Sometimes it was as high as one-seventh, sometimes very much less; a rough estimate of the average amount over the whole country is one-thirteenth. The agricultural products which were subject to tithe varied greatly too. It was always levied on cereals; in certain districts cattle, sheep and vineyards might also be subject to it.

The amount which the individual peasant had to pay in tithes inevitably varied very considerably, but, in general, it may be said that this tax represented a considerable drain on the income which he might derive from his land. Often the amount which he had to pay in tithes was nearly as great as the amount of his *taille*; Vauban quotes the example of fifty parishes in Burgundy where the *taille* amounted to 45,000 *livres*, and the tithe to 37,000. Indeed, the amount paid to the Church could exceed the amount paid in direct taxes to the state: witness the fifty parishes in Normandy mentioned by Vauban as paying 46,000 *livres* in *taille* and 73,000 in tithes (*Dîme royale*, pp. 118-24). It is therefore hardly surprising if the tithes did not add to the popularity of the clergy. Moreover, the method of collection was an additional source of grievance. As the tithe was a first charge on the crop, the collectors had to be informed in advance of the day when it was to be harvested. Meanwhile, until they arrived, the peasant was forbidden to remove his crop. When they came, they proceeded to take the pick of his produce and even carried off the straw, which the peasant could not well do without. To add to the peasant's resentment, tithes were often collected by a wealthy chapter or abbey, instead of going to maintain the poor *curé* and keep the parish church in a proper state of repair. Occasionally, indeed, the tithe (it was known then as *dîme inféodée*) went to a layman.

From tithes, rents and feudal dues the clergy derived an income which, considering the small proportion of the population which it represented, made it the wealthiest body in France. It must not be imagined, however, that this income was equitably distributed among the different sections of the clergy. There were in fact gross inequalities. The regular clergy (i.e. the members of the various religious orders) was, on paper at least, much wealthier than the secular clergy (bishops, canons and parish priests). Moreover, the income of the higher ranks of the clergy was out of all proportion to the meagre pittance earned by the parish priests.

Since the Concordat of 1516 the disposal of a considerable part of the wealth of the Church lay in the hands of the King, who appointed to all the higher ecclesiastical posts. This right of appointing all archbishops, bishops, abbots and so on, conferred great power on the Crown, for it meant that the King could appoint men who he knew would be obedient to his wishes, and that he had in his hands a means of rewarding the loyalty and obedience of the great noble families by providing their younger sons, and sometimes too their daughters, with lucrative sinecures. As a contemporary put it:

> Le pouvoir du roi de nommer aux bénéfices . . . fait un des plus beaux droits de sa couronne et lui met en main de quoi donner non seulement des récompenses considérables à ceux qu'il juge à propos d'en gratifier, mais de récompenser même par là, dans les enfants, les services que les pères lui rendent dans les affaires du gouvernement de l'État, des finances, de la justice, ou de la guerre, ou d'ailleurs dans les services domestiques et de cour auprès de sa personne, et ce, sans qu'il en sorte rien de ses trésors et de son Épargne.[1] (Ézéchiel Spanheim, *Relation de la Cour de France*, pp. 33-4.)

The result was that in the seventeenth century practically all the archbishoprics and bishoprics were in the hands of great noblemen or of the sons of the King's ministers; indeed, they often remained in the same family for generations, as the holder might persuade the King to appoint his nephew or some other relative as his successor.

The hold of the nobility on the highest posts in the Church was not limited to the bishoprics and archbishoprics of France. There were, besides, several hundred chapters whose canons had, nominally at least, the task of relieving their bishop of the temporal administration of the diocese. Entry into these chapters was often restricted to those who could prove that they had several generations of noble ancestors. Indeed, many of the canons remained laymen; the Kings of France were actually canons of several chapters! There existed also chapters composed of women; sometimes only those of noble birth were admitted, after taking vows which required merely temporary celibacy, and allowed them to live in great state, secluded only from the vulgar.

As for the regular clergy, the wealthiest section of the Church, the King had once more at his disposal several

[1] Treasury.

hundreds of posts of abbots and priors. Many of these were given to younger sons of noblemen; others were held by bishops who regarded the revenue as an addition to their income from their diocese. It was, in fact, an exception for a nobleman actually to reside in his abbey, though he normally had a house there, separated off from the parts of the building occupied by the monks. Generally, the abbey was put *en commende*, that is, the titular abbot drew a certain proportion of the revenues of the abbey (generally a third, sometimes more), and left the spiritual side of affairs to another abbot, chosen by the monks. In the seventeenth century many of these titular abbots (*abbés commendataires*) were not even in holy orders. At the beginning of the period when abuses were at their worst, not only laymen, but children, women, even Protestants drew the revenues attached to such posts. This was a legacy from the preceding century when Desportes's love-poetry was rewarded with several abbeys; Henry IV's minister, Sully, a well-known Protestant, continued to hold four abbeys which brought him the handsome income of 45,000 *livres*. The practice of appointing laymen to such posts did not altogether die out in the course of the century, though abuses were by then less startling. Yet even in the 1660's we find the example of Racine, a layman, worse still a poet, and worst of all a dramatist, being given a priory, though he did not actually hold the post for long. And it still happened that the most worldly noblemen, whose connection with the Church was of the flimsiest, were rewarded by the King with abbeys and priories.

In a word, if the nobles had not yet obtained, as they were to do in the eighteenth century, a virtual monopoly of all the highest posts in the Church, they were already well on the way to doing so. In a nobleman's family it was the recognized thing that the younger sons and daughters should be found a safe and comfortable existence in the Church. The eldest son, who would in due course inherit his father's title and the lion's share of his estates, naturally went in for a career in the army and at court. One or two of the daughters might perhaps be married, if the family fortune could stand the strain of providing the necessary dowries. It was taken for granted that the younger children would enter the Church. A contemporary satirist tells us how the fate of children was decided almost from the cradle:

> Un père a trois enfants: à peine sont-ils nés
> Qu'ils sont à quelque état aussitôt destinés.
> L'aîné, c'est pour Thémis [1]; le second, pour Bellone [2];
> A celui qui le suit un bréviaire l'on donne,
> Et, contre toutes lois et contre le bon sens,
> On fait Monsieur l'abbé d'un enfant de deux ans.
> Que si ce père aussi l'est de plus d'une fille,
> La laide ou la boiteuse est toujours pour la grille [3];
> Dès l'enfance on l'y met, qu'elle le veuille ou non;
> On lui fait épouser une sainte prison . . .
>
> (Louis Petit, *Satire VI.*)

The children of noblemen did not enter the Church because they felt it to be their true vocation. For the daughters the question of marriage or the convent was decided by their place in the family and by the number of dowries which their father could provide. Similarly, the question whether a young nobleman was to be destined for the army or the Church, the only two careers open to him, depended on the size of the family fortune, and whether he was an elder or a younger son. The result was that the highest posts in the Church were often filled by extraordinary misfits. Saint-Simon writes of one of his friends who ended up as an archbishop: 'Sa mère l'avait fait prêtre à coups de bâton' (*Mémoires*, iv. 349). Or take the case of another younger son, the notorious Cardinal de Retz, who entered the Church simply because he was born after his elder brother, and because the Archbishopric of Paris had been in the Retz family for three generations. In his memoirs, after relating various love-affairs and duels of his youth, he goes on:

> Je ne crois pas qu'il y eût au monde un meilleur cœur que celui de mon père et je puis dire que sa trempe était celle de la vertu. . . . Cependant et ces duels et ces galanteries ne l'empêchèrent pas de faire tous ses efforts pour attacher à l'Église l'âme peut-être la moins ecclésiastique qui fût dans l'univers. La prédilection pour son aîné et la vue de l'archevêché de Paris, qui était dans sa maison,[4] produisirent cet effet. (*Œuvres*, i. 89-90.)

[1] The goddess of justice.
[2] The goddess of war.
[3] The convent.
[4] Family.

The memoirs of Saint-Simon offer an extraordinary gallery of portraits of the higher clergy of his age. Archbishops and bishops, with few exceptions, were first and foremost *grands seigneurs*. They entered the Church, not from choice, but at the bidding of their fathers, because they were younger sons, often because there was a bishopric or archbishopric in the family. Like other *grands seigneurs*, they were irresistibly attracted to the court, both because it was the centre of all social life for men of their class, and because, by keeping themselves constantly in the King's eye, they could hope to snap up posts and honours as they fell vacant. With rare exceptions, their lives were thoroughly worldly. Two or three specimens from Saint-Simon's collection of portraits will make this only too clear.

Let us take first the example of a highly respected bishop, distinguished both for an apparently exceptional piety and for his independence in refusing to acclaim the Revocation of the Edict of Nantes. Pierre de Coislin (1635-1706), the younger son of the Marquis de Coislin, was presented with an abbey at the early age of six. Two years later he exchanged this toy for the wealthy abbey of Saint-Victor. At eighteen he was appointed to the post of *premier aumônier du roi*, and at twenty-one he became Bishop of Orleans. Ten years before his death he obtained the coveted cardinal's hat. This prelate stands out as an exception in Saint-Simon's eyes, because one had to be careful of one's language in his presence, because he devoted a considerable part of his income to charitable works, lived in his diocese for at least six months of the year, and adopted a relatively modest scale of living. Yet, even so, despite all these rare virtues, our Cardinal-Bishop spent a great deal of his time at court, frequented the best society and gave up a great part of the day to entertaining:

> Il avait passé sa vie à la cour; mais sa jeunesse y avait été si pure qu'elle était non seulement demeurée sans soupçon, mais que jeunes et vieux n'osaient dire devant lui une parole trop libre, et cependant le recherchaient tous, en sorte qu'il avait toujours vécu dans la meilleure compagnie de la cour. Il était riche en abbayes et en prieurés, dont il faisait de grandes aumônes,

et dont il vivait. De son évêché qu'il eut fort jeune, il n'en toucha jamais rien, et en mit le revenu entier tous les ans en bonnes œuvres.[1] Il y passait au moins six mois de l'année, le visitait soigneusement, et faisait toutes les fonctions épiscopales avec un grand soin, et un grand discernement à choisir d'excellents sujets pour le gouvernement et pour l'instruction de son diocèse. Son équipage, ses meubles, sa table sentaient la frugalité et la modestie épiscopales, et quoiqu'il eût toujours grande compagnie à dîner et à souper, et de la plus distinguée, elle était servie de bons vivres, mais sans profusion et sans rien de recherché. (*Mémoires*, ii. 356-7.)

Other examples in the memoirs of Saint-Simon are less edifying. Let us look for a moment at the portrait of the Bishop of Langres (1625-95):

> C'était un vrai gentilhomme et le meilleur homme du monde, que tout le monde aimait, répandu dans le grand monde[2] et avec le plus distingué. On l'appelait volontiers *le bon Langres*. Il n'avait rien de mauvais, même pour les mœurs, mais il n'était pas fait pour être évêque; il jouait à toutes sortes de jeux et le plus gros jeu du monde. M. de Vendôme, Monsieur le Grand[3] et quelques autres de cette volée[4] lui attrapèrent gros deux ou trois fois au billard. Il ne dit mot, et s'en alla à Langres où il se mit à étudier les adresses du billard, et s'enfermait bien pour cela, de peur qu'on le sût. De retour à Paris, voilà ces messieurs à le presser de jouer au billard, et lui à s'en défendre comme un homme déjà battu, et qui, depuis six mois de séjour à Langres, n'a vu que des chanoines et des curés. Quand il se fut bien fait importuner, il céda enfin. Il joua d'abord médiocrement, puis mieux, et fit grossir la partie; enfin il les gagna tout de suite, puis se moqua d'eux, après avoir regagné beaucoup plus qu'il n'avait perdu. (*Ibid.*, ii. 365-6.)

One more portrait from Saint-Simon must suffice, that of the Bishop of Troyes (1641-1731), who acquired at an early age two abbeys, three priories and a bishopric. After praising him for his knowledge of the temporal affairs of the clergy, Saint-Simon continues:

[1] He could well afford to do this, as the income from his bishopric amounted to only one-fifth of his total income, most of which he derived from his abbeys, priories and other posts in the Church.

[2] High society. [3] *Le grand Écuyer*. [4] Rank.

Il avait de plus bien de l'esprit, et plus que tout, l'esprit du monde, le badinage des femmes, le ton de la bonne compagnie, et passa sa vie dans la meilleure et la plus distinguée de la cour et de la ville, recherché de tout le monde, et surtout dans le gros jeu et à travers toutes les dames; c'était leur favori; elles ne l'appelaient que *le Troyen*, et *chien d'évêque* et *chien de Troyen* quand il leur gagnait leur argent. Il s'allait de temps en temps ennuyer à Troyes, où, pour la bienséance et faute de mieux, il ne laissait pas de faire ses fonctions; mais il n'y demeurait guère, et, une fois de retour, il ne se pouvait arracher. (*Ibid.*, iv. 116.)

From another source we obtain an interesting account of the way in which some of these aristocratic bishops could behave when they were in their dioceses. The subject of this portrait is the blind bishop of Clermont in Auvergne in the first half of the century:

S'il n'eût eu que de la fermeté, c'eût été une vertu épiscopale; mais il avait des faiblesses qui n'édifiaient pas trop son peuple, et des abaissements qui le rendaient presque méprisable. Tous les bals se tenaient chez lui, et sa maison, qui devait être une maison de prières et de pénitence, était une maison de réjouissances et de festins; toutes les assemblées se faisaient dans la salle de son évêché où il ne paraissait point comme évêque pour instruire son peuple, mais comme un gentilhomme en habit violet qui disait des douceurs aux dames comme les autres. Il saluait toutes les dames plus que paternellement, . . . et ne se trompait point sur le jugement de leur beauté, quelque aveugle qu'il fût, . . . connaissant comme bon pasteur toutes les brebis. . . .

Jugez, monsieur, si le clergé pouvait être bien réglé sous un prélat de cet exemple; aussi l'on voyait des chanoines ordinairement vêtus de couleur, qui quittaient leur habit ecclésiastique après le sermon, et paraissaient couverts de rubans des couleurs les plus éclatantes. On les voyait courir aux comédies [1] avec des dames, dès qu'ils étaient sortis du sermon, et faire un mélange de la vanité du monde avec la piété extérieure que leur état leur imposait. (Fléchier, *Mémoires sur les grands jours d'Auvergne en 1665*, pp. 110-11.)

Beneath the archbishops and bishops came the canons and the *abbés*. Many of the latter were younger sons who lacked

[1] Plays.

18. *Sébastien Leclerc*, Conseiller au Parlement

19. *Sébastien Leclerc*, Président à mortier

20. Château de Maisons (built 1642–50, for a wealthy judge)

21. *Antoine Le Nain*, La réunion de famille

22. *Mathieu Le Nain*, Le repas de famille

any religious vocation and merely found in the Church a convenient livelihood. Often a young nobleman would hold several lucrative abbeys while still a child, and would continue all his life to live a worldly existence in Paris, drawing the revenues of these different posts. *Abbés* are satirized in innumerable works of the period. La Bruyère, for instance, speaks with indignation of the contrast between the real functions of an abbot and the frivolous and useless existence led by many of the *abbés* of his time :

> Il y a des choses qui, ramenées à leurs principes et à leur première institution, sont étonnantes et incompréhensibles. Qui peut concevoir, en effet, que certains abbés, à qui il ne manque rien de l'ajustement, de la mollesse et de la vanité des sexes et des conditions, qui entrent auprès des femmes en concurrence avec le marquis et le financier, et qui l'emportent sur tous les deux, qu'eux-mêmes soient originairement, et dans l'étymologie de leur nom, les pères et les chefs de saints moines et d'humbles solitaires, et qu'ils en devraient être l'exemple? Quelle force, quel empire, quelle tyrannie de l'usage! Et, sans parler de plus grands désordres, ne doit-on pas craindre de voir un jour un jeune abbé en velours gris et à ramages [1] comme une Éminence, ou avec des mouches [2] et du rouge comme une femme? (*Les Caractères*, xiv. 16.)

Another abuse which is frequently mentioned in the literature of the period was the practice of parents sending their daughters into a convent for purely selfish reasons, without consulting their feelings and desires. Many a girl was thus sacrificed to the career of a brother or the dowry of an elder sister.

The theme is treated in the following paragraphs from La Bruyère, one of solemn warning, the other bitterly satirical:

> Une mère, je ne dis pas qui cède et qui se rend à la vocation de sa fille, mais qui la fait religieuse, se charge d'une âme avec la sienne, en répond à Dieu même, en est la caution. Afin qu'une telle mère ne se perde pas, il faut que sa fille se sauve.
>
> Un homme joue et se ruine: il marie néanmoins l'aînée de ses deux filles de ce qu'il a pu sauver des mains d'un Ambreville [3];

[1] Velvet embroidered with figures.

[2] Patches of black taffetas worn on their faces by women to show up the whiteness of their skin.

[3] A criminal of the time, executed in 1686.

la cadette est sur le point de faire ses vœux, qui n'a point d'autre vocation que le jeu de son père. (*Les Caractères*, xiv. 29, 30.)

Many abbesses who, because of their noble rank, stepped into their position at a very early age, led extremely worldly lives, and inevitably their example was frequently followed by their nuns, many of whom were also of noble birth. For instance, in 1664 Bossuet was sent to reform a convent in Metz where he found grave abuses. Admission to this particular convent was restricted to women of noble birth, who took the title of *chanoinesses*, and lived in their own quarters, behaving pretty well as they liked. The Abbess led the way in dissipation: the convent was the scene of dancing, gaming, concerts and entertainments to which officers and musicians from the town were invited. When the Abbess left the convent to pay her social calls, she was accompanied by a young *pensionnaire* dressed as a page, who carried her train. The administration of the temporal affairs of the convent was in great confusion: the revenues had been squandered, and enormous debts contracted; ornaments, bells, the ancient treasure of the foundress, even relics of saints, had been sold. The internal government of the convent was highly tyrannical; nuns were beaten and threatened with imprisonment. Yet, despite this scandalous state of affairs, it took Bossuet sixteen years to overcome the resistance of the aristocratic Abbess and to reform the convent.

An interesting example of the sort of life which a girl of aristocratic family could lead in a convent is to be found in a letter of Mme de Sévigné in which she advises Mme de Grignan to send one of her daughters into a convent where her aunt is Abbess:

> Pour moi, je mettrais la petite avec sa tante; elle serait abbesse, quelque chose; cette place est toute propre aux vocations un peu équivoques: on accorde la gloire et les plaisirs. . . . On a mille consolations dans une abbaye; on peut aller avec sa tante voir quelquefois la maison paternelle; on va aux eaux, on est la nièce de Madame. (9 June 1680.)

Altogether, a girl of noble birth who was forced by her parents to enter a convent seems to have done much to make the best of a bad job, and particularly to retain as far as possible the outlook and the prerogatives of a woman of her rank. The result, however, can hardly have been edifying from the point of view of religion.

So far we have dealt only with the aristocratic recruits to the clergy, who naturally formed a minority of that body. The Church was in a real sense a mirror of the society of the age. Just as in the outside world there was an abyss between the *noble* and *roturier*, between the privileged classes of society and the unprivileged, so inside the Church the wealthy bishop or *abbé*, generally of aristocratic origin, looked down with contempt upon the humble parish clergy. The best posts in the Church, those which were well paid and had only nominal duties, were almost a monopoly of a privileged minority. The poorly paid and arduous work of the parish priests might well be left to plebeians. It is true that the lot of the *curés* and *vicaires* varied considerably. In general, in the towns the *curés* enjoyed a fair social standing; but in the country, and the majority of priests, like the majority of the population of France at that time, were to be found there, things were usually very different. There the *curé* or *vicaire*, often, it is true, very ignorant and sometimes less interested in looking after his flock than in hunting or in even more worldly occupations, lived in conditions almost indistinguishable from those of the peasants.

Yet, whatever their shortcomings, the parish priests formed the vast majority of the French clergy, and on them lay the obligations of preaching, relieving the sufferings of the sick and poor, and playing their part in the administration of local affairs. In return, the great majority of *curés* and *vicaires* received a miserable stipend. In many cases country churches had been founded by monasteries, or had later been put under their control. If this was so, the *curé* did not himself collect the tithes, which were originally destined for the payment of his stipend and the upkeep of the parish church. They were collected by agents of the convent, who paid the *curé* a mere pittance, called *portion congrue*. The significance acquired by the term is interesting. Literally, *portion congrue* implies that the stipend was adequate for the needs of the priest; that in practice it was very inadequate is seen in the modern meaning of the term, *réduire quelqu'un à la portion congrue*, which might be translated as 'to put someone on short commons'.

In the matter of taxation we see once more how closely the organization of the clergy in seventeenth century France resembled that of secular society. Like the nobility, the clergy enjoyed the privilege of exemption from the *taille*. As an archbishop of the time put it, 'L'ancien usage de l'Église pendant sa vigueur était que le peuple contribuât par ses biens, la noblesse par son sang et le clergé par ses prières aux nécessités de l'état.' However, the complete exemption from taxation here claimed had been lost in the second half of the sixteenth century when the clergy as a body was obliged to make a contribution to the Treasury. Nevertheless, they still retained the important privilege of holding at regular intervals an Assembly which negotiated with the King the amount of their contribution to the exchequer. This contribution bore the name of *don gratuit*. At first, the Assembly would haggle with the King as to the amount to be paid, but from the time of Louis XIV onwards it ceased to offer any resistance to the demands of the Crown. It was perhaps the wiser course to follow, as the *don gratuit* was a relatively modest contribution to the needs of the Treasury. In order to raise the money, a tax called *décimes* was levied on all the clergy by the Church itself. Here again, just as the privileged orders left the main burden of taxation on the shoulders of the unprivileged classes, so the aristocratic section of the clergy paid a relatively small part of the *décimes* in proportion to their wealth, while the *curés* and *vicaires* were correspondingly overtaxed.

The feelings of resentment aroused in the parish clergy at the spectacle of the wealth of so many indolent bishops and other members of the higher clergy occasionally find expression in the writings of the age, as for instance in the following lines from an anonymous poem of the end of the century:

> Tandis que le prélat dans la fleur de ses jours
> Presse le mol duvet d'un fauteuil de velours
> Ou, remplissant de loin les devoirs de sa crosse,
> Fait rouler dans Paris le superbe carrosse,

D'avides receveurs et de riches fermiers
Lui comptent tous les jours des écus à milliers.
Pour fournir aux plaisirs où nos abbés s'adonnent,
Mille et mille colons [1] de toutes parts moissonnent.
D'un *Benedicamus* entonné faiblement
L'inutile chanoine est payé grassement.
Voilà les forts appuis, les épaules robustes,
Sur qui doivent tomber les décimes si justes.
Mais pour s'en garantir ensemble conjurés,
Tout tombe sur le dos des malheureux curés:
Pour tout bien on nous laisse, en nous coupant la bourse,
Du triste *Requiem* [2] la honteuse ressource.

(*Chansonnier Clairambault*, 1695. *Epître au roi Louis XIV . . . au sujet de la capitation.*)

Such open expressions of resentment were, however, rare in our period. A century later, when the States General were summoned to Versailles, this gap between the higher clergy, recruited more and more exclusively from the aristocracy, and the plebeian parish clergy, was to have important political consequences, when the greater part of this order went over to the Third Estate and helped to form the National Assembly. But in the seventeenth century it was taken for granted that the majority of the higher posts should be filled by members of the aristocracy, and that in their outlook and way of living they should often be noblemen first and churchmen second.

Of this fact the letters of Mme de Sévigné once more bring evidence, for instance in the whole tone of the following letter to her daughter:

> M. le coadjuteur de Reims . . . s'en est allé à Reims, et Mme de Coulanges lui disait: 'Quelle folie d'aller à Reims! et qu'allez-vous faire là? Vous vous y ennuierez comme un chien; demeurez ici, nous nous promènerons.' Ce discours à un archevêque nous fit rire, et elle aussi; nous ne le trouvâmes nullement canonique, et nous comprîmes pourtant que si plusieurs dames le faisaient à des prélats, elles ne perdraient peut-être pas leurs paroles. (20 March 1671.)

Another highly significant story about the same ecclesiastic,

[1] Peasants. [2] Prayers for the dead.

promoted to the rank of Archbishop, brings out the pride and arrogance of these aristocratic prelates. It ought to be added that this one's tendency towards such vices must have been increased by the fact that he was a *parvenu*, the brother of Louvois, one of the most famous ministers of Louis XIV.

> L'archevêque de Reims revenait hier fort vite de Saint-Germain, comme un tourbillon. S'il croit être grand seigneur, ses gens [1] le croient encore plus que lui. Ils passaient au travers de Nanterre, *tra*, *tra*, *tra*; ils rencontrent un homme à cheval, *gare*, *gare*; ce pauvre homme se veut ranger, son cheval ne le veut pas; enfin le carrosse et les six chevaux renversent le pauvre homme et le cheval, et passent par-dessus, et si bien par-dessus que le carrosse en fut versé et renversé; en même temps l'homme et le cheval, au lieu de s'amuser à être roués et estropiés, se relèvent miraculeusement, et remontent l'un sur l'autre, et s'enfuient et courent encore, pendant que les laquais et le cocher, et l'archevêque même, se mettent à crier: 'Arrête, arrête le coquin, qu'on lui donne cent coups.' L'archevêque, en racontant ceci, disait: 'Si j'avais tenu ce maraud-là je lui aurais rompu les bras et coupé les oreilles.' (5 Feb. 1674.)

No doubt the attitude of the Archbishop on this occasion could scarcely be considered in harmony with the Christian conception of charity. But the wealth and pride of the higher clergy was part and parcel of the gross inequality which marked the society of the age, an inequality which gave rise to one of the most moving passages in La Bruyère:

> Ce garçon si frais, si fleuri, et d'une si belle santé, est seigneur d'une abbaye et de dix autres bénéfices: tous ensemble lui rapportent six vingt mille livres de revenu, dont il n'est payé qu'en médailles d'or. Il y a ailleurs six vingt familles indigentes qui ne se chauffent point pendant l'hiver, qui n'ont point d'habits pour se couvrir, et qui souvent manquent de pain; leur pauvreté est extrême et honteuse. Quel partage! [2] Et cela ne prouve-t-il pas clairement un avenir? [3] (*Les Caractères*, vi. 26.)

No doubt it may be said that in the course of the century the most glaring abuses within the Catholic Church tended to disappear. Yet that Church could not escape from the

[1] Servants. [2] Division of wealth. [3] A future life.

limitations imposed upon it by the structure of the society within which it worked. In the ranks of the clergy, which itself formed one of the privileged orders in the state, there was reproduced in broad outline the same distinction between *noble* and *roturier* which divided secular society under the *ancien régime*. No amount of piety and virtue could efface the abuses inherent in the method of recruitment of the higher clergy which arose out of the very nature of the society of the time.

CHAPTER V

THE DEVELOPMENT OF ABSOLUTISM, 1600-1661

THE internal history of France in the seventeenth century is mainly the story of the establishment of absolute monarchy by Richelieu, Mazarin and Louis XIV. The success which they achieved in strengthening the power of the Crown in the very period when absolutism was being broken on this side of the Channel, was not merely due to their personal talents, but was the outcome of certain historical forces. The establishment of absolutism in France in the seventeenth century was the culmination of a long historical process going back to the Middle Ages. To see their achievements in proper perspective it is once again essential to go back for a moment to the state of France in feudal times.

If we study a map of France round about the year A.D. 1000, when feudalism was at its height, we see that not only was the country (with the exception of a small piece of Spain and of modern Belgium) considerably smaller than it is today, but that it was divided into a number of large fiefs or principalities. Not only were these principalities independent of one another, their Dukes or Counts were sovereign princes. They were not the *subjects* of the King of France; they were merely his *vassals*. Moreover, the King of France was not a hereditary monarch; he was merely an overlord elected to that position by other equal overlords. Like them he possessed lands, castles and towns inherited from his ancestors; the only difference was that his territory, the *domaine royal* as it was called, was smaller than that of his great vassals. It consisted merely of a narrow strip of territory (the equivalent of two modern French departments) running from north of Paris to just south of Orleans. In other words, the King of France was at that time the poorest and least powerful of the great overlords of France. Moreover, it must be remembered that he exercised no authority over the territory of these powerful vassals; his administrative powers were limited to his own Domain.

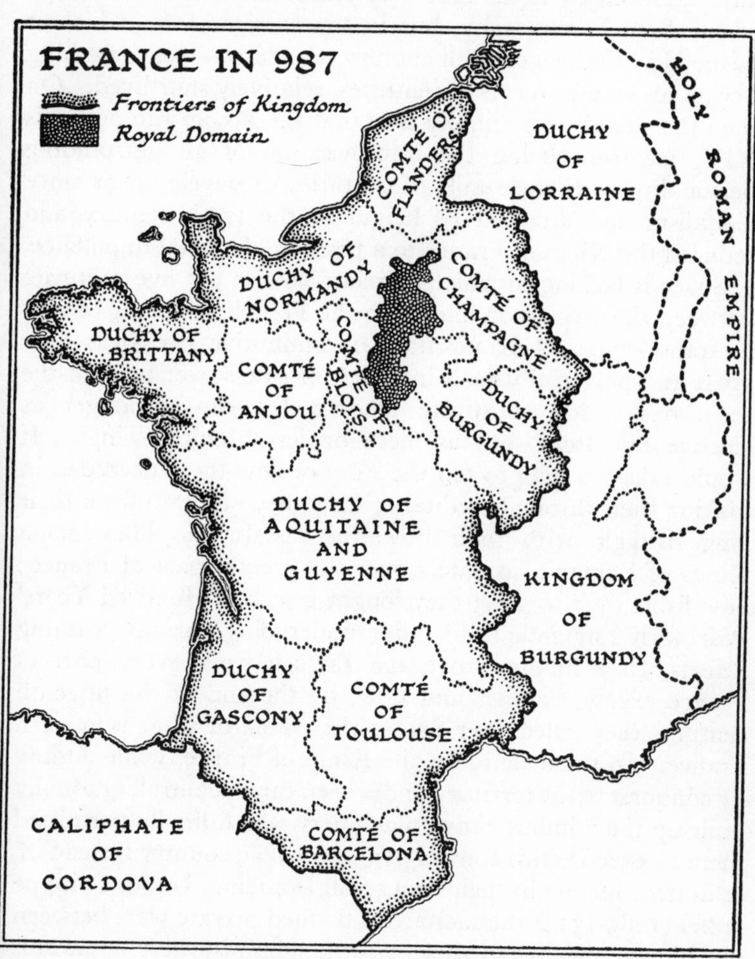

It was from these modest beginnings that the French monarchy moved slowly forward, with many rebuffs and setbacks, towards the absolutism which was to reach its culminating point in the second half of the seventeenth century in the person of Louis XIV, and to be swept away a century later in the Revolution of 1789. Absolute monarchy of the kind achieved by Louis XIV was thus not the traditional type of the French monarchy, but in the extreme form which it assumed in the seventeenth century, absolutism was something new, and, seen in terms of centuries, relatively shortlived. On the other hand, it is equally true that the absolutism of Louis XIV, far from being the improvisation of an outstanding personality, was the result of centuries of development since feudalism had attained its height in the tenth century and reduced the Kings of France to a position of virtual impotence.

Space is lacking in which to relate how in the five centuries between the year 1000 and 1500 the French Kings succeeded in transforming their position as diminutive overlords over great and powerful vassals into that of rulers over most of the territories which constitute modern France—no longer as elective monarchs, but as more or less absolute kings. It would take too long to tell the story of how they succeeded in making their throne hereditary; how they emerged from their long struggle with their powerful vassals, the Plantagenet Kings of England, as rulers over the greater part of France; how from 1337 to 1453 they fought a second Hundred Years' War with England, until, after undergoing various crushing defeats, they finally drove the English from every part of France except Calais; and how, by the end of the fifteenth century, they ruled over nearly the whole of what is modern France. In these centuries the Kings of France, while adding by conquest to the territory under their direct control, gradually built up the administrative machinery which finally permitted them to exercise this control over the whole country instead of, as at first, merely in their own small Domain. Under Philippe le Bel (1285-1314) the monarchy banned private wars between the barons and began to set up the administrative apparatus required for governing the country, and to collect from all parts of France the taxes necessary for the upkeep of the machinery of government. The Crown gradually established the taxes (the *taille*, *gabelle*, and so forth) which were essential for the maintenance of its power, and which were to last through the centuries down to the Revolution of 1789; and finally, in the fifteenth century, this regular income from taxation made it possible for it to set up a standing army.

By the beginning of the sixteenth century the unification of France was almost complete; and at the same time, through the crushing of the great vassals, the French Kings were almost absolute rulers over the country. Francis I (1515-1547) and his son, Henry II (1547-1559), if they were not yet as powerful as their descendant Louis XIV was to be, may be described as absolute monarchs. The great nobles were no longer rivals of the King; the undermining of their economic position was gradually driving them into a state of complete dependence on their royal master. They were now attracted to the court of the French Kings by the hope of obtaining the money with which to lead a life of luxury such as the dwindling incomes from their estates could no longer provide. In order to pay for their wars, their court, the expenses of government and of pensions to their favourites, the French Kings needed a large revenue; in order to obtain it they turned to the section of society which had in its hands the main wealth of the country, the middle classes. From the time of Francis I we see more and more clearly how the continued progress of the monarchy towards absolutism depended on the financial aid of the middle classes, for it was mainly from this source that it could obtain the necessary money. Thus in 1522 the first French public loan, the famous *rentes*, was raised by the Crown which offered an interest of eight per cent. to its subjects. Another method of tapping the wealth of the middle classes was the sale of official posts; we have already seen how eagerly the pecuniary and social advantages which they offered were sought after by the middle classes. In its century-long struggle for supremacy over the great nobles and then for the establishment of absolutism, the Crown owed its victory largely to the wealth which the middle classes had accumulated in trade and industry.

By the middle of the sixteenth century an absolute monarchy had clearly emerged in France; then the growth in the power of the Crown was violently interrupted by the Wars of Religion which for thirty years (1563-1593) devastated the country. In the struggle between Catholics and Huguenots the authority of the Crown disappeared at times almost completely. The state of mind of the various classes of society towards the end of the civil wars, when disorder was at its very height, is described thus by a contemporary: 'Une grande partie de la noblesse ne veut plus de roi; le peuple ne veut ni souverain, ni noblesse, et ne reconnaît ni prince, ni gentilshommes. Il n'y a pas jusqu'aux moindres habitants des campagnes qui ne veulent se dérober à leur domination.'

In the crumbling both of the royal authority and of the existing social order, theorists were not wanting to denounce the absolutist tendencies of the Crown, and to demand the re-establishment of such institutions as had in earlier days tempered the power of the monarchy. Catholic, and particularly Jesuit, writers wrote apologies for regicide, should the King oppress the Church or fail to carry out his oath to exterminate all heretics in his domains. In 1589 Henry III fell a victim to the dagger of a Dominican friar: and for the next four years until he abjured Calvinism and was at last able to enter Paris, his successor, Henry IV, had to carry on an apparently interminable war in order to secure his throne. Even when he was at last established in Paris and had accepted the religion of the majority of his subjects, his power was not secure until he had bribed into submission the great noblemen who led the ultra-Catholic party.

Over thirty years of civil war had made the financial position of the Crown, which was difficult even in normal times, almost desperate. In the provinces the governors, nominally the King's agents, exercised power for their own ends. The whole nation indeed seemed to be on the point of disintegrating into a loose form of federation, which would have meant the end both of national unity and absolutism.

The French Royal Family in the Seventeenth Century

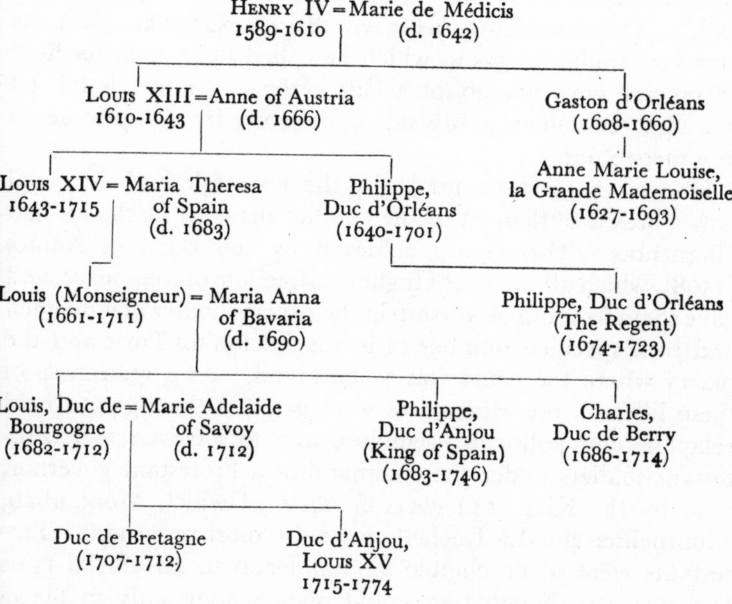

Such was the situation which confronted Henry IV on the morrow of his abjuration in 1593. Yet he finally emerged the most popular of all French Kings, because he proved that the monarchy was at that time the only form of government capable of assuring peace and order. A soldier for the greater part of his life (he was born in 1553), he succeeded in restoring absolute monarchy, without, however, surrounding himself with all the pomp of formal etiquette and king-worship which his grandson, Louis XIV, was to employ. He always remained accessible, and familiar, not to say free, in language and manners. He was determined to be absolute ruler over his subjects, and yet his courtiers were never struck dumb with terror in his presence as were later those of Louis XIV:

witness the anecdote of a nobleman who asked him for a favour in the following terms: 'Sire, vous faites du bien à des traîtres, et n'en faites pas à vos véritables serviteurs.—Pardieu, dit le roi en colère, je fais du bien à qui il me plaît.—Il est vrai, sire, mais il vous doit plaire d'en faire à des gens comme moi.' (Tallemant, *Historiettes*, viii. 81-2.) Or take again the firm yet familiar terms in which he called upon a disobedient provincial governor to obey his orders: 'Votre lettre est d'homme en colère, je n'y suis pas encore, je vous prie de ne m'y mettre pas.'

One of the first essentials for the restoration of the royal power was a settlement of the conflict between Catholics and Huguenots. This Henry achieved by the Edict of Nantes (1598), which allowed the Huguenots freedom of conscience, and gave them freedom of worship in the private houses of noblemen and in a specified number of towns, excluding Paris and the places where the court was to be found. As a guarantee of these liberties the Huguenots were granted the right to hold religious and political assemblies, and to garrison with Protestant soldiers under the command of a Protestant governor, paid by the King, 142 *places de sûreté*, of which Montauban, Montpellier and La Rochelle were the most important. Protestants were to be eligible for admission to all official posts and degrees, though they could open schools only in places where the exercise of their religion was permitted. Special law-courts were to be set up to include a certain number of Protestant judges, so that justice should be administered impartially. The Protestants thus obtained considerable privileges—civil and political, as well as religious—from the Edict of Nantes. The Crown was not yet strong enough, at the end of the Wars of Religion, to attempt to enforce religious uniformity, as it was to do under Louis XIV. The only words in the edict which looked forward to such a future, were those which expressed the hope that Frenchmen would worship 'd'une même intention, s'il n'a plu à Dieu que ce soit *pour lors* [1] en une même forme de religion.'

Having overcome the opposition of both Catholics and

[1] At present.

Huguenots to this compromise solution to the religious question, Henry was free to devote himself to the restoration of the royal power and of the economic position of France, both gravely impaired by the long years of civil war. The latter was the indispensable condition for the former, since without economic recovery the monarchy would have been unable to secure the support of the social classes on which its existence depended. In this work of economic reconstruction Henry was aided by two collaborators of very unequal fame, the Duc de Sully, a Protestant nobleman who devoted himself to the finances and the improvement of agriculture, and Barthélemy de Laffemas, a Protestant merchant attached to the personal service of the King, who was interested in the development of industry.

By a policy of strict economy Sully succeeded in wiping out a large part of the national debt. Not merely did he avoid a deficit in the Treasury accounts, in itself a very considerable achievement for any French minister under the *ancien régime*; he also succeeded in building up a reserve of gold which was stored in the Bastille. Yet he did nothing to reform the systems of taxation which he had inherited from his predecessors. All he attempted to do was to get the best possible results out of a thoroughly bad system. Thus he remitted to the peasants the payment of certain arrears of taxes, and reduced the amount of the *taille*, though at the same time he increased the amount of the *gabelle*. He also reduced the number of privileged persons who enjoyed exemption from taxation, by making those people pay who had usurped the privilege during the disorders of the Wars of Religion. At the same time he was compelled by the Treasury's urgent need for money to take a step which greatly diminished the power of the Crown over its own officials, for he allowed them to make their posts hereditary in return for the payment of an annual tax (*paulette*, after the name of the *financier* Paulet, who invented it).

In order to fill the coffers of the Treasury, Henry had to improve the condition of agriculture, trade and industry. In Sully's eyes agriculture was the most important source of wealth for France. 'Pâturage et labourage', he wrote, 'sont les deux mamelles dont la France est alimentée, les vraies mines et trésors de Pérou.' In a country whose economic life was so dominated by agriculture as was France in the seventeenth century, the peasantry, who produced the greater part of the national income and paid the greatest part of the taxes, deserved all the protection the monarchy could give them. Sully accordingly put in force various measures to assist them; but the most important benefit which the reign of Henry IV procured for the peasant was over a decade of peace both at home and abroad.

Trade and industry were not, however, neglected during the reign, for they too, however small in scale judged by modern standards, were important both in the economic life of the country and in providing money for the Treasury. The economic policy of the various governments of the *ancien régime* had as its first aim the raising of money through taxation. Thus the edict of 1597 by which Henry attempted, in vain, to organize all trades into guilds (*métiers jurés*), was inspired not merely by a desire to exercise control over trade and industry, but also by the aim of raising money from the members and officials of the guilds. The general economic policy of Henry and his adviser, Laffemas, was that system associated with the name of Louis XIV's minister, Colbert, but actually formulated a century earlier by the middle classes during the Wars of Religion. Mercantilism, which sought to conserve the national stock of gold and silver by using tariffs to secure the home market for French industries against the competition of foreign manufactured goods, was the economic policy of the French monarchy from the very beginning of the seventeenth century, for this policy seemed to promise the country greater power and influence in Europe. It was also in keeping with the desires of the French middle classes at this stage in their development: just as they looked to the monarchy for the maintenance of internal peace and order, so they looked to it for protection in the economic field against the invasion of the home market by foreign goods. The monarchy, for its part, was anxious to encourage French industry so as to increase the national wealth and consequently the yield from taxation.

23. *A. Bosse*, La galerie du Palais

24. *A. Bosse*, Le bal

25. Courtyard of th
Hôtel de Sully, Pari
(built in 1624)

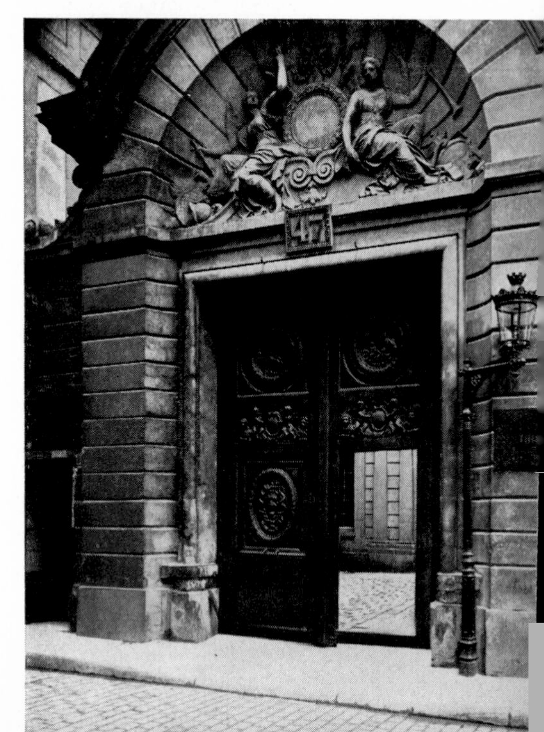

26. Entrance to the Hôtel des Ambassadeurs de Hollande, Paris

Thus we see Henry IV attempting to revive French industries, like cloth-making, and introducing such new industries as the manufacture of silk and velvet, all with the object of preventing French money being spent abroad to purchase foreign goods.

With the revival of the economic life of the nation, the monarchy was once more in a position to make itself all-powerful. Henry was resolved to wield absolute power and to crush any resistance to his will. He conveniently forgot the promise to summon the *États Généraux* which he had made at the beginning of his reign when his position was still insecure. He kept a close eye on the behaviour of the provincial governors. Marshal de Biran, Governor of Burgundy, and one of his oldest friends, indulged in various plots with foreign rulers; his first offence was pardoned, the second punished with death. Yet, with all his absolutist spirit, Henry IV made no essential changes in the administrative machine which he inherited from his predecessors; he was satisfied so long as he was obeyed. The result was that the power of the Crown rested less on strong institutions and habits of obedience than on the personality and strong will of the monarch. When in 1610 he was murdered in the streets of Paris and left a boy of nine to succeed him, the French monarchy, which lacked both his dominating personality and strong institutions, received a severe setback in its development towards absolutism.

Louis XIII (1610-1643)

Marie de Médicis, the widow of Henry IV, assumed the office of Regent during the minority of her son, Louis XIII. Now that the strong hand of Henry had gone, the great nobles, with the *Princes du sang* such as Condé at their head, began to reassert themselves, believing that their hour had come. 'Le temps des rois est passé, et celui des grands et des princes est venu.' They had long been accustomed to profit from periods when the monarchy was weak. Supported by a crowd of lesser noblemen who had attached themselves to their service, they constantly threatened to leave the court and to rouse to revolt the provinces under their control as governors. Yet, even at this early period in the seventeenth century, we can see that things had changed since the time when the great nobles presented a serious menace to the monarchy. By now they had ceased to cherish hopes of regaining their former power; their aim in revolting was to extract as much money as possible from the Regent in the form of pensions and lucrative sinecures. Their policy of blackmail met with some success, as the Regent was only too ready to comply with their demands for money in order to keep the peace.

The Huguenots began to cause trouble after the assassination of Henry, as they were alarmed by the ultra-Catholic influences by which the Regent was surrounded, and were also stirred to action by various ambitious great noblemen among them. For the next few years both these parties made things difficult for the Regent, as their appetite grew with concessions and bribes. In 1614 affairs reached a crisis. Supported by a number of great noblemen, Condé left the court and raised the standard of revolt in the provinces, covering up his purely selfish aims with a declaration in which he maintained that the Regent's policy was oppressive to all sections of the community. 'Et ce qui était le meilleur', Richelieu was later to point out, 'est qu'il se plaignit des profusions et prodigalités qui se faisaient des finances du Roi, comme si ce n'était pas lui et les siens qui les eussent toutes reçues, et que, pour gagner du temps avec eux, la Reine n'y eût pas été forcée.' (*Mémoires*, i. 275.) Finally, they demanded the summoning of the *États Généraux*. The Queen was compelled to accede to this demand; and also to hand over further liberal bribes.

This meeting of the *États Généraux*, which lasted into 1615, is interesting, not merely because it was to be the last meeting of that body before 1789, but because it reveals very clearly why absolutism was at last firmly established in France in the seventeenth century. The reason was simply that there was at that time no alternative form of government: no one section of the community was strong enough to resist the march of absolutism, nor could the various classes unite on any common programme of opposition to the monarchy. The *États Généraux* were an assembly of the three orders or estates of the kingdom, the Clergy, the Nobility and the Third Estate (*tiers état*) or non-privileged classes. Though in its composition it was not altogether unlike the English Parliament, it never possessed anything like the same power or prestige. Its meetings took place at long intervals. Indeed, it was only summoned in times of difficulty, during wars and minorities, and the meetings never led to any fruitful results. There were no definite rules about its summoning, its composition or the length of its meetings; above all, it possessed no real power, as it was a purely consultative body, whose functions were limited to making humble representations to the King on the grievances of the different orders of his subjects.

The meeting of the *États Généraux* in 1614 proved a complete fiasco, as the three orders, which met, as was the custom, as separate bodies, could not agree on any common programme. There was bitter hostility between the Nobility and the Third Estate. The deputies of the *tiers état* represented chiefly the wealthy middle class who had used their wealth to acquire official posts in the law-courts, financial administration and local government of France. The old nobility, who looked with envious eyes on the contrast between their own financial difficulties and the wealth of these *parvenus* which had often enabled them to buy titles and estates and to persuade impecunious noblemen to marry their daughters, were determined to keep them in their place. 'Il y a autant de différence entre eux et nous', declared one of the spokesmen of the Nobility, 'qu'entre le maître et le valet.' The best method of keeping down these insolent *officiers* was to strike at one of the main sources of their power, the *paulette,* which made their posts hereditary and so increased their value. The Nobility and Clergy therefore joined together to ask the Third Estate to petition the King, who had meanwhile reached the age of thirteen, his legal majority, to abolish the *paulette*. After some debate the Third Estate decided to accede to this request, but on two conditions. First, they demanded that, in return, the Clergy and Nobility should support a petition for a reduction in the *taille*. The second condition, a very cunning proposal which allowed them to get their own back on the privileged orders, was that they should couple with their petition for the abolition of the *paulette* one for a reduction of the King's expenditure on pensions. A spokesman of the Third Estate, addressing the King, made scathing reference to the enormous sums paid in pensions to the great nobles. 'Il y a de grands et puissants royaumes', he declared, 'qui n'ont pas tant de revenus que celui que vous donnez à vos sujets *pour acheter leur fidélité.*'

After this clash with the Nobility, the Third Estate also came into conflict with the Clergy. Finally, after the three orders had presented their separate petitions, they were sent home without having achieved any practical results. The divisions between the three orders, combined with the fact that intermittent meetings of the *États Généraux* in times of crisis had not allowed of the formation of a tradition of limiting the power of the Crown, made it easy for the monarchy to emerge from this meeting with its power of action unscathed.

Needless to say, the real power was not at this moment in the hands of a boy of thirteen, even if he had attained his legal majority. France was governed nominally by the Queen-Mother, but in reality by her Italian favourite, Leonora Galigaï, and her husband Concini, who had acquired the title of Maréchal d'Ancre. These two favourites were much hated, as public opinion regarded them as responsible for all the unpopular measures taken by the government. And now the Paris *Parlement*, which was thoroughly alarmed by the possibility of the *paulette* being abolished, went into open opposition.

Despite the resemblance in name with the English Parliament, we have seen that the composition of the *Parlements* was entirely different, since they consisted of judges who had inherited or purchased their posts, and whose primary function was to try the more important civil and criminal cases. But it would be a mistake to look upon the *Parlements*, particularly the Paris *Parlement*, as merely so many courts of justice, for their members laid claim to even more important functions. The Paris *Parlement*, which had jurisdiction over a large part of France, traced its history back through the centuries to the Royal Council of the mediaeval kings. Among its many extrajudicial functions was included the right of registering all royal edicts before they could come into force. Out of this practice grew the right of addressing remonstrances to the King (*droit de remontrance*) if the *Parlement* should disapprove of an edict. This right lay in the foreground of the political claims of the *parlementaires*; and during the *ancien régime*, whenever the monarchy was weak, it was always asserted. During the minority of Louis XIV, for instance, we shall again see the *Parlements* playing an important political role. Although it was very different in composition from the English Parliament, which was then conducting its struggle against the despotism of the Stuarts, the absence of any other form of national representation after the last meeting of the *États Généraux* in 1614, gave a certain colour to its claim to speak on behalf of the nation, and to oppose in its name the absolutist tendencies of the monarchy.

In 1615, under the cloak of defending the fundamental laws of the monarchy against the misrule of the ministers then in power, the Paris *Parlement* presented remonstrances in which it affirmed its right to intervene in affairs of state, denounced the disorder in the finances of the country, and made a thinly veiled attack on the Concini. For the first time in its history the *Parlement* openly attacked the monarchy for the abuses in the régime; in defending its own interests as a caste, it gave expression to the discontents of all the different social classes. Such was the use which it made of the independence which the Crown had conferred upon it by allowing the posts of its members to become hereditary. During the next two centuries, whenever the monarchy was weak, it was to find itself opposed by the *Parlements*, which, despite their selfish interests, were nevertheless the only bodies which could claim to speak for the nation.

If the meeting of the *États Généraux* and the protests of the *Parlement* led to no practical results, the position of the monarchy was still difficult. In 1616 the great noblemen and the Protestants again gave proofs of serious insubordination, as they knew that the government was weak and unpopular. Marie de Médicis carefully kept her son from taking any part in affairs of state, despite the fact that he was now technically of age. The real power continued in the hands of Concini, who had made himself governor of a number of very important frontier-fortresses. Then in 1617 he was murdered in the courtyard of the Louvre, and the Queen-Mother was compelled to exchange power for exile in the provinces. 'Je suis roi maintenant,' Louis XIII exclaimed. In practice, he allowed all real power to fall into the hands of a favourite of his own, the Duc de Luynes, who proceeded to cover up his very slight noble birth with various high-sounding posts and titles. The next four years, which ended with the death of the new favourite in 1621, saw the unedifying spectacle of two revolts made by the Queen-Mother, supported by various great noblemen, against her own son, and an armed rising of the Huguenots. The monarchy was still far from master of the situation at home. Indeed, its position did not begin to be restored until Richelieu came to power in 1624.

Around the figure of Richelieu have clustered all sorts of legends which it is difficult to remove. Born in 1585, the son of a nobleman who had married into the wealthy Paris bourgeoisie, he was educated for a career in the army, but, as a younger son, he was finally compelled to enter the Church in order to keep a bishopric in the family. Bishop of Luçon at the age of twenty-two, he was yet dissatisfied with so humble a diocese, since it was, in his own words, 'le plus vilain évêché de France, le plus crotté et le plus désagréable'. He sought other outlets for his great ambition, and at the meeting of the *États Généraux* in 1614, he distinguished himself as the spokesman of the Clergy. Later he was for a few months a member of the government, but soon followed the Queen-Mother, to whom he had attached himself, into exile in the provinces. It was through his position as intermediary between Louis XIII and Marie de Médicis that Richelieu finally gained his Cardinal's hat and succeeded in attaining power in 1624.

In the later years of his life, in his *Testament politique*, Richelieu summed up his aims in a simple formula. He promised the King, he declares, to employ all his efforts and all the authority conferred upon him to 'ruiner le parti huguenot, rabaisser l'orgueil des grands, réduire tous ses sujets en leur devoir et relever son nom dans les nations étrangères au point où il devait être' (p. 95). All these aims were complementary, but during his eighteen years of power, down to his death in 1642, most of Richelieu's energy was in fact devoted to foreign affairs, so that his achievements at home, important as they were, were dwarfed by his preoccupation with diplomatic and military matters.

When he came to power in 1624, the Thirty Years' War was raging in Germany. The Emperor was striving to win back to Catholicism those parts of the country which since the Reformation had gone over to Protestantism, and at the same time to transform the loose federation of some four hundred states known as the Holy Roman Empire into a hereditary, centralized monarchy on the French model. The Habsburgs of Vienna were in close alliance with the Habsburgs of Madrid, and even if the power of Spain was now in decline, it still continued to threaten France since the Low Countries, Franche-Comté and parts of Italy were under its control. In face of the threat of encirclement from Madrid and Vienna, French opinion was divided. There were devout Catholics who placed their faith above the political interests of France and demanded an alliance with the Habsburgs in their crusade against Protestantism; but there were others—and Richelieu, devout Catholic and cardinal as he was, was among them—who, despite their religious views, favoured an alliance with the Protestant states in order to combat the threat of Habsburg power to France's position in Europe.

Beginning in 1618 as a civil war between the Emperor and certain German states, the Thirty Years' War gradually developed into a general European conflict. In the opening years of the struggle the Protestant party in Germany suffered defeat after defeat, and by 1624 the victorious Emperor was on the point of making himself master of the whole country. Instead of facing a weak and disunited Germany, France would have been threatened with encirclement by a combination of two powerful Habsburg empires. Yet it was at first difficult for Richelieu to intervene in the conflict, however menacing the situation was becoming for France, because of the threat to the monarchy from both Protestants and great nobles at home.

'Lorsque Votre Majesté', Richelieu began his *Testament politique*, 'se résolut de me donner en même temps et l'entrée

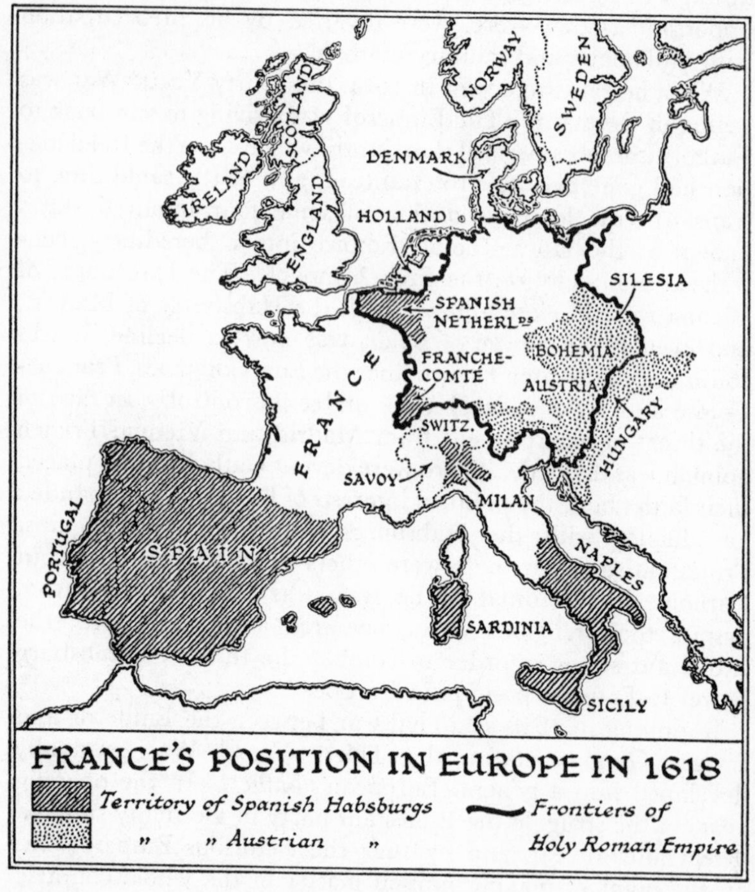

FRANCE'S POSITION IN EUROPE IN 1618

de ses Conseils et grande part en sa confiance pour la direction de ses affaires, je puis dire avec vérité que les Huguenots partageaient l'état avec Elle, que les grands se conduisaient comme s'ils n'eussent pas été ses sujets, et les plus puissants gouverneurs des provinces comme s'ils eussent été souverains en leurs charges.' Of these two internal dangers the Protestant was the more pressing, for in 1625, at a moment when Richelieu was engaged in a delicate diplomatic manœuvre, the Huguenots seized the opportunity to revolt. 'Tant que les Huguenots auront le pied en France,' Richelieu wrote in that year, 'le roi ne sera jamais le maître au dedans et ne pourra entreprendre aucune action glorieuse au dehors.' In other words, in order to have his hands free to intervene in the European war, Richelieu was determined to take away from the Huguenots the political power which made them 'a state within the state'.

His chance came in 1627 when La Rochelle, the most important of the Huguenot *places de sûreté*, revolted and sought help from Protestant England. After a siege lasting nearly a year, La Rochelle fell, and by 1629 all the Protestant strongholds in the South of France had also capitulated. This time the King refused to regulate his future relations with his Huguenot subjects by means of a treaty: their new status was defined by an *édit de grâce* (La Grâce d'Alais) whereby the Huguenots retained their freedom of conscience and restricted freedom of worship, but lost all the political privileges which the Edict of Nantes had conferred upon them. The Huguenots' political power was finally broken.

In his treatment of the opposition which he had to face both from members of the royal family and from the great noblemen, Richelieu did not immediately attain such final results. Not only was he opposed by the great noblemen, and by their ladies who were at least equally anxious to play a part in the intrigues against him. He had also to reckon with the hostility of the Queen, Anne of Austria, a Spanish princess; of the Queen-Mother, who was furious at being deprived by her former *domestique* of the political power which she considered to be hers by right; and of the King's brother, Gaston, Duke of Orleans, who in the absence of any children from the marriage of Louis XIII and Anne of Austria, remained until the birth of a Dauphin in 1638 heir-presumptive to the throne. In 1626 Gaston d'Orléans, urged on by his favourites and various great noblemen, was the figurehead of a conspiracy to assassinate Richelieu, in which various great ladies and even the Queen were implicated. As usual, Gaston submitted when the conspiracy was discovered, and betrayed his accomplices, one of whom, a young nobleman named Chalais, was tried by special commissioners appointed for the purpose by Richelieu, and executed. Several others were imprisoned. This was the first time since the beginning of the reign of Louis XIII that an aristocratic conspiracy was punished with such severity; a new master was at work.

Yet Richelieu's position still remained far from secure, for it was dependent all the time on the continuance of the King's good graces, of which he might at any moment be deprived. Until 1631, when Louis finally broke with his mother, Richelieu had to carry with him, not one ruler, but two; and his relations with Marie de Médicis became increasingly strained. The Queen-Mother came out more and more openly on the side of her favourite son, Gaston, and more and more openly against Richelieu. Things came to a head in 1630 when, after a serious illness, Louis, always a devoted son, was persuaded by his mother to dismiss Richelieu. However, at the very moment when she and her supporters were exulting at his imminent downfall, Richelieu swung the King round again, to their general discomfiture: hence the name of the *journée des dupes*.

A few months later Gaston insulted Richelieu, left the court and finally fled to the Low Countries where he was shortly to be joined by Marie de Médicis. Their accomplices were punished with exile, imprisonment or death, and the Queen-Mother was to spend the last ten years of her life abroad. Meanwhile Gaston returned to France in 1632, accompanied by Spanish levies, in order to join up with the revolt organized in Languedoc by its governor, the Duc de Montmorency, who had a considerable following there. The revolt failed, and Montmorency was defeated in battle, taken prisoner and executed. Leaving his supporters to the tender mercies of Richelieu, Gaston took fright and fled to Brussels, where he spent two years in exile. In 1634 he returned at last to France, but only on the most humiliating terms; if Richelieu could not punish the heir-presumptive as severely as he did other rebels, he took care on each occasion to make Gaston appear more and more contemptible.

Meanwhile events abroad were moving rapidly towards war with the Habsburg powers. The clash of French and Spanish interests in Italy led to fighting there, although not yet to war. After Denmark had been knocked out of the Thirty Years' War in 1629, the Protestant states in Germany had found a new protector in the King of Sweden, Gustavus Adolphus. In 1630 Gustavus entered Germany, and, supported by subsidies from Richelieu, won a series of brilliant victories over the Catholic forces, only to lose his life at the last one, at Lützen, in 1632, by which time his ambitions were beginning to clash with those of Catholic France. Two years later the Swedish army received a crushing defeat at the Battle of Nördlingen, and the Emperor appeared once more to be master of Germany. In face of this danger to France, Richelieu began to prepare to intervene in the war in more direct fashion. He proceeded to sign a series of alliances with such Protestant countries as Sweden and Holland as well as with certain Protestant states in Germany. In 1635 France declared war on Spain, although, despite her intervention in the Thirty Years' War, she still nominally remained at peace with the Austrian Habsburgs and the Empire. Notwithstanding various setbacks in the opening years of the war, Richelieu died in the belief that peace would soon be secured. However, the war in Germany was to last until the Treaty of Westphalia in 1648, while the war with Spain dragged on until the Treaty of the Pyrenees in 1659.

Richelieu's preoccupation with diplomatic and military affairs must be taken into account if we are to understand the limitations of his policy at home. As prime minister and real ruler of France for a period of eighteen years, he is generally regarded as the chief architect of French absolutism. Yet, if his work is examined closely, it will be seen that this view is somewhat exaggerated. Foreign affairs not only engaged the greater part of his time and energy in these years; they also prevented him from putting into effect many of his plans at home. For instance, he had projects for a reform of the finances, one of the weakest points of the French monarchy under the *ancien régime*. He would have liked to put an end to the selling of official posts and to have bought out as many as possible of the existing holders. In practice, this and similar good intentions were rendered impossible of execution by the urgent necessity of raising money to carry on the wars which were the consequence of his active foreign policy. In fact, far from achieving a reform of the French finances, Richelieu made the position worse than ever. He was compelled to have resort to such devices as the selling of ridiculous and useless public offices, merely in order to raise money; and his period of rule was a golden age for the tax-farmers, who reaped tremendous fortunes. Again, he wished to encourage trade and industry. He conferred noble rank on wholesale merchants; above all, he set up companies to engage in trade with foreign countries and the French colonies. Although these were provided with great privileges and a monopoly of trade in their particular field, none of them was a success, partly because the weight of taxation made it hard to raise the necessary capital. Again, Richelieu cannot be said to have been deterred from taxing the poorer sections of the community by excessive sentimentality. 'Si les peuples étaient trop à leur aise', he wrote in the *Testament politique*, 'il serait impossible de les contenir dans les règles de leur devoir.' (p. 253.) However, his policy occasionally had opposite results from those which he appears to have anticipated, for the burden of taxation led to a series of local revolts, both in town and country, all of which were pitilessly suppressed.

If Richelieu made no really important changes in the government machinery of France, this was simply because he had no new conception of government to offer. He was determined that the King (and the King's chief minister) should everywhere be obeyed. He crushed the resistance of the Huguenots and deprived them of all their political rights. He drove the Queen-Mother into exile; he repeatedly humiliated the Queen and the King's brother, Gaston d'Orléans. Although to the end of his life he was never free from the danger of aristocratic plots against him, he treated all conspirators, however exalted in rank, with ruthless severity; those who escaped a hasty trial and the scaffold, were condemned to prison or exile. He razed to the ground the fortresses of rebellious noblemen and did his best to put an end to duelling, another feudal survival, by enforcing severe edicts against the practice. The impression which his ruthless treatment of the rebellious members of the aristocracy produced on his contemporaries is well described by the phrase of Cardinal de Retz, 'l'âpre et redoutable Richelieu avait foudroyé plutôt que gouverné les humains'. (*Œuvres*, i. 232.)

Yet, however omnipotent Richelieu may have been in the last years of his life, however determined that the King's will should everywhere be carried out, and however ruthless he might be in breaking any form of open resistance to his authority, he did not create the strongly centralized form of government upon which the absolute monarchy of Louis XIV was to rest. In a word, he did nothing to change the fundamental institutions of France. Though Louis XIII told the members of the Paris *Parlement* in straight terms, 'Vous n'êtes établis que pour juger entre maître Pierre et maître Jean', and forbade them to intervene in affairs of state, Richelieu, who needed their assent to his financial edicts, did not attempt to deprive them of their *droit de remontrance*. Nor did he change the status of the governors of provinces, whose influence among the nobles and other notabilities of their district often made them dangerous to the Crown, as, for instance, in Montmorency's revolt in Languedoc. All he did was to punish such governors as revolted, and to replace them by men on whose loyalty he could rely. More important still, he did nothing to put an end to the existing system of decentralization whereby the provinces were governed less by the King and his ministers than by such local bodies as the Provincial Estates, the *Parlements*, the town-councils, and various groups of government officials whose purchase or inheritance of their posts gave them a certain independence. From all these Richelieu would demand, and obtain, complete obedience, if necessary by force; but he sought neither to abolish them nor to modify their powers in any way. In the seventeenth century the Crown gradually succeeded in putting an end to this decentralization by sending its own agents, the *Intendants*, to govern the provinces, to supervise the administration of justice, local government, and the collection of taxes. Under Louis XIV these agents became permanent officials, who were fixed in a province for a number of years, and as the King's representatives imposed obedience on the Nobles, Clergy, *Parlement* and local officials of the province. Under Richelieu such agents were already at work, but their missions were both temporary and limited to a small number of provinces: and there is no evidence (rather the contrary) to show that Richelieu wished to make their position permanent or to enlarge their powers to the degree which they were to attain later in the century.

Yet, even if Richelieu did not create the institutions on which the absolute monarchy of Louis XIV was to rest, his eighteen years as prime minister left their mark on the history of France. His death, in 1642, followed the year after by that of his master, marked the close of an extremely important period in French history. Abroad he had begun a war which, besides bringing to France important territorial accessions, brought to an end the hegemony of Spain in Europe, and defeated the plans of the Emperor to create a united Germany under his control. He thus prepared the way for the dominant position which France was to occupy in Europe under Louis XIV. At home, if he did not establish a strongly centralized government, his ruthless policy so cowed the aristocracy and all the other sections opposed to absolutism that, although during the minority which followed they were to make one last attempt to arrest the progress of the monarchy towards absolutism, he had laid the foundations of the unchallenged power which Louis XIV was to wield.

The Minority of Louis XIV. Mazarin. (1643-1661)

For the second time in just over thirty years the French monarchy had to undergo the test of a minority, with the usual setbacks to the establishment of absolutism. The young King, Louis XIV, was a child of five. Power was nominally in the hands of Anne of Austria, the Queen-Mother and Regent; in practice, the real ruler of the country, and a minister far more assured of the royal favour than ever Richelieu had been, since he could count on the affection of the Regent, was an Italian, Cardinal Mazarin (1602-1661). Yet, in other respects the new administration was inevitably weaker than that of Richelieu. First, Mazarin lacked the ferocious ruthlessness of his predecessor, both in his policy and in his manner; he relied less on force than on intrigue and soft words. Cardinal de Retz summed up the contrast between the two men when he wrote that Richelieu had 'un successeur doux, bénin, qui ne voulait rien, qui était au désespoir que sa dignité de cardinal ne lui permettait de s'humilier autant qu'il l'eût souhaité devant tout le monde, qui marchait dans les rues avec deux petits laquais derrière son carrosse'. (*Œuvres*, i. 232.)

It was, as we have seen, the recognized thing that during a minority the great nobles and other bodies in the state should reassert themselves. After the repression which they had suffered during the rule of Richelieu, it was inevitable that their reaction should this time be more than usually violent. The difficulties of Mazarin were still further increased by the legacy which he inherited from his predecessor. He was left with an apparently interminable war on his hands, and with all the financial difficulties which Richelieu had been unable to solve. The result was that the first ten years of Mazarin's administration were very disturbed. At times it seemed as if the monarchy had united against itself all sections of the community, and even that it was in danger of sharing the fate which in these very years overtook the Stuarts in England. Nevertheless the monarchy was finally to emerge from these long years of crisis more powerful than ever before in its history. The forces which had attempted to arrest its development towards absolutism were neither strong enough nor united enough to succeed in the attempt.

It is difficult to summarize briefly the causes and development of the civil war, known as the Fronde,[1] which finally

[1] *Fronde* ('a sling') gave rise to the expressions *Fronde* and *frondeurs*—those that were 'agin the government'.

broke out in 1648 and lasted until 1653. Broadly speaking, it may be said to have been brought about by two different but not entirely distinct causes. The middle classes and the mass of the people of France were angered by the ruinous level of taxation which was due to the requirements of the foreign war, and also, in part, to the depredations of the tax-farmers: this was the heyday of the *traitants*, who at this period were entrusted, not only with the collection of the indirect taxes, but even with that of the *taille*. The second cause of the revolt was the inevitable reaction against the progress which the monarchy had made towards absolutism under Richelieu, and the desire for a return to the state of affairs when the power of the Crown was tempered by that of other bodies in the state. 'Il y a plus de douze cents ans que la France a des rois,' wrote de Retz, one of the chief troublemakers of the Fronde, 'mais ces rois n'ont pas toujours été absolus au point qu'ils le sont.' In earlier ages France had known a form of government which represented 'un sage milieu . . . entre la licence des rois et le libertinage [1] du peuple'. All that had been changed when Richelieu came to power: 'Il forma dans la plus légitime des monarchies la plus scandaleuse et la plus dangereuse tyrannie qui ait jamais peut-être asservi un état' (*Œuvres*, i. 271-5). The reaction against the policy of Richelieu led in the Fronde even to a questioning of the very basis of absolute monarchy. In the words of Retz, 'le peuple entra dans le sanctuaire: il leva le voile qui doit toujours couvrir tout ce que l'on peut dire, tout ce que l'on peut croire du droit des peuples et de celui des rois, qui ne s'accordent jamais si bien ensemble que dans le silence' (*Ibid.*, p. 294). The revolt against absolutism is perhaps best reflected in the *Recueil de maximes véritables et importantes pour l'institution* [2] *du roi* of Claude Joly (1653), which expounds the theory of government by consent and denounces those who try to persuade kings that they are complete masters of the lives and property of their subjects:

> C'est une fausseté bien dangereuse que l'intérêt des ministres avares et ambitieux a voulu établir et insinuer aux rois: qu'ils sont maîtres des vies et des biens de leurs sujets, et par conséquent

[1] Insubordination. [2] Education.

27. *François Pourbus,*
Henri IV

8. *François Pourbus,*
Marie de Médicis

29.
Philippe de Champa
Louis XIII courc
par la Victoire

30. *Peter Paul Rubens*,
Anne d'Authrice

> que tout ce qui nous appartient est à eux, et qu'ils ont droit de le prendre et de le donner à qui ils veulent, et appliquer où bon leur semble. . . . Puisqu'ils ne sont pas les maîtres de nos biens, ils n'ont pas droit de les prendre, ni de mettre aucuns impôts sur nous sans notre volonté et consentement. (pp. 432-7.)

Such subversive sentiments were not to appear again in print in France for many a decade.

The blending of these two causes of discontent led first to a period of tension, and finally, in the years from 1648 onwards, to civil war. The great noblemen, barely kept in check by all the ruthless energy of Richelieu, began once more to reassert themselves under a minority, to seek for more power, and, above all, for more honours, pensions and sinecures. The middle classes and the people of Paris were discontented because of increases in the already high level of taxation, and because the interest on the *rentes* was paid only after interminable delays, and even then only in part. The *Parlements* too were affected by the financial difficulties of the Treasury, for the urgent need for money compelled the government to raise the amount of the *paulette*, the tax in return for which the *Parlementaires* were permitted to hand on their posts to their sons. Moreover, in addition to its own grievances about the fiscal policy of the government, and those of the mass of the people whom it claimed to represent, the *Parlements* and the mass of *officiers* were hostile to Absolutism, and especially to the system of sending *Intendants* to govern the provinces. If the *Intendants* were not yet permanently established in the provinces as agents of the central government, intervening in every sphere of local administration, they were already beginning to threaten the power of the *Parlements* and other local officials in this domain. In attacking Mazarin, the *Parlements* were not merely asserting their claim to intervene in affairs of state, especially during a minority, or defending themselves and the people against the demands of the Treasury. They aimed, above all, at arresting the development of a strong, centralized monarchy which would deprive *officiers* of many of their powers, and thus in the long run reduce the value of their posts.

The threat to their power and pockets drew together all the highest tribunals in France; the Paris *Parlement*, the *Grand Conseil*, *Chambre des Comptes* and *Cour des Aides*, despite the express ban of the Regent, assembled together in the Palais de Justice in June 1648. There they drew up a series of demands which they presented to Anne of Austria. Some of their proposals were of a fairly general nature, such as the demand that no subject should be imprisoned without trial for longer than twenty-four hours. But most significant, because they reveal clearly the real motives of the *Parlementaires* in their revolt against the Crown, were the demands that the *Intendants* should be abolished and that the rights and powers of all *officiers* should be secured. Because they put their own selfish interests first, the *Parlements* were, in fact, incapable of leading a serious movement of resistance to the development of absolutism. As a contemporary saw very clearly, if they spoke of the necessity of reforms, particularly in the finances of the country, it was only in order to gain popular support: 'Jugeant bien que ce qui les regardait en particulier ne ferait pas assez d'effet dans l'esprit du peuple, et ne serait pas assez appuyé s'ils ne prenaient le prétexte du bien public et de la réformation des finances, ils résolurent de ne point parler d'autres choses.' (Guy Joly, *Mémoires*, i. 67.) The presentation of these demands was followed by riots in the streets of Paris; Mazarin unwillingly agreed to a number of the proposals put forward by the *Parlement* in order to gain time.

It is impossible to deal here in any detail with the complicated events of the Fronde. In the first revolt, known not altogether inappropriately as the *Fronde parlementaire*, the Paris *Parlement*, after its first movement of resistance to the Crown, was soon only too anxious to make peace with Mazarin, as it was uneasy in its alliance with certain great noblemen and with the people of Paris. Order had no sooner been restored than the second Fronde, the *Fronde princière*, broke out. The backbone of this second revolt were the *princes du sang*, with Condé at their head; assisted by various great noblemen and ladies, they raised armies and tried to drive out Mazarin. The aim of the princes and great noblemen was not so much to achieve any definite political ends as rather to acquire honours and sinecures for themselves, their families and their followers. The memoirs of the time offer a revealing picture of the troubled atmosphere of these years; the background to these revolts was an astonishing series of intrigues, both political and amorous, and a fierce lust for power, and still more for prestige and money. Nothing was more frequent than changes of side, which took place according as love, or more frequently self-interest and prospects of material gain, dictated. The character and methods of Mazarin facilitated this corruption; he strove to maintain his position less by the use of force than by intrigue and vague promises which served to gain time when the situation was difficult. Something of the motives which actuated the members of the aristocracy in their revolt can be discerned in the following passage from the memoirs of a lady of the court:

> Les princes et les grands seigneurs . . . se souciaient beaucoup plus d'obtenir du ministre ce qu'ils désiraient, que de le chasser ni de s'amuser [1] à réformer l'État. Tous disaient qu'ils voulaient y travailler, et les dupes seules entraient dans cette tromperie; mais alors, ni bien longtemps depuis chacun ne cherchait que son intérêt particulier, et fort peu celui du public. . . . Tous voulaient maltraiter le Cardinal pour l'humilier, et lui faire des affaires qui pussent l'embarrasser; et presque tous voulaient qu'il demeurât, pour en pouvoir tirer leurs avantages. Il donnait volontiers quand il était en mauvais état; et ils ne savaient que trop qu'il n'épargnait ni dignités ni argent pour se retirer de péril. (Mme de Motteville, *Mémoires*, p. 239.)

The second Fronde, which lasted from 1650 to 1653, spread over a great part of the country. Mazarin was twice compelled to retire over the frontier into Germany, and the revolt appeared to threaten gravely the power and prestige of the monarchy. Yet in the second part of 1652 the young King, now no longer a minor, returned in triumph to Paris, to be followed a few months later, in February 1653, by Mazarin. The Fronde was over. Neither the great noblemen nor the *Parlements* had succeeded in putting the clock back, in arresting

[1] Waste their time.

the evolution of the French monarchy towards absolutism. Indeed, the principal result of the Fronde was to plunge a great part of France into terrible distress. All that the great mass of the people now wanted was peace and order.

In the years between the collapse of the Fronde and his death in 1661, Mazarin wielded immense power. A less impressive and forceful personality than Richelieu, he yet came to possess in these years a greater degree of authority and security than his predecessor had ever enjoyed in his eighteen years of rule. The Queen-Mother left affairs of state entirely in his hands, while the young King was occupied in pursuits more congenial to an adolescent. Despite their discontents, the different classes of society were exhausted by the Fronde, and preferred their present state of subservience to a repetition of the futilities of the civil war. No class or union of classes was capable of resisting the further development of absolutism; the last revolt had ended in dismal failure. However heavy the burden of taxation might be, the peasants were willing to endure it rather than face a return to the misery and destruction caused by the Fronde. The middle classes desired only peace and order in which to carry on their occupations, and felt a fierce hatred for all those who had been responsible for the Fronde. And though the great noblemen might still grumble at the rule of Mazarin, stern economic necessity drove them to court to the Cardinal's feet, for he could give or withhold at pleasure the pensions and lucrative posts which they so greatly needed.

In the following passage from a contemporary description of the political state of France in 1655, we see very clearly the causes which made possible the final establishment of absolutism after the collapse of the Fronde:

> Présentement il n'y a nul changement à attendre en ce royaume. Les peuples sont accablés de misère, de taille et de toute sorte d'impositions qu'ils aiment mieux souffrir que la guerre.
>
> La noblesse est tellement ruinée qu'elle n'est pas capable de monter à cheval pour aucune exécution, quelque apparence qui leur puisse être présentée d'une plus avantageuse condition.

Les Parlements sont tous asservis et ceux qui les composent n'oseraient parler ni rien dire contre le présent gouvernement.

Les grandes villes ne respirent que le repos et détestent [1] ceux qui ont été les auteurs des derniers troubles.

L'ordre ecclésiastique est tout dépendant de la cour et du favori de qui ils ont reçu leurs bénéfices.

Tous les gouverneurs des places sont attachés de même à la cour et au Cardinal.

Tous les grands seigneurs se plaignent et je n'en connais pas un seul qui fût capable de rien.

Pour Paris tout le peuple déteste le présent gouvernement et s'y assujettit pourtant volontairement. . . . On voit clairement que dans Paris on veut le repos et qu'on ne veut plus entendre à aucun remuement; cela est certain.

Quant aux courtisans ils sont toujours malcontents, mais avec tout cela il découle toujours quelque douceur [3] qui les apaise, et nul n'est capable de rien.

Le maréchal de Turenne qui seul a sens, courage et expérience, est asservi à la faveur, car depuis qu'il est marié, il a si grande peur de perdre la fortune de sa famille, qu'il est le valet des valets du Cardinal. Les autres courtisans sont pires que valets, car ce sont des esclaves. . . . (Public Record Office: State Papers Foreign, France (SP 78), vol. 113, ff. 48-9.)

Mazarin had been equally successful in his foreign policy. In 1648 he brought to an end by the Treaty of Westphalia the war with the Emperor begun by Richelieu. Not only did France acquire the new province of Alsace; but the attempt of the Austrian Habsburgs to make themselves rulers over a united Germany had been foiled, and Germany was long to remain a weak and divided neighbour of France. If the war with Spain dragged on for another eleven years until the Treaty of the Pyrenees, that treaty was to mark the end of the Spanish hegemony in Europe and the threat to France of encirclement by the alliance of Spanish and Austrian Habsburgs. Under the terms of the treaty France annexed the province of Roussillon and part of the province of Artois, so important to the defence of France because of its proximity to Paris. He had thus brought to a successful conclusion the

[1] Execrate. [2] Hear of. [3] i.e. pensions, gifts of money, etc.

foreign policy of Richelieu and completed the foundations of the hegemony which France was to exercise in Europe under the personal reign of Louis XIV.

Despite the importance of the achievements of Mazarin, historians have so far failed to discover exactly how he governed France. We know that on the morrow of the Fronde, French absolutism was to attain its highest point during the personal reign of Louis XIV; but we know little or nothing of the intervening period, from 1653 to 1661, when Mazarin's power was firmly secured. Yet it must have been during this period that the way was prepared for the authoritarian government of Louis XIV. Already before Mazarin's death much of the administrative machinery, on which the royal power was to rest, must have been built up. This is particularly true of the use of *Intendants* to govern the provinces. In any case the years in which Mazarin enjoyed power had seen the failure of the last revolt against absolutism; when at his death in 1661 power at last passed to a somewhat impatient Louis XIV, the way was open for the most absolute reign in the whole of French history.

CHAPTER VI

ABSOLUTISM AT ITS HEIGHT, 1661-1685

THE long reign of Louis XIV covered nearly three-quarters of a century, from 1643 to 1715. Its most brilliant period dates from the death of Mazarin in 1661 to a point somewhere between 1680 and 1690, when the first symptoms of decline became visible. It was at the age of twenty-two, after the Regency of his mother and the rule of Mazarin, that Louis XIV assumed power. He was not a man of exceptional gifts. Yet he possessed the qualities of industry and self-control, a rough sense of justice, a knowledge of men and an ability to hide his true feelings. Physically he was endowed with a tough constitution as well as with a handsome presence which made him every inch a king:

> En quelque obscurité que le sort l'eût fait naître,
> Le monde, en le voyant, eût reconnu son maître.

These lines from Racine's *Bérénice* (1670) are generally taken to refer to the King, then at the height of his powers.

From the first the young King was determined to be master in his own kingdom. He was King by the grace of God, and responsible to God alone. His views on the exalted position of the monarch are summed up in striking fashion in the memoirs which he composed for the Dauphin:

> Il faut assurément demeurer d'accord que, pour mauvais que puisse être un prince, la révolte de ses sujets est toujours infiniment criminelle. Celui qui a donné des rois aux hommes a voulu qu'on les respectât comme ses lieutenants, se réservant à lui seul le droit d'examiner leur conduite. Sa volonté est que, quiconque est né sujet, obéisse sans discernement. . . . Il n'est point de maxime plus établie par le christianisme que cette humble soumission des sujets envers ceux qui leur sont préposés. (*Mémoires*, pp. 254-5.)

In the same work he drew the logical conclusion from this belief in the sacred and unlimited power of the monarchy:

the property of all his subjects, whether lay or ecclesiastical, was at his disposal to use as he thought fit in the interests of the state: 'Les rois sont seigneurs absolus et ont naturellement la disposition pleine et libre de tous les biens, tant des séculiers que des ecclésiastiques, pour en user comme sages économes,[1] c'est-à-dire, selon les besoins de leur état.' (*Ibid.*, p. 197.)

The King must not only reign; he must also govern. In 1671 Louis described, not without some illusions, the way in which he considered he had governed France in the ten years since he had taken over the reins of power from Mazarin, and had set himself to work regularly every day with his ministers:

> La plupart regardaient l'assiduité de mon travail comme une chaleur[2] qui devait bientôt se ralentir; et ceux qui voulaient en juger plus favorablement, attendaient à se déterminer par les suites.
>
> Le temps a fait voir ce qu'il en fallait croire, et c'est ici la dixième année que je marche, il me semble, assez constamment dans la même route, ne relâchant rien de mon application; informé de tout; écoutant mes moindres sujets; sachant à toute heure le nombre et la qualité de mes troupes, et l'état de mes places[3]; donnant incessamment mes ordres pour tous leurs besoins; traitant immédiatement avec les ministres[4] étrangers; recevant et lisant les dépêches; faisant moi-même une partie des réponses, et donnant à mes secrétaires la substance des autres; réglant la recette et la dépense de mon État; me faisant rendre compte directement par ceux que je mets dans les emplois importants; tenant mes affaires aussi secrètes qu'aucun autre l'ait fait avant moi; distribuant les grâces par mon propre choix, et retenant, si je ne me trompe, ceux qui me servent, quoique comblés de bienfaits pour eux-mêmes et pour les leurs, dans une modestie[5] fort éloignée de l'élévation et du pouvoir des premiers ministres. (*Ibid.*, pp. 30-1.)

This last principle—not to allow any one minister to monopolize power and thus to follow in the footsteps of Richelieu and Mazarin—was throughout his long reign one of the main preoccupations of Louis XIV. 'Quant aux personnes qui devaient seconder mon travail,' he wrote in his advice to his

[1] Stewards. [2] Zeal. [3] Fortresses. [4] Envoys. [5] Modest position.

son, 'je résolus sur toutes choses de ne point prendre de premier ministre, et si vous m'en croyez, mon fils, et tous vos successeurs après vous, le nom en sera à jamais aboli en France, rien n'étant plus indigne que de voir d'un côté toutes les fonctions, et de l'autre le seul titre de roi.' (*Ibid.*, p. 25.)

The ministers whom he admitted to his counsels were men of relatively humble origin, who owed their position entirely to his favour, and could therefore be relied upon to show unquestioning loyalty. On his accession to power Louis broke entirely with the ancient traditions of the French monarchy. In his councils there was no place for any member of the royal family, not even for the Queen-Mother who, during her son's minority, had at least nominally governed France. When Louis's only brother, Monsieur, asked for the post of governor of Languedoc, the request was refused on the grounds that 'c'était manque de prévoyance et de raison que de mettre les grands gouvernements entre les mains des Fils de France,[1] lesquels, pour le bien de l'État, ne doivent jamais avoir d'autre retraite que la Cour, ni d'autre place de sûreté que dans le cœur de leur frère'. (*Ibid.*, p. 155.) In fact, Monsieur was all his life excluded from any position of authority in the government, and was compelled to fritter away his days at court, indulging in amusements which were not always highly edifying. A foreign envoy described him as of a disposition 'toute portée aux plaisirs, éloignée d'aucune application sérieuse,' and added:

> Comme il est curieux à l'excès de sa parure et de son ajustement, aussi met-il en usage tout ce qui peut y contribuer, jusqu'à porter dans les bras des bracelets de pierreries, et à ne rien omettre de ce qui peut entretenir la fraîcheur ou l'éclat de son teint. . . . Ses entretiens, après tout, ne partent pas d'un génie [2] fort éclairé, ni rempli d'autres idées que de celles qui se peuvent trouver conformes au train ordinaire de la Cour de France et aux conjonctures qui s'y présentent. Et, comme on ne le tient pas propre à garder un secret, il arrive qu'on ne lui en confie guère: aussi n'a-t-il aucune part aux affaires d'État ou du gouvernement, ni même entrée ou séance dans aucun Conseil, que purement

[1] Sons of a King of France.

[2] Mind.

dans celui qu'on appelle *des dépêches.*[1] . . . (Ézéchiel Spanheim, *Relation de la Cour de France*, pp. 140-1.)

Louis also excluded from his councils the *princes du sang*, at whose head was Condé, one of the greatest generals of the age; all prelates, for Louis did not want to see a repetition of the rule of the two cardinals, Richelieu and Mazarin; and all great noblemen, even Turenne, to whose generalship the monarchy owed many victories, both in foreign wars and in critical periods of the Fronde.

To the disgust of the courtiers the ministers who composed the *Conseil d'en haut*, the most important of the royal councils, were all bourgeois who, through their inherited wealth, had been able to purchase government posts, and had risen to high positions in the administration. 'Les grands de la cour,' a contemporary wrote, 'et, entre autres, M. de Turenne, n'en étaient pas fort satisfaits, et demandèrent s'il se pourrait bien faire que trois bourgeois eussent la principale part dans le gouvernement de l'État.' Except in war-time, when their military reputation gave men like Condé and Turenne a place in the royal counsels, the great noblemen and princes of the blood had now lost every shred of power. The new King ruled with the help of members of the middle class which, thanks to its economic power, was already well on the way to supplanting the nobility as the most important section of society.

These bourgeois ministers were dependent on the King both for their position and for the continuation of his favours to them and to their families. Their faithfulness was rewarded by their master with all sorts of honours and favours; their sons were allowed to succeed them and to cover up their middle-class origins by the purchase of estates and titles. Yet Louis was resolved to limit their power; none of them was to be allowed a predominant place which might make of him a second Richelieu or Mazarin. This end, so he imagined, was secured by taking none of them entirely into his confidence, and by encouraging a keen spirit of rivalry between his ministers and also between the different families of ministers. Every day he

[1] One of the less important royal councils.

worked solidly for several hours with his ministers, either separately or in council; but all decisions were to be taken by him alone, for, as he put it, 'la décision a besoin d'un esprit de maître'. That at least was the theory. The practice is perhaps best described by a foreign envoy writing in 1690 who, after speaking of the king's 'génie naturellement borné', goes on:

> Il s'est fait un art de régner, moins par science et par réflexion, que par les conjonctures et par habitude, en sorte qu'on peut dire, sans offenser le Roi, et malgré les éloges outrés de ses panégyristes, que ce n'est pas un de ces génies [1] de premier ordre qui voit, qui pénètre, qui résout, qui entreprend tout par lui-même, qui en forme le plan et en exécute le projet, et ce qui fait le véritable caractère des héros donnés pour la gloire de leur siècle et pour la félicité publique. De là vient aussi une suffisance [2] du Roi assez bornée dans le fonds des affaires, qui s'en contente d'en savoir les dehors, sans les approfondir suffisamment, aisée par là à être préoccupée [3] par les personnes où il prend confiance et qu'il en croit aucunement [4] instruites et, après tout, un attachement, ou, pour mieux dire, un entêtement, qui n'est pas moins grand, pour l'exécution des desseins ou des projets formés ou conseillés par un ministère violent ou artificieux.

Thus, despite his pride in carrying the whole government on his shoulders, his decisions were often inspired by his ministers.

> C'est qu'en effet il juge moins des affaires et des intérêts publics par ses propres lumières que par celles qu'on lui en donne. . . . Après tout, s'il a assez de talent pour comprendre les grandes affaires, on peut dire qu'il ne s'en occupe pas assez pour les digérer et pour les envisager par tous les biais [5] qu'elles peuvent avoir: en sorte que son assiduité qu'on lui voit aux Conseils et sa grande application est bornée le plus souvent à donner lieu au rapport intéressé ou altéré qu'on lui fait, aux délibérations conformes qui s'en prennent en sa présence et au choix qui s'y résout des moyens ou des personnes pour les faire réussir. Jaloux au dernier point de son autorité, sensible outre mesure à tout ce qui la regarde ou qui la peut blesser, il s'en laisse entraîner aisément à embrasser les conseils qu'on lui donne et les mesures

[1] Minds. [2] Competence, intelligence. [3] Biassed, prejudiced.
[4] To some degree. [5] Sides.

qu'on lui propose pour la soutenir. (Ézéchiel Spanheim, *Relation de la Cour de France*, pp. 70-2.)

This relatively fair and objective contemporary account of Louis's gifts and weaknesses as a King would seem to have the ring of truth: it is far less severe than the verdict of another writer of the time, the violently partial Duc de Saint-Simon, the author of the famous memoirs of the reign.

In Louis's eyes the government of France was to be in the hands of the King, aided by a small number of ministers subordinate to him. But in order that the decisions of the King and his three or four ministers at the centre might be carried out all over the country, an administrative machine was necessary. The second feature of the absolute form of government established by Louis was that it constituted a highly centralized bureaucracy; the decisions of the central government were carried out in the provinces by the *Intendants*, who, like the ministers, were of middle-class origin, and, since they were at any moment subject to recall, could be depended upon to fulfil loyally their role as agents of the royal authority.

We have seen that the *Intendants* had already played a certain part in the government of France under Richelieu, and especially Mazarin; but it was with Louis XIV and his minister Colbert that the central government systematically established its authority in all the provinces of France by the use of these agents on a permanent footing. As always under the *Ancien Régime*, it was only gradually that this institution grew up, that the *Intendants* were assigned a definite district to be administered until such time as they were recalled or sent elsewhere, and were given specific duties.

'L'intendant, c'est le Roi présent dans les provinces'; that is how a famous historian sums up the position of the *Intendant* in his province. His functions may be fairly simply deduced from his official designation: *Intendant de Justice, de Police et de Finances*. His first task was to keep a watchful eye on the influential persons in his district, the nobles, clergy and officials, who might abuse their influence to resist the royal power. He was also responsible for the maintenance of order in his province. In addition, he had to watch over the administration of justice, so as to prevent abuses. He had the right to preside over any court within his province, and in certain circumstances he could try cases himself. Again, the *Intendant*, aided by a number of assistants (*subdélégués*), gradually took over a great many of the functions of the officials who were concerned with the assessment and collection of the *taille*; for he came in time to direct the assessment of the different parishes in his province, to examine the lists of collectors, and to assess people who had used their influence to obtain unauthorized exemptions from the *taille*, or too light assessments. Finally, the *Intendant* intervened more and more in local government, for the monarchy took advantage of the state of indebtedness of the towns and villages to assume control over their administration.

The new form of strongly centralized monarchy which grew up in the 1660's did not change fundamentally the social organization of France. It was superimposed upon the existing social structure and political institutions; it did not destroy them. Though shorn of much of their power, the old institutions which had imposed some check on the power of the Crown, still lingered on. The *États Généraux*, it is true, were never summoned; but they were simply forgotten, not abolished. The *Parlements*, which during Louis's minority had attempted to take upon themselves the role of representatives of the nation, were not allowed to intervene in affairs of state. Yet Louis did not deprive them of their right to make remonstrances when royal edicts were submitted to them for registration; what he did was to strip this right of any real significance by insisting that such remonstrances could only be made *after* the edicts had been registered, that is to say, too late to secure their withdrawal or even their revision.

The provinces had, up to this time, enjoyed varying degrees of autonomy which might stand in the way of the royal power. Their governors had, in the past, been able to build up a dangerous degree of influence and prestige, which had sometimes been turned against the royal authority. To avoid this happening, Louis decided 'de ne plus donner nul gouvernement vacant que pour trois ans, me réservant seulement de pouvoir prolonger ce terme par de nouvelles provisions,[1] toutes les fois que je le trouverais à propos' (*Mémoires*, p. 125). From now onwards governors were not likely to attempt to stir up trouble in their provinces, as they had done under Richelieu and Mazarin, since the renewal of their appointment was conditional on exemplary conduct. Indeed, to be doubly sure, it was Louis's practice to keep the governors of provinces most of the time at court where they would be under his eye. What remained of their former functions was gradually taken over by the *Intendants*. Yet once again Louis did not abolish the old institutions to make way for the new; he merely rendered the old institution harmless to his power, by reducing the post of governor to a lucrative, and therefore sought after, honour.

Although the towns had already lost much of the freedom which they had at one time enjoyed, they still possessed varying degrees of self-government. The development of the power of the *Intendants* meant, as we have seen, a growth of interference by the central government in local affairs. Certain of the forms of self-government were permitted to survive in the towns, but most of the substance had gone. In the end even the formal election of Mayors ceased in many cities, for they now became permanent officials who acquired their posts by purchase.

Certain provinces which bore the name of *Pays d'états* still retained their Estates or Provincial Assemblies, to which the nobility, clergy and Third Estate sent deputies. The most important of the *Pays d'états*, among which were Brittany and Burgundy, was the province of Languedoc, in the South of France. The privileges of these provinces were greatly envied by outsiders, because in general the amount of taxes which they were called upon to pay was less in proportion to their population than in other provinces. Yet it is doubtful whether in practice conditions were substantially better there than elsewhere. The *Pays d'états* were never a model of democratic government, because affairs were largely in the hands of a wealthy oligarchy; and the taxes were levied with as great

[1] Letters confirming an appointment.

inequalities as elsewhere. The *Pays d'états* did, however, possess the important privilege of assessing and collecting taxes themselves, and paying the province's share of taxation to the central government in the form of a *don gratuit*, the amount of which was fixed by negotiation with the King's agents.

Such remnants of provincial autonomy were hardly likely to appeal to Louis XIV. Yet once again he did not abolish the institution outright. What he did was to deprive the Provincial Estates of any real power. To this end the deputies were bullied or bribed into submission by the threat to withhold, or the promise to confer, favours which they might possibly receive from the King. Moreover, Louis abandoned the old system of allowing the deputies to present the grievances of the province before they proceeded to vote the *don gratuit*. More important, he gave up the custom of asking for more than he expected to receive, and then haggling with the deputies about the final amount to be paid over. Now the King demanded a definite sum which the deputies had to vote immediately; and from this time onwards the amount demanded constantly rose, without anyone daring to make the slightest protest. A vivid picture of the state of impotence to which the Estates of Brittany were reduced by the absolutism of Louis XIV is provided by the letters of Mme de Sévigné. Her accounts of the meetings are mainly concerned with relating the various amusements (balls, plays, banquets and so forth) which were offered to the deputies. As for the serious side of their business, the question of taxes, Mme de Sévigné writes: 'Les états ne doivent pas être longs; il n'y a qu'à demander ce que veut le Roi; on ne dit pas un mot: voilà qui est fait.' (5 Aug. 1671.)

Thus under Louis XIV all those institutions which might curb in some degree the power of the Crown—the *Parlements*, the governors of provinces, Provincial Estates and town councils—were gradually stripped of any effective power. The government was supreme both in the centre and in the provinces. No one class, no combination of classes could impose any effective check on the government machine. The common people—the peasants, the artisans, all those below the level of the well-to-do middle class—had no place in the social or political life of the period. Though by far the most numerous section of the community, they did not count in the eyes of their rulers or of the upper classes. It is amusing to see this blindness in the way in which the peasantry are mentioned in the semi-official handbook of seventeenth century France, the *État de la France*. After listing the various posts held by the nobility and clergy, and dealing with the only sections of the Third Estate who really counted—the judges, members of the University and merchants—all that the author can find to say on the subject of the peasantry, which after all formed the vast majority of the population of France at that time, is one short sentence: 'On pourrait faire un quatrième membre du tiers état, qui est le paysan, *mais il n'y a rien à dire de considérable*.' (N. Besongne, *État de la France*, ii. 462.)

The Third Estate, in practice if not in theory, was limited to the wealthier sections of the middle classes: the *rentiers*, (*bourgeois vivant noblement* as they were called), the *officiers* who held posts in the administration of justice and finances, the bankers, tax-farmers and merchants. It is true that the most important *officiers*, the *Parlementaires*, had no cause to love Louis, for he had deprived them of all say in matters of state, but they had to obey the demands of a strong King. Even when he proceeded to hit them where it hurt them most, by reducing the value of their hereditary posts, they did not dare to make the slightest protest. The Ambassador of Savoy reported in 1669 when this blow had just fallen: 'Ce coup a mis dans un abattement qui n'est pas concevable, tous les parlements; ils en murmurent étrangement [1] en secret et en sont outrés de désespoir, et s'ils avaient l'autorité et crédit des autres fois, ils feraient éclater tout leur dépit, mais ils n'ont plus ni force ni crédit et sont réduits à une soumise obéissance.' (Marquis de Saint-Maurice, *Lettres de la cour de Louis XIV*, i. 302.)

It is likewise true that the minor *officiers* who were concerned with the collection of taxes and the administration of justice in the lower courts had been deprived of much of their power by the growing importance of the *Intendants*; but their discon-

[1] Terribly.

31.
lippe de Champaigne,
Richelieu

32.
lippe de Champaigne,
Mazarin

33. *R. Nanteuil*, Louis XIV

34. *R. Nanteuil*, Colbert

35. *R. Nanteuil*, Louvois

tent was too unimportant to matter. In general, the middle classes were the firmest supporters of absolute monarchy in seventeenth century France. They remembered the age-long alliance between middle classes and Crown which had finally broken the power of the feudal nobility. Their bitter experience of the futility of the Fronde had increased their feelings of loyalty towards the institution which alone at that time could give them security and stability. Their outlook was very different from that of their descendants, who after another century of economic advance were to sweep away absolutism and to claim a degree of political power proportionate to their importance in the economic life of the nation. Far from harbouring such subversive thoughts, the seventeenth century French bourgeois accepted absolutism as a necessity for securing a stable country, and the social hierarchy as something divinely ordained: the one thought of an ambitious bourgeois was to make enough money to enable himself or his children to rise up the social ladder into the ranks of the aristocracy.

Of the two privileged orders, the clergy alone possessed some remnants of independence. Every five years its elected representatives met in the *Assemblée du Clergé*. It paid no direct taxes, except a voluntary payment, the *don gratuit*, the amount of which was fixed by negotiations between the King and the Assembly. Yet such independence as the clergy possessed was strictly limited. Ever since the Concordat of 1516 had conferred upon the King the right of disposing of all ecclesiastical posts of any importance, nobody who wished to make a career in the Church could afford to incur the royal displeasure. The result was that, far from offering opposition to his desires, the upper clergy were only too ready to play the role of courtiers.

As for the nobility, we have seen in an earlier chapter how their state of impoverishment drove them to a position of increasing dependence on the favours of the King, and how this finally completed the transformation of the French aristocracy from turbulent, semi-feudal lords, ever ready to profit from any weakness in the government, into docile courtiers. The great noblemen had had their last fling in the Fronde; already during the last years of Mazarin's rule we have seen how they became his *esclaves*. By the time the personal reign of Louis XIV began, the *Princes du sang* and great nobles had ceased to possess the bands of noble retainers and the small armies which, earlier in the century, had allowed them to make war on the monarchy. Under Louis XIV the great noblemen were no longer in a position to blackmail the King by threatening to leave the court and to set up the standard of revolt in the provinces under their control. In 1670 the Ambassador of Savoy reported to his master that Monsieur, the King's brother, was in a bad temper and threatening to leave the court, a step which, he considers, would be very ill-advised now that times have changed:

> Il n'est plus le temps d'autrefois que, quand un fils de France [1] se retirait de la Cour mal satisfait et était une fois à trois lieues de Paris, l'on croyait le royaume bouleversé et en péril; chacun armait pour son parti et les mécontents levaient le masque. Présentement personne ne bougera, tout le monde est soumis dans le devoir et dans la crainte, le Roi dans la souveraine puissance, fort en argent et en troupes, maître des Parlements, des places et de tout ce qui est dans son royaume. (Saint-Maurice, *Lettres*, i. 387-8.)

Indeed, if a nobleman left the court of Louis XIV, it was because the King had exiled him to his estates—a dreaded punishment which meant the end of all favours and a life of utter boredom. 'Le chef-d'œuvre de Louis XIV, le complément du système de Richelieu,' wrote Stendhal, 'fut de créer cet ennui de l'exil.'

To keep the nobles out of any mischief the King insisted on their coming to court. And the nobles came, not only because the life at court suited their tastes for luxury and amusement, but because it was the only way of obtaining all the favours which the King had at his disposal. They knew that if they did not come to court, they had no chance of obtaining any assistance from the King.

> Non seulement il était sensible à la présence continuelle de ce qu'il y avait de distingué, mais il l'était aussi aux étages [2] in-

[1] Son of a King of France.

[2] Ranks.

ferieurs. Il regardait à droite et à gauche à son lever, à son coucher, à ses repas, en passant dans les appartements, dans les jardins de Versailles, où seulement les courtisans avaient la liberté de le suivre; il voyait et remarquait tout le monde; aucun ne lui échappait, jusqu'à ceux qui n'espéraient pas même être vus. Il distinguait très bien en lui-même les absences de ceux qui étaient toujours à la cour, celles des passagers qui y venaient plus ou moins souvent; les causes générales ou particulières de ces absences, il les combinait, et ne perdait pas la plus légère occasion d'agir à leur égard en conséquence. C'était un démérite aux uns, et à tout ce qu'il y avait de distingué, de ne faire pas de la cour son séjour ordinaire, aux autres d'y venir rarement, et une disgrâce sûre pour qui n'y venait jamais, ou comme jamais. Quand il s'agissait de quelque chose pour eux: 'Je ne le connais point,' répondait-il fièrement. Sur ceux qui se présentaient rarement: 'C'est un homme que je ne vois jamais.' (Saint-Simon, *Mémoires*, xxviii. 134-5.)

A foreign eye-witness describes their obsequious attendance on the King in the following words:

. . . La Cour de France, sur le pied où elle est sous ce règne, est dans une grande soumission pour son roi, en sorte qu'on ne saurait voir, ni plus d'empressement à lui marquer son zèle et à lui faire sa cour, ni plus d'attachement à s'y acquitter, avec une régularité entière et exacte, des fonctions où chacun est appelé. Ce qu'on n'avait pas vu sous les règnes précédents, ni même sous celui-ci durant sa minorité et lorsque le pouvoir absolu du gouvernement était entre les mains d'un premier ministre, comme du cardinal Mazarin, et du cardinal de Richelieu sous le règne passé. En sorte que tous les courtisans, jusques aux moindres, se font une application particulière de voir le Roi, et d'en être vus dans toutes les occasions qui s'en présentent, comme à son lever, quand il sort du Conseil et va à l'église, ou quand il prend ses repas, et ce qu'il fait ordinairement en public. Et ce qui, outre le génie [1] de la nation, assez portée naturellement, ou par devoir, ou par intérêt, ou par curiosité, à voir leur roi, ce qui, outre cela, dis-je, ne peut venir que de ce qu'il s'est rendu maître de toutes les grâces, et ainsi de tout ce qui a du rapport à l'état politique, ou militaire, ou ecclésiastique. (Ézéchiel Spanheim, *Relation de la Cour de France*, pp. 282-3.)

[1] Character.

Crippled by their debts, often reduced to seeking a living by gaming, the nobles would spend all their time at court on the lookout for some post or pension which would bring them financial relief. The greater part of a courtier's life was spent in the antechamber of the King or his ministers. One veteran is said to have given the following advice to a newcomer: 'Dites du bien de tout le monde, demandez tout ce qui vaquera, et asseyez-vous quand vous le pouvez.' Writing to her daughter on an occasion when the King happened to be in a particularly generous mood, Mme de Sévigné sums up in forceful if inelegant language the attitude of the courtiers to the royal bounty: 'Le roi fait des libéralités immenses; en vérité il ne faut point se désespérer; . . . il peut arriver qu'en faisant sa cour, *on se trouvera sous ce qu'il jette*.' (12 Jan. 1680.)

To keep the nobles in order Louis drew them to court and 'domesticated' them. The proudest honour which a great nobleman could now receive was to possess one of the high posts in the King's Household. At the beginning of his personal reign Louis had as *Grand Maître* of his Household the first *prince du sang*, Condé; as *Grand chambellan* the Duc de Bouillon; other great noblemen held the posts of *Premier maître d'hôtel*, *Premiers gentilshommes de la Chambre*, *Grand Maître de la Garderobe*, *Grand Écuyer*, *Grand Veneur*, *Grand Fauconnier*, to quote only a few of the more important posts. Hundreds of other noblemen held posts of varying importance in the King's Household and in his Guards. Similar posts were also held by noblemen, their wives and daughters in the Queen's Household. At his birth the Dauphin was provided with a household, which was greatly expanded when he grew up and married; there was, of course, a great scramble for these posts as they became available. Besides giving such posts as a reward for assiduity and obedience, the King would also confer pensions upon courtiers, or give them lucrative sinecures, provide their daughters with dowries, even pay their debts. In addition, there were rich bishoprics and other high posts in the Church with which he could provide their younger sons. A foreigner contrasts the great noblemen of the personal reign of Louis XIV with those of an earlier generation: at court they

ne subsistent presque que des libéralités du Roi et des appointements[1] de leur charge, et ainsi . . . sont plus réservés dans la dépense, moins élevés dans les manières, et d'ailleurs dans une dépendance soumise et aveuglée pour les volontés de la Cour. Il n'en était pas de même sous le feu règne et au commencement de celui-ci, qu'il y avait de grands seigneurs en France, et d'un grand air . . . qui, ou par l'élévation de leur génie et la fierté de leur naturel, ou par le nombre de leurs créatures, et de leurs pensionnaires qu'ils avaient soin de s'attirer et d'entretenir, ou par les grands biens qu'ils possédaient, ou enfin par la faveur des peuples et les agréments particuliers de leurs personnes, soutenaient avec hauteur et avec fierté dans les occasions la dignité de leur rang, de leurs emplois ou de leur naissance. (Ézéchiel Spanheim, *Relation de la Cour de France*, pp. 292-3.)

The result was that the nobles were now entirely disciplined. Mme de Sévigné, who still had vivid memories of the Fronde and of the days when the monarchy had been less powerful, describes in 1675 the striking contrast between the omnipotence of the King and the abject state to which the nobility had now been reduced:

La royauté est établie au delà de ce que vous pouvez vous imaginer; on ne se lève plus, et on ne regarde personne. L'autre jour, une pauvre mère toute en pleurs, qui a perdu le plus joli garçon du monde, demanda sa charge à Sa Majesté. Elle passa; ensuite, et toute à genoux, cette pauvre Mme Froulai se traîna à ses pieds, lui demandant avec des cris et des sanglots qu'elle eût pitié d'elle; elle passa sans s'arrêter. (21 Aug. 1675.)

In her next letter she returns to the same subject, showing incidentally the tremendous competition which there was for every post which fell vacant. 'Sa pauvre mère demande sa charge de grand maréchal des logis, qu'elle a achetée; elle crie et pleure, et ne parle qu'à genoux; on lui répond qu'on verra; et vingt-deux ou vingt-trois hommes demandent cette charge.' (26 Aug. 1675.)

The King was not always so hard-hearted towards courtiers when they sought favours from him. Indeed, he could be exceedingly gracious with those who had served him faithfully,

[1] Salary.

and would go out of his way to help them in their financial difficulties, of which, of course, he was fully aware. Three years before, Mme de Sévigné had been charmed by his kindness towards Marshal de Bellefonds, who was on the point of giving up his post of *Premier maître d'hôtel* because of his debts:

> Mais écoutez la bonté du Roi, et le plaisir de servir un si aimable maître. Il a fait appeler le maréchal de Bellefonds dans son cabinet, et lui a dit: 'Monsieur le maréchal, je veux savoir pourquoi vous me voulez quitter. Est-ce dévotion? Est-ce envie de vous retirer? Est-ce l'accablement de vos dettes? Si c'est le dernier, j'y veux donner ordre, et entrer dans le détail de vos affaires.' Le maréchal fut sensiblement touché de cette bonté: 'Sire, dit-il, ce sont mes dettes; je suis abîmé; je ne puis voir souffrir quelques-uns des amis qui m'ont assisté, à qui je ne puis satisfaire.—Eh bien, dit le Roi, il faut assurer leur dette. Je vous donne cent mille francs de votre maison de Versailles, et un brevet de retenue de quatre cent mille francs,[1] qui servira d'assurance si vous veniez à mourir. Vous payerez les arrérages [2] avec les cent mille francs; cela étant, vous demeurerez à mon service.' En vérité, il faudrait avoir le cœur bien dur pour ne pas obéir à un maître qui entre dans les intérêts d'un de ses domestiques avec tant de bonté; aussi le maréchal ne résista pas; et le voilà remis à sa place et surchargé d'obligations. (13 Jan. 1672.)

From this famous letter we obtain a most vivid picture of the state of dependence in which the nobility was placed by its debts, and of the way in which the King was able to use his power to gain their gratitude and obedience.

The great object of the courtier was to keep himself in the King's eye, to be noticed by him as he passed, even on rare occasions to have a word or two addressed to him. When in 1690 Mme de Sévigné's grandson, the young Marquis de Grignan, paid a visit to Versailles, she complains to her daughter of the meagre account which he had given of his doings there, and in particular of his failure to give any information on the vital point: Had the King given any sign of having noticed his presence, or perhaps even said a word or

[1] This meant that when he or his heirs disposed of his post at court, they would be certain to get 400,000 francs.

[2] Back-interest.

two to him? 'Ce marquis devait bien vous faire un peu plus en détail le récit de son premier voyage de Versailles; c'est ce qu'on veut savoir, et si *le Roi ne lui a point fait mine, ou dit quelque parole.*' (19 Feb. 1690.)

It is amusing to see in another of her letters how thrilled Mme de Sévigné herself was when, on being invited to see Racine's *Esther* performed by the girls of the school of St. Cyr, she had the privilege of having three perfectly banal sentences addressed to her by Louis himself at the end of the performance. In her letter to her daughter she can scarcely conceal her pride and delight at being so greatly honoured:

> Je ne puis vous dire l'excès de l'agrément de cette pièce. . . . J'en fus charmée, et le maréchal aussi, qui sortit de sa place pour aller dire au Roi combien il était content, et qu'il était auprès d'une dame qui était bien digne d'avoir vu *Esther*. Le Roi vint vers nos places, et après avoir tourné, il s'adressa à moi, et me dit: 'Madame, je suis assuré que vous êtes contente.' Moi, sans m'étonner,[1] je répondis: 'Sire, je suis charmée; ce que je sens est au-dessus des paroles.' Le Roi me dit: 'Racine a bien de l'esprit.' Je lui dis: 'Sire, il en a beaucoup; mais en vérité ces jeunes personnes en ont beaucoup aussi; elles entrent dans le sujet comme si elles n'avaient jamais fait autre chose.' Il me dit: 'Ah, pour cela, il est vrai.' Et puis Sa Majesté s'en alla, et me laissa l'objet de l'envie. (21 Feb. 1689.)

A vivid picture of the trials and disappointments which often awaited the courtier before the King rewarded his assiduity is to be found in a volume of memoirs of the time. The Duc de La Feuillade, one of the great favourites and flatterers of Louis, almost lost patience before he received a courtier's reward. The author of the following passage relates a conversation between the Duke and his mother:

> 'Non, je n'y puis plus tenir; je suis percé de coups, j'ai eu trois freres tués à son service: il sait que je n'ai pas un sou, et que c'est Prudhomme qui me fait subsister, et il ne me donne rien. Adieu, ma bonne amie, disait-il en s'adressant à ma mère, qui était dans son lit[2]; adieu, je m'en vais chez moi, et j'y trouverai encore des choux.' Ma mère lui dit: 'Vous êtes fou. Ne

[1] Getting flustered.

[2] See p. 62 n.1.

connaissez-vous pas le Roi? C'est le plus habile homme de son royaume: il ne veut pas que les courtisans se rebutent; il les fait quelquefois attendre longtemps, mais heureux ceux dont il a exercé la patience. Il les accable de bienfaits. Attendez encore un peu, et il vous donnera assurément, puisque vos services méritent qu'il vous donne; mais, au nom de Dieu, renouvelez d'assiduité, paraissez gai, demandez tout ce qui vaquera[1]; si une fois il rompt sa gourmette de politique,[2] s'il vous donne une pension de mille écus, vous êtes grand seigneur avant qu'il soit deux ans.' Il la crut, fit sa cour à l'ordinaire, et s'en trouva bien: sa fortune égala celle de M. de La Rochefoucauld[3] . . . qui, après avour été quinze ans de tous les plaisirs du Roi, et presque son favori, sans avoir de chausses,[4] passa tout d'un coup de la souveraine indigence à la souveraine opulence, par la source intarissable des grâces que le Roi fit couler chez lui dans le temps qu'il s'y attendait le moins, et qu'il commençait aussi à désespérer. (Abbé de Choisy, *Mémoires*, ii. 62-3.)

The 'domestication' of the nobility was seen most clearly in the sumptuous setting which Louis created for his court at Versailles. He had always disliked Paris because he remembered the turbulent scenes which had taken place there during the Fronde when he was a child. From the outset of his personal reign, and especially from 1675 onwards, he began to spend more and more of his time at Versailles, gradually transforming the modest hunting-lodge which his father had built there into a magnificent palace, surrounded by vast gardens and an entirely artificial town. If he lavished immense sums of money on the buildings and grounds, it was not only that his taste ran to the magnificent, but because at Versailles he could keep the great noblemen immersed in splendid but harmless occupations. In 1682 he settled there permanently, and from that date until 1789 Versailles was to be the centre of the French monarchy and government, and the envy of all European kings and princes.

The pomp and splendour of Versailles must not make us forget the everyday life of the mass of French people in these

[1] 'Every post that falls vacant.'
[2] 'If he once changes his policy towards you.'
[3] The son of the author of the *Maximes*.
[4] 'Without having a shirt to his back.'

years. From 1661 until his death in 1683 economic affairs were under the direction of Colbert, a merchant's son who had gradually raised himself to high office among the ministers of Louis XIV. He wanted a prosperous France in which the wealth and well-being of the people would assure the greatness of the King. He was a mercantilist of the most extreme and doctrinaire type, holding that the greater a country's stock of gold and silver, the greater would be its power. 'Autant augmenterons-nous l'argent comptant,' he declared, 'autant augmenterons-nous la puissance, la grandeur et l'abondance de l'État.' He was particularly impressed by the commercial power of Holland, a small country compared with France, which none the less enjoyed great prosperity, thanks to its merchant navy. Colbert aimed at wresting this commercial supremacy from the Dutch by building a large merchant fleet, by setting up new industries in France and excluding as far as possible imports from foreign countries, while at the same time selling abroad and transporting on French ships the largest possible quantity of French goods.

Colbert saw with a clear eye the disabilities from which France suffered in the sphere of trade and industry: the bad communications, the internal customs-barriers, the diversity of laws and weights and measures, and, above all, the crushing burden of taxation. Yet, although he was in some respects ahead of his time, his practical achievements were limited by the obstacles to reform presented by the society in which he lived. As *Contrôleur général*, he directed all his efforts towards restoring the financial situation, which was a running sore in the monarchy of the *Ancien Régime*. The legacy which he inherited from Richelieu and Mazarin was a deplorable one: at the latter's death in 1661 the revenues for the following year and even part of those for 1663 had been used up in advance. Out of 83 million *livres* paid by the taxpayer, only 31 millions found their way to the Treasury; the difference went for the most part into the pockets of the tax-farmers. In order to remedy this state of affairs, Colbert made the *financiers* disgorge part of their profits, and also redeemed a large proportion of the *rentes*, to the great advantage of the Treasury. The *rentiers* protested to the King against this measure, but were compelled to give way.

By 1667 the gross national revenue had been raised to 95½ millions, and the net revenue to 63: that is to say, in six years Colbert had succeeded in doubling the effective part of the King's revenues. This result was achieved by a variety of reforms. Colbert tried to bring some order into the Treasury accounts; and he increased enormously the income from the royal *domaine*, particularly from its forests. He had ambitious schemes for the reform of the abuses in the assessment and collection of the *taille*. He dreamed, for instance, of extending the *taille réelle* to the whole of France, and of carrying out a survey of the whole country so as to be able to assess the value of the land on a fair basis; but the plan could never be realized, and he was compelled to confine himself to reforms of detail. He did his utmost to root out the *faux nobles* and to make them pay the *taille*. He instructed the *Intendants* to see that the rich did not use their influence to put the main burden of the tax on the shoulders of the less wealthy; and that the nobles did not have the *taille* of their tenants reduced so as to be able to extract a higher rent from them. These efforts met with only partial success, for the nobles and the wealthier peasants had long been accustomed to make full use of their influence to secure unfair reductions in the *taille*. Indeed, so common was the practice, that we find Colbert himself thanking one of his *Intendants* for reducing the amount of *taille* levied on the peasants on his son's estates! He would also have liked to do something to mitigate the harsh methods by which this tax was collected, but here too his efforts bore no fruit. Finally he reduced the amount of the *taille*. Yet this brought little real advantage to the peasantry, who had to bear the main burden, as indirect taxes were increased to an even greater extent.

In short, Colbert was full of good intentions and grandiose plans for a reform of the fiscal system; but in practice he could achieve little. The abuses were too deeply rooted in the existing social system, and the wars which arose out of Louis's expansionist ambitions and Colbert's own economic policy called for heavier and heavier taxation. As soon as the wars of the reign started in 1667, taxation began to rise and soon reached a ruinous level, thus defeating his plans for increasing the economic prosperity of France. Again, he failed to abolish the internal customs-barriers which stood in the way of trade, particularly the grain-trade, for these obstacles to the free passage of goods from one province to another often led to a food-shortage in one part of the country at a time when other regions might be only too willing to dispose of their surplus.

If old-established French industries were to be expanded and new ones introduced, Colbert saw that it was necessary to have industrial undertakings possessing more capital and greater productive power than the industries organized in guilds. He therefore favoured the development of domestic industry, employing cheap labour in the country districts round the large towns, and producing for export large quantities of silk, cloth and linen. Above all, he encouraged and protected the *manufactures royales*, factories employing relatively large numbers of workers and belonging either to the State (as the Gobelins tapestry-works in Paris) or subsidized by it, as was the famous cloth-factory at Abbeville, run by a Dutchman, Van Robais. Colbert strove by every conceivable method to increase both the range and the output of French industry. He recruited skilled workers from abroad and tried to force the poor into working in the new industries. He even reduced the abnormally large number of Church festivals which interfered very considerably with work, to the annoyance of La Fontaine's cobbler. In order to improve the quality of French manufactured goods, he laid down minute regulations concerning methods of production, and formed a body of inspectors to see that they were observed. Thus we find him writing in 1670 to the *Inspecteur général des manufactures*:

> Je vous envoie cette lettre à Abbeville. Ne manquez pas d'examiner, lorsque vous y serez, tous les moyens pour perfectionner la manufacture de draps qui y est établie et pour faire en sorte que l'on y fasse d'aussi beaux et bons draps gris-mêlé qu'en Angleterre et qu'en Hollande. Et comme vous aurez pu con-

naître [1] qu'il y a une très grande différence entre la fabrique de France et celle d'Angleterre, il faut nous appliquer, par tous moyens possibles, à rendre nos draps égaux en beauté et en bonté à ceux de ce royaume-là. (*Lettres, instructions et mémoires*, ii. 576.)

Two years later we find him writing to the *Intendant* of the province:

> Je suis bien aise que la manufacture de Van Robais aille fort bien. Je vous prie de vous informer bien en détail de la quantité de pièces de drap qu'elle fait tous les ans, et de faire tout ce qui dépendra de vous pour la faire augmenter et même pour la perfectionner, n'y ayant rien de si grande conséquence et qui importe tant au bien de la ville d'Abbeville que de faire en sorte, par le moyen de la dite manufacture, d'exclure tous les draps de Hollande et d'Angleterre. (*Ibid.*, ii. 669.)

Ten years later, only a few months before his death, we see him still watching over the progress of this establishment when he writes to the *Intendant*:

> J'apprends, par votre lettre du 22, les conférences que vous avez eues avec le sieur Van Robais. Comme sa manufacture réussit fort bien, il ne reste qu'à l'obliger à faire des draps de la même finesse que ceux d'Angleterre et de la même largeur. C'est à quoi je vous prie de tenir la main. Je vous prie aussi de faire visiter tous les deux mois, ou par vous-même, lorsque vous passerez à Abbeville, ou par quelque officier de cette ville-là en qui vous ayez une entière confiance, tout ce qui dépend de cette manufacture, particulièrement le nombre de métiers et d'ouvriers qui y travaillent et des pièces de draps qu'ils fabriquent, et même de quelle qualité ils sont, parce que si cette fabrique augmente en nombre de métiers et en nombre d'ouvriers qui y travaillent, je ferai de temps en temps quelques gratifications au sieur Van Robais pour l'obliger de l'augmenter toujours, ces manufactures étant d'une grande utilité à l'état. (*Ibid.*, ii. 743.)

In order to protect these new industries against foreign competition, Colbert placed fresh tariffs on imported goods. These first tariffs of 1664 were relatively moderate, too moderate indeed for a man in such a hurry as Colbert. Three

[1] Perceive.

years later he doubled them in order to ruin the Dutch, the great commercial rivals of France. The latter at once proceeded to return the compliment by placing heavy duties on French goods; and this economic war finally led to armed conflict between the two countries in 1672. The long war which ensued (it lasted for six years) contributed to a considerable degree to the failure of Colbert's economic policy. And in the end, at the Treaty of Nimeguen, Colbert was forced to withdraw his tariffs.

Colbert saw with a jealous eye the wealth which England and Holland derived from their great trading companies, such as the English East India Company. Like Richelieu before him, he attempted to imitate their example by setting up similar bodies in France. In 1664 he founded the *Compagnie des Indes Orientales*, which was given a monopoly of French trade with the Far East. Other companies were set up on similar lines to trade with the Levant and Northern Europe. Yet, despite the example set by the King and the *Princes du sang* who subscribed to their capital, the French middle classes were unwilling to risk their money in what seemed to them speculative ventures. In the end the monopoly of the *Compagnie des Indes Orientales* was withdrawn, and trade with the Indies was left open to all merchants, on condition that they used the company's ships and depots. This company was the only one to survive Colbert.

Despite the failure of the privileged companies and the withdrawal of his high tariff system of 1667, despite, too, his inability to reform the taxation system, Colbert did obtain some results, even though they proved to be much more modest than those which he had dreamed of. He succeeded in increasing very considerably the industrial production of France, and if there were some setbacks during the latter part of the reign of Louis XIV, he had built for the future, since many of his dreams of a greater and more powerful French industry were to be realized in the course of the eighteenth century. The subsidies which he gave to shipowners resulted in a considerable increase in shipbuilding, and in course of time France developed a substantial merchant navy, with the result that overseas trade, especially with Northern Europe, Spain, the Levant and the French colonies, greatly expanded. France thus took her place alongside the great commercial countries, England and Holland.

Yet in many ways Colbert was too far in advance of his time for his policy to be successful in the prevailing social and economic conditions. The middle classes were not prepared to support a bold policy of commercial expansion. They were afraid of the highly speculative risks involved in foreign trade. Above all, their eyes were fixed on the steady income and social prestige enjoyed by the holders of *rentes* and, especially, *offices*. Moreover, as we saw in an earlier chapter, the period in which he tried to apply his programme of economic expansion was one in which France's chief industry, agriculture, was far from prosperous. His years of office coincided with a marked fall in the price of agricultural products; as their incomes fell, the peasants were less and less able to bear the crushing burden of taxation. Like the small peasants, especially those who owned little or no land and were compelled to work for wages, the minor noblemen were very hard hit. No doubt the classes engaged in trade and industry continued to enjoy considerable prosperity, but at the death of Colbert in 1683 great masses of the population, both of town and country, were in a poverty-stricken condition, which was to be aggravated still further by wars and the consequent increases in taxation.

Colbert never had things all his own way as minister. Quite apart from the difficulty of winning the King's approval for his policies, he was faced with the rivalry and often open hostility of other ministers. This was especially the case towards the end of his life, when he found himself supplanted in the King's favour by his chief rival, Louvois, who, as Secretary of State for War, exercised a great influence over Louis and indeed for a period virtually controlled the foreign policy of France. Under his influence Louis's policy towards his neighbours became, as we shall see, increasingly brutal and aggressive. The result was further wars, and further misery for a great proportion of the population of France. The power and prestige of *Le Roi Soleil* were purchased at a heavy price. The splendours of Versailles, the military triumphs of the first half of the personal reign of Louis XIV, cannot conceal this misery. If the world of birth and privilege, clustered around the court in Paris or Versailles, was the centre of a brilliant intellectual and, above all, artistic life, the lot of the great mass of Frenchmen who lived and toiled outside that narrow circle must never be lost sight of if we are to attain a balanced picture of the glories and wrongs of the age.

When Louis established himself permanently at Versailles, in 1682, France was at the very height of her power in Europe. In the two decades since the beginning of his personal reign Louis had achieved for her that dominating position which her population and wealth and the foreign policy of his predecessors seemed to promise her. The first step in his policy of expansion was to lay claim to the Low Countries and the province of Franche-Comté, both of which were then in Spanish hands, on the grounds that they were part of the inheritance of his Queen, Maria Theresa, a Spanish princess. In 1667 he invaded Flanders and captured a large number of fortresses, and in the following year he seized the province of Franche-Comté in a lightning campaign. The conquest of Flanders so alarmed Holland and England that, together with Sweden, they signed at The Hague a Triple Alliance to guard against the danger of French domination of Europe. France thereupon quickly made peace with Spain at Aix-la-Chapelle in 1668, returning Franche-Comté, but retaining part of the province of Flanders, including eleven fortified towns which further strengthened her very vulnerable north-eastern frontier.

Louis did not forgive the Dutch for their insolence in daring to interfere with his plans for annexing the Spanish Low Countries. Moreover, relations were further poisoned by the tariff-war between France and Holland which had been brought on by the protectionist policy of Colbert, who was jealous of the dominant position in international trade which their huge merchant navy gave the Dutch. 'Comme nous avons anéanti l'Espagne sur terre', he wrote, 'il faut anéantir la Hollande sur mer. Les Hollandais n'ont pas le droit d'usurper tout le commerce, sur lequel ils ont établi leur état.' Louis carefully prepared for war by carrying on a series of negotiations to isolate Holland and to secure the neutrality of England, Sweden and the German princes on the Rhine. Mme de Sévigné gives a vivid picture of the haughty and overbearing attitude of Louis towards the Dutch when at the beginning of 1672 his preparations for the attack were almost complete:

> Le Roi donna hier 4e janvier audience à l'ambassadeur de Hollande: il voulut que M. le Prince, M. de Turenne, M. de Bouillon et M. de Créquy fussent témoins de ce qui se passerait. L'ambassadeur présenta sa lettre au Roi, qui ne la lut pas, quoique le Hollandais proposât d'en faire la lecture. Le Roi lui dit qu'il savait ce qu'il y avait dans la lettre, et qu'il en avait une copie dans sa poche. L'ambassadeur s'étendit fort au long sur les justifications qui étaient dans sa lettre, et que Messieurs les États [1] s'étaient examinés scrupuleusement, pour voir ce qu'ils avaient pu faire qui déplût à Sa Majesté; qu'ils n'avaient jamais manqué de respect, et que cependant ils entendaient dire que tout ce grand armement n'était fait que pour fondre sur eux; qu'ils étaient prêts de satisfaire Sa Majesté dans tout ce qu'il lui plairait ordonner, et qu'ils la suppliaient de se souvenir des bontés que les rois ses prédécesseurs avaient eues pour eux, auxquelles ils devaient toute leur grandeur. Le Roi prit la parole, et, avec une majesté et une grâce merveilleuse, dit 'qu'il savait qu'on excitait ses ennemis contre lui; qu'il avait cru qu'il était de sa prudence de ne pas se laisser surprendre, et que c'est ce qui l'avait obligé de se rendre si puissant sur la mer et sur la terre, afin qu'il fût en état de se défendre; qu'il lui restait encore quelques ordres à donner, et qu'au printemps il ferait ce qu'il trouverait le plus avantageux pour sa gloire et pour le bien de son État'; et fit un signe de tête à l'ambassadeur, qui lui fit comprendre qu'il ne voulait pas de réplique. La lettre s'est trouvée conforme au discours de l'ambassadeur, hormis qu'elle finissait par assurer Sa Majesté qu'ils feraient tout ce qu'elle ordonnerait, pourvu qu'il ne leur en coûtât point de se brouiller avec leurs alliés. (5 Jan. 1672.)

In this scene and the invasion of Holland which followed there is something reminiscent of events nearer our own time. The

[1] The States of Holland.

36. *H. Rigaud*, Louis XIV

victorious progress of Louis's armies was finally halted by systematic flooding, and once again a coalition was formed to stem the menace of French power. Louis had in the end to face both the Emperor and Spain, as well as Holland and numerous German states. In the war against Spain his armies once more occupied Franche-Comté and undertook the conquest of the Spanish Low Countries, fortress by fortress. Despite many brilliant victories, Louis was soon anxious to make peace, a desire shared by the opposing coalition, although negotiations and fighting dragged on until 1678. By the Treaty of Nimeguen Spain was forced to cede Franche-Comté and eleven fortified towns in Flanders, thus giving France an additional cover of fortresses to shield Paris against invasion from the North-East.

These victories made Louis XIV—'Louis le Grand'—master of western Europe for the next ten years. On the flimsiest of pretexts he proceeded to extend his kingdom by annexing various towns and territories on her eastern frontier, and particularly the city of Strasbourg, important as a bridgehead over the Rhine into Germany. The other European powers were for the moment unable to prevent these annexations, but such arbitrary acts led in the end to the formation of another more powerful coalition to put an end to the threat of French domination in Europe.

But all this lay in the future when in 1682 Louis finally moved into the new palace of Versailles, the abode of a monarch who was at once absolute at home and, by his recent victories, supreme in Europe. Versailles was the abode of *Le Roi Soleil* with his proud motto, *Nec pluribus impar*; the very doors bore in gold the emblem of his greatness. The palace was, in the eyes of his worshipping contemporaries, the symbol of his semi-divinity, a temple dedicated to the worship of *Le Roi Soleil.* The daily life of the King, and therefore of the royal family and the courtiers, was regulated by the strictest etiquette, one which, as historians have pointed out, was, like the King himself, as much Spanish as French in origin. Gone were the familiarity and simplicity, not to say coarseness of the court of his grandfather, Henry IV, and the relatively free and easy atmosphere of the court of his father, Louis XIII.

Under Louis XIV the greatest attention was paid to the regulation of the most minute details of ceremonial. In the King's eyes this tedious insistence upon points of etiquette was no idle waste of time: everything contributed to one great end, the exaltation of the King above the rest of mankind. He was equally strict in maintaining the hierarchy of ranks among the aristocracy, particularly where behaviour in his presence was concerned; witness the amusing account given by Saint-Simon of the King's anger when at a concert a rather pert girl failed to give up her seat on the arrival of a Duchess:

> A une musique [1] où le Roi était, à Versailles, Mlle de Melun, qui s'accoutumait à n'être plus si polie, se trouva la première après la dernière duchesse. Bientôt après il en arriva une autre, qui alla pour se placer, et à qui tout fit place en se baissant,[2] comme cela se faisait toujours. Mlle de Melun ne branla pas, et ne fit que se lever et se rasseoir. C'était la première fois que femme ou fille non titrée, même maréchale de France, n'eût pas donné sa place en ces lieux-là aux duchesses et aux princesses étrangères. . . . Le Roi qui le vit, rougit, le montra à Monsieur, et, comme il se tournait de l'autre côté où était Mlle de Melun, en levant la voix, Monsieur l'interrompit, et, le prenant par le genou, se leva et lui demanda, tout effrayé, ce qu'il allait faire. 'La faire ôter de là!' dit le Roi en colère. Monsieur redoubla d'instances pour éviter l'affront, et se donna pour caution que cela n'arriverait jamais.[3] Le Roi eut peine à se contenir le reste de la musique. Tout ce qui y était, voyait bien de quoi il était question, et la fille, entre deux duchesses, se pâmait de honte et de frayeur jusqu'à perdre toute contenance. Au sortir de là, Monsieur lui lava bien la tête, et la rendit sage pour l'avenir. (*Mémoires*, v. 339.)

But it was on the person of the King that the most formidable apparatus of etiquette was concentrated. If we take a typical day in his life, we can recreate for ourselves the atmosphere of worship in which he lived, fawned upon and served by descendants of the once so proud great noblemen. The King's rising in the morning (*le lever du Roi*) was surrounded with the

[1] Concert.
[2] Moving down a place.
[3] 'That it would never happen again.'

most complicated ceremonial. Admission to this solemn rite was regulated by one's place in the court hierarchy. The first *entrée* consisting of the King's immediate family and the *Princes du sang*, and the second, composed of the high officials of the King's Household and any other noblemen to whom the King gave permission, had the privilege of being admitted while the King was still in bed. After he had risen, and had been helped into his dressing-gown by the Great Chamberlain or the First Gentleman of the Chamber, the other courtiers who had the right to attend the *lever* were gradually admitted, in four successive 'waves'. Meanwhile, the great noblemen who held posts in the Royal Household carried out their functions of aiding the King to dress. The Master of the Wardrobe pulled off the King's nightshirt by the right sleeve, and the First Valet of the Wardrobe pulled it by the left sleeve. The honour of presenting the King with his shirt belonged to Monsieur, failing him to a *prince du sang*, and failing him to the Great Chamberlain; the first *Valet de chambre* held out the right sleeve, and the First Valet of the Wardrobe the left. To the Master of the Wardrobe fell the honour of helping His Majesty to pull on his breeches. And so the ceremony went on. . . .

After his *lever* the King announced his programme for the day, and then went to hear Mass in the chapel. Here, as La Bruyère pointed out in a famous passage, it was the King, rather than God, that the courtiers worshipped:

> . . . Ces peuples d'ailleurs ont leur Dieu et leur roi. Les grands de la nation s'assemblent tous les jours, à une certaine heure, dans un temple qu'ils nomment église. Il y a au fond de ce temple un autel consacré à leur dieu, où un prêtre célèbre des mystères qu'ils appellent saints, sacrés et redoutables. Les grands forment un vaste cercle au pied de cet autel, et paraissent debout, le dos tourné directement au prêtre et aux saints mystères, et les faces élevées vers leur roi, que l'on voit à genoux sur une tribune, et à qui ils semblent avoir tout l'esprit et tout le cœur appliqués. On ne laisse pas de voir dans cet usage une espèce de subordination,[1] car ce peuple paraît adorer le prince, et le prince adorer Dieu. . . . (*Les Caractères*, viii. 74.)

[1] Hierarchy.

After this act of worship the King spent the morning working with his ministers, and then dined alone in his own room with elaborate ceremony. On special occasions he would dine in state with his family and a few favoured great nobles and ladies: at such times the presence of a chaplain, the captain of the *Gardes du corps* and eighteen soldiers was considered necessary.

After dinner the King would take a walk in the grounds of Versailles, or more often go hunting. The ceremony of changing his clothes and footgear on his return from such excursions —*le débotté du Roi*—was again carefully regulated, and was attended by the same privileged groups of courtiers who were admitted to the *lever*. After a second meeting between the King and his ministers in the afternoon, the evening entertainment would begin at six. Three times a week there were theatrical performances; and on Mondays, Wednesdays and Thursdays what was known as the *Appartement*. This institution is perhaps best described in the following passage:

> Le roi permet l'entrée de son appartment de Versailles, le lundi, le mercredi et le jeudi de chaque semaine pour y jouer à toutes sortes de jeux depuis six heures du soir jusqu'à dix, et ces jours-là sont nommés *jours d'appartement*. . . . Chacun se présente à l'heure marquée pour être reçu dans ses superbes appartements. Aucun ne se présente qu'il n'ait su auparavant que l'entrée lui est permise. Les uns choisissent un jeu et les autres s'arrêtent à un autre. D'autres ne veulent que regarder jouer, et d'autres que se promener pour admirer l'assemblée et la richesse de ces grands appartements. Quoiqu'ils soient remplis de monde, on n'y voit personne qui ne soit d'un rang distingué, tant hommes que femmes. La liberté de parler y est entière, et l'on s'entretient les uns les autres selon qu'on se plaît à la conversation. Cependant le respect fait que, personne ne haussant trop la voix, le bruit qu'on entend n'est point incommode . . . Lorsque l'on est las d'un jeu, on joue à un autre. On entend ensuite la symphonie [1] ou l'on voit danser. On fait conversation. On passe à la chambre des liqueurs [2] ou à celle de la collation.[3] La manière dont on est servi a des agréments qu'on ne saurait concevoir.

[1] Concert of instrumental music.
[2] Liquid refreshments.
[3] Light meals.

On y voit ceux qui servent qui ont des justaucorps bleus avec des galons or et argent. Ils sont derrière toutes les tables de joueurs, et ont soin de donner des cartes, des jetons et les autres choses dont on peut avoir besoin. Même selon les jeux où l'on joue, ils épargnent aux joueurs la peine de compter, comme au *Trou-Madame*, où ils calculent les points qu'on en a faits et les écrivent. . . . Dans le salon où sont dressés les buffets, des bas-reliefs représentant l'Abondance sont au-dessus de la porte de marbre. . . . Plusieurs guéridons or et azur qui portent des girandoles éclairent ce salon, aussi bien qu'un lustre d'argent qui pend au milieu. Trois grands buffets sont aux côtés du même salon. Celui du milieu, au-dessus duquel on voit une grande coquille d'argent, est pour les boissons chaudes, comme café, chocolat, etc. Les autres buffets sont pour les liqueurs, les sorbets et les eaux de plusieurs sortes de fruits. On donne de très excellent vin à ceux qui en souhaitent, et chacun s'empresse à servir ceux qui entrent dans ce lieu, ce qui se fait avec beaucoup d'ordre et de propreté.[1] (*Mercure*, Dec. 1682.)

After this period of relative relaxation, though even then Louis never completely unbent, for in public he was always the King, he proceeded to sup in state with the members of the royal family. In due course he retired to bed, which was the occasion of another solemn ceremony, with the same spectators as at his rising. The greatest privilege which could be conferred upon one of the courtiers in attendance at the *coucher du Roi*, was that of holding the King's candlestick. The precious object was solemnly passed from the hands of the chaplain to those of the *Premier valet de chambre*, and from thence to the great nobleman upon whom the King wished on that occasion to confer the honour of holding it. Saint-Simon offers an account of this apparently futile ceremony, which nevertheless symbolizes a great historical process, the 'domestication' of the great nobles:

Quoique le lieu où il se déshabillait fût fort éclairé, l'aumônier du jour qui tenait, à sa prière du soir, un bougeoir allumé, le rendait après au premier valet de chambre, qui le portait devant le Roi venant à son fauteuil. Il jeta un coup d'œil tout autour, et nommait tout haut un de ceux qui y étaient, à qui le premier

[1] Elegance.

valet de chambre donnait le bougeoir. C'était une distinction et une faveur qui se comptait, tant le Roi avait l'art de donner l'être à des riens. Il ne le donnait qu'à ce qui était là de plus distingué en dignité et en naissance, extrêmement rarement à des gens moindres en qui l'âge et les emplois suppléaient. Souvent il me le donnait, rarement à des ambassadeurs, si ce n'est au Nonce, et, dans les derniers temps, à l'ambassadeur d'Espagne. On ôtait son gant, on s'avançait, on tenait ce bougeoir pendant le coucher, qui était fort court, puis on le rendait au premier valet de chambre, qui, à son choix, le rendait à quelqu'un du petit coucher. (*Mémoires*, x. 61-3.)

One might imagine that the nobles were not too well pleased with the abject state of dependence on the King to which they were reduced at Versailles. Yet, whatever they may have said or thought in private, in public they were all flattery, so as to curry favour with the King. Indeed, this adulation was often carried to the most absurd and degrading extremes. When in his old age Louis complained of lacking teeth to masticate his food properly, a Cardinal exclaimed: 'Des dents, Sire, eh! qui est-ce qui en a?' (*Ibid.*, xxv. 182.) One of the most notorious flatterers was the Duc de La Feuillade, who had a statue of Louis XIV erected in Paris, in the new Place des Victoires. A contemporary describes the ceremony of its unveiling in the following terms:

On vit à Paris la même année, à la face de Dieu et des hommes, une cérémonie fort extraordinaire. Le maréchal de La Feuillade fit la consécration de la statue du Roi qu'il avait fait élever dans la place nommée des Victoires. Le Roi est à pied, et la Renommée lui porte une couronne de laurier sur la tête. C'est le plus beau jet de bronze qu'on ait encore vu. La Feuillade fit trois tours à cheval autour de la statue, à la tête du régiment des gardes dont il était colonel, et fit toutes les prosternations que les païens faisaient autrefois devant les statues de leurs empereurs. Le prévôt des marchands et les échevins [1] étaient présents. Il y eut le soir un feu d'artifice devant l'hôtel de ville, et des feux par toutes les rues. . . . On dit que La Feuillade avait dessein d'acheter une cave dans l'église des Petits-Pères, et qu'il prétendait la pousser par-dessous terre jusqu'au milieu de la place

[1] The nearest equivalent would be 'Lord Mayor and Aldermen'.

des Victoires afin de se faire enterrer sous la statue du Roi. Il avait eu aussi la vision [1] de fonder des lampes perpétuelles qui auraient éclairé la statue nuit et jour. On lui retrancha le jour. (Abbé de Choisy, *Mémoires*, ii. 59-61.)

The idolatrous nature of the ceremony also aroused the sarcasm of Saint-Simon:

Le duc de Gesvres, gouverneur de Paris, à cheval à la tête du corps de ville,[2] y firent les tours, les révérences et les autres cérémonies tirées et imitées de la consécration de celles [3] des empereurs romains. Il n'y eut à la vérité ni encens, ni victimes; il fallait bien donner[4] quelque chose au titre de roi Très-Chrétien.[5] (*Mémoires*, vi. 244.)

In order to curry favour with the King, the great nobles were compelled to buy magnificent costumes for themselves and their wives for every great court ceremony, as Louis liked the splendour of his palace to be enhanced on these occasions by the magnificence of the costumes. He had other reasons, too, according to Saint-Simon:

Il aima en tout la splendeur, la magnificence, la profusion. Ce goût, il le tourna en maxime par politique, et l'inspira en tout à sa cour. . . . Le fond était qu'il tendit et parvint par là à épuiser tout le monde en mettant le luxe en honneur, et pour certaines parties en nécessité, et réduisit ainsi peu à peu tout le monde à dépendre entièrement de ses bienfaits pour subsister. (*Ibid.* xxv. 154-5.)

Thus, despite their financial troubles, the courtiers were compelled to satisfy the desires of their royal master and get still further into debt. When his grandson, the Duc de Bourgogne, married in 1697, Louis asked his courtiers to procure magnificent costumes for the ceremonies connected with the marriage. Saint-Simon, who suffered on this occasion both for himself and for his wife, tells the whole story in amusing detail:

[Le Roi] s'était expliqué qu'il serait bien aise que la cour y fût magnifique, et lui-même, qui depuis longtemps ne portait plus que des habits fort simples, en voulut des plus superbes. C'en

[1] Ridiculous notion. [2] Again approximately 'Lord Mayor and Aldermen'. [3] 'Les statues.' [4] Concede. [5] Title given to the King of France.

fut assez pour qu'il ne fût plus question de consulter sa bourse, ni presque son état,[1] pour tout ce qui n'était ni ecclésiastique, ni de robe. Ce fut à qui se surpasserait en richesse et en invention; l'or et l'argent suffirent à peine; les boutiques des marchands se vidèrent en très peu de jours; en un mot, le luxe le plus effréné domina la cour et la ville, car la fête eut une grande foule de spectateurs. Les choses allèrent à un point que le Roi se repentit d'y avoir donné lieu, et dit qu'il ne comprenait pas comment il y avait des maris assez fous pour se laisser ruiner par les habits de leurs femmes; il pouvait ajouter: et par les leurs. Mais la bride était lâchée, il n'était plus temps d'y remédier; et, au fond, je ne sais si le Roi en eût été fort aise, car il se plut fort, pendant les fêtes, à considérer tous les habits. . . . Ce n'est pas la dernière fois que la même chose lui est arrivée; il aimait passionnément toute sorte de somptuosité à sa cour, et surtout aux occasions marquées, et qui se serait tenu à ce qu'il avait dit, lui eût très mal fait sa cour.

Il n'y avait donc pas moyen d'être sage parmi tant de folie; il fallut plusieurs habits; entre Mme de Saint-Simon et moi, il nous en coûta vingt mille livres [approx. £1500]. (*Ibid.*, iv. 306-8.)

The ruined state of the aristocracy is well illustrated in a contemporary *chanson*, according to which the finery in which the great nobles and great ladies paraded on this occasion, was never paid for:

Chacun, pour mieux paraître,[2]
A l'envi travaillant,
L'on fit sa cour au maître
Aux dépens du marchand.

Another interesting document on the contrast between the impoverished state of the aristocracy and the expense which the luxury of court life demanded is to be found in a well-known letter of Mme de Sévigné, who upbraids her daughter for the extravagant life which she and her husband lead in the provinces, and compares it to the 'black magic' by which the impoverished courtiers manage to indulge in all the expenses required of men of their rank:

Cela me paraît une sorte de magie noire, comme la gueuserie des

[1] Rank. [2] 'To cut a better figure.'

courtisans; il n'ont jamais un sou, et font tous les voyages, toutes les campagnes, suivent toutes les modes, sont de tous les bals, de toutes les courses de bague,[1] de toutes les loteries, et vont toujours, quoiqu'ils soient abîmés; j'oubliais le jeu, qui est un bel article; leurs terres diminuent; il n'importe, ils vont toujours. (21 Aug. 1680.)

At court the nobles were thus condemned to a life of futility and extravagance, which, with all its attractions and splendour, was not always a happy one. Beneath the polished exterior and refined manners of the courtiers there reigned fierce competition for the King's favours. The courtier's days were spent in the attempt to snatch up any of the pensions, posts or favours which might become available. He lived in an atmosphere of intrigue and hypocrisy, vividly portrayed by La Bruyère:

> L'on se couche à la cour et l'on se lève sur l'intérèt: c'est ce que l'on digère [2] le matin et le soir, le jour et la nuit; c'est ce qui fait que l'on pense, que l'on parle, que l'on se tait, que l'on agit; c'est dans cet esprit qu'on aborde les uns, et qu'on néglige les autres, que l'on monte et que l'on descend; c'est sur cette règle que l'on mesure ses soins, ses complaisances, son estime, son indifférence, son mépris . . . . (*Les Caractères*, viii. 22.)

It was a hard life calling for patience, dissimulation and infinite tact; and often when a courtier had carefully laid his plans with a view to attaining some post or honour, despite all his skill and perseverance in carrying them out, his whole scheme might be a failure. At other times they might be rewarded by success. Or is it all just luck? asks La Bruyère in another famous passage:

> La vie de la cour est un jeu sérieux, mélancolique, qui applique.[3] Il faut arranger ses pièces et ses batteries, avoir un dessein, le suivre, parer celui de son adversaire, hasarder quelquefois, et jouer de caprice[4]; et, après toutes ses rêveries[5] et toutes ses mesures, on est échec, quelquefois mat. Souvent, avec des pions qu'on ménage bien, on va à dame,[6] et l'on gagne la partie; le plus habile l'emporte, ou le plus heureux. (*Ibid.*, viii. 64.)

[1] Tilting at the ring.
[2] Meditates upon.
[3] 'Absorbs all one's attention.'
[4] By inspiration.
[5] Careful thought.
[6] (Chess) 'one queens a pawn'.

There was, too, a certain monotony about the ceaseless round of rather artificial pleasures which the court offered to those who frequented it. The outward signs of happiness often merely served to mask passionate self-interest, anxiety and unhappiness. To quote La Bruyère again:

> Il y a un pays [1] où les joies sont visibles, mais fausses, et les chagrins cachés, mais réels. Qui croirait que l'empressement pour les spectacles, que les éclats [2] et les applaudissements aux théâtres de *Molière* et d'*Arlequin*,[3] les repas, la chasse, les ballets, les carrousels,[4] couvrissent tant d'inquiétudes, de soins et de divers intérêts, tant de craintes et d'espérances, des passions si vives et des affaires si sérieuses? (*Ibid.*, viii. 63.)

The moralist's rather gloomy picture of court-life is confirmed by many who had first-hand experience of its pleasures and sorrows. Mme de La Fayette sums up in one phrase the inevitable monotony of a round of rather artificial pleasures: 'Toujours les mêmes plaisirs, toujours aux mêmes heures, et toujours avec les mêmes gens.' (*Mémoires de la Cour de France*, p. 101.) Even more striking is the testimony of Mme de Maintenon to the emptiness and final boredom produced by such a life:

> Il y a de la peine dans tous les états,[5] cela est bien vrai, et à commencer par celui des gens de la cour, qui, selon le monde, paraissent si heureux, il n'y a rien de si gênant que la vie qu'ils mènent; pour faire sa cour, il en coûte bien de la peine, de la contrainte, de la dépense et de l'ennui, et, au bout de tout cela, on trouve un homme qui dit: Ah! que je suis fâché, je suis debout depuis ce matin, et je ne crois pas seulement que le Roi m'ait vu! On se lève de grand matin, on s'habille avec soin, on est tout le jour sur ses pieds, pour attendre un moment favorable, pour se faire voir, pour se présenter, et souvent on revient comme on était allé, excepté que l'on est au désespoir d'avoir perdu son temps et sa peine. Mais je voudrais que vous puissiez voir l'état des plus heureux, c'est-à-dire, de ceux qui voient le Roi, et qui ont l'honneur d'être dans sa familiarité; il n'y a rien de pareil à l'ennui qui les dévore. Nous sommes à présent à Meudon, qui est un palais magnifique; eh bien! il faut s'aller promener,

[1] Place.
[2] *Éclats de rire.*
[3] The Italian actors in Paris.
[4] Tournaments.
[5] Ranks of society.

sans en avoir envie, par un vent effroyable, par respect pour le Roi; on revient très fatigué, et on voit quantité de femmes qui se plaignent et qui disent: 'Que je suis lasse! Voilà une maison qui nous fera mourir!'—'Je ne puis plus durer,[1] dit une autre; encore si je m'étais promenée avec quelqu'un qui m'eût fait plaisir, mais non, je me suis trouvée enfilée avec un tel, qui m'a fait mourir d'ennui.' Car on ne choisit pas là qui on veut, non plus qu'ici, il faut demeurer avec celle qui se présente. M. le Dauphin a fait faire un appartement, depuis peu, qui est admirable; il n'y a rien de si beau, mais il est si éloigné, et il y a un si grand nombre de degrés à monter pour y aller, que l'on y arrive à demi fatigué; quand on y est: 'Voilà un beau lieu', dit-on; on se regarde: 'Eh bien, que ferons-nous?' et on demeure là, sans savoir, en effet, à quoi s'amuser. (Marcel Langlois, *Madame de Maintenon*, pp. 210-11.)

Yet, despite all its disadvantages and its fundamental futility, Versailles and the life it offered exercised an irresistible attraction for the aristocracy, because there alone could they hope to gain honours, dignities and—to quote the words of Mme de Sévigné's exiled cousin, Bussy-Rabutin—'quelque chose de solide dont j'ai plus besoin que d'honneurs', pensions and other money gifts. Besides, material reasons apart, the court was the centre of all social life; to be sent into exile in the provinces was the greatest calamity which could befall a seventeenth century courtier. 'Sire,' said one nobleman to Louis XIV, on returning to the court after twenty years of exile, 'quand on est assez misérable pour être éloigné de vous, non seulement on est malheureux, mais on est ridicule'. There spoke the skilful courtier, and yet, on this occasion at least, he was speaking from the heart.

The monarchy had thus succeeded in reducing to utter impotence the descendants of the great noblemen who had once been its most dangerous enemies. In fact, the very dimensions of its victory over the aristocracy were one of the main causes of its final undoing. The impoverished state and the uselessness of the nobility as a social class came in the end to present a great danger to the monarchy. Living a life of luxury at court, partly on the King's bounty, partly on their

[1] 'Bear it any longer.'

rents and on such feudal dues as they could wring out of their peasants, in return for precisely nothing, the nobility became increasingly unpopular. Surrounded by nobles at Versailles, and cut off, both physically and socially, from the rest of the French people, the monarchy appeared in the eyes of the nation to identify itself with the maintenance of aristocratic privilege. The final result of this policy was that in 1789 the Revolution swept away at one blow both absolutism and aristocracy. Yet, a hundred years earlier, all these remote consequences were hidden away in the future. Versailles enshrined the greatness of Louis XIV, his absolute power at home and the preponderant position which, under his leadership, France had acquired in Europe. Something of the enchantment which was felt by contemporaries—at least among the aristocracy—at the spectacle of the new palace of Versailles, is reflected in the following lines, written by Mme de Sévigné to her daughter in 1683, to describe her impressions of an *Appartement*:

> Je reviens de Versailles; j'ai vu ces beaux appartements, j'en suis charmée. Si j'avais lu cela dans quelque roman, je me ferais un château en Espagne d'en voir la vérité. Je l'ai vue et maniée; c'est un enchantement, c'est une véritable liberté, ce n'est point une illusion comme je le pensais. Tout est grand, tout est magnifique, et la musique et la danse sont dans leur perfection. . . . Mais ce qui plaît souverainement, c'est de vivre quatre heures entières avec le souverain, être dans ses plaisirs et lui dans les nôtres: c'est assez pour contenter tout un royaume qui aime passionnément à voir son maître. (12 February 1683.)

The spell was to last for just over a hundred years, until the day in October 1789 when Louis XVI and his family were dragged from the palace and taken off to Paris by the Revolutionary crowds.

CHAPTER VII

THE WRITER AND HIS PUBLIC

THE literary journals of our time are filled with the lamentations of writers about the hardness of their lot. We hear of the impossibility of earning a living with one's pen if one tries to produce work of any artistic value, of the depredations of the Commissioners of Inland Revenue, of brilliant careers frustrated by the necessity of earning a living in more humdrum occupations. Justified as many of these complaints are, they have their comic side for the student of seventeenth century French literature. Naturally then as now (though today the taxation of inherited wealth and unearned incomes is making the species rarer) there were men of independent means who were wealthy enough merely to write for their own pleasure without any thought of attempting to make a career with their pen. Some of the great names of the age—La Rochefoucauld, Pascal, Mme de La Fayette, to mention only three—came into this category. Again there were men—as there are today—who managed to combine writing with the exercise of some other profession. There were actor-playwrights like Molière, and many minor writers who were civil servants, judges or professional men. To these any earnings from their pen were no doubt welcome, but not indispensable.

But what of that band of writers—many of them obscure, but others as famous as Corneille, Racine and La Fontaine—who, lacking either inherited wealth or a profession which would give them a comfortable living, sought to make a career with their pen? Undoubtedly they were very much worse off than the writers of the present-day with all their legitimate grievances. The reading-public of seventeenth century France, in a society where illiteracy was still widespread, was extremely small. There were none of the additional sources of income upon which the contemporary man of letters can draw: no B.B.C., no film rights, no literary journalism, for the daily newspaper was as yet unknown, and the periodical press in general was only in its infancy. The first weekly newspaper—the *Gazette de France*—was founded in 1631, and the first learned and scientific journal, the *Journal des Savants*, in 1665. In 1672 appeared the first French periodical which gave most of its attention to literary matters, the *Mercure Galant*, and while its editors seem to have extracted large pensions from Louis XIV in return for boosting the wonders of his reign, that did not help any of their fellow-writers, and indeed they themselves died in poverty when cuts in government expenditure dried up this source of wealth in the hard opening years of the eighteenth century.

The seventeenth century French writer was thus driven back on the tender mercies of publishers, and if publishers today tend to be regarded by writers as fairly stonyhearted, they are the soul of generosity compared with their seventeenth century predecessors. Then publishers had, of course, the excuse that the size of the reading-public made the sale of books very small. Editions were thus extremely limited in size—500 or 1000 copies was quite a common figure for a literary work—and anything above 1500 or 2000 was quite exceptional. It is true that a successful book might go through quite a number of editions in a relatively short number of years. But many of these would be brought out by other publishers. The trouble was that, once a book was successful, publishers abroad—especially in Holland—brought out pirated editions which naturally reduced the sales of the original publisher, and in the absence of any international copyright convention there was no redress. Other publishers in France itself often exploited the success of a new book by bringing out surreptitious editions, and though they could sometimes be prosecuted and compelled to compensate the original publisher, this was not always easy.

The result was that when a publisher negotiated with an author for his manuscript, if he gave him anything at all for it —and in earlier times it had often not been his habit to do so —he gave him only a small sum, calculated on the cost of producing the first edition, since even if the book proved to be successful, there was no certainty that pirated versions of it would not prevent him from making profits out of later editions. It is unfortunate that relatively few agreements between authors and publishers in seventeenth century France have come down to us, but the few that have, show clearly that writers of the time earned very little from their works. It is true that, if we convert the following figures into English money at the rate of exchange which prevailed in the period (13 *livres* to the pound), one gets a somewhat exaggerated impression of the smallness of the earnings of seventeenth century writers; yet, even if we make allowance for the tremendous fall in the purchasing-power of money in the last three centuries, it will still be seen that their earnings were very meagre.

Plays, especially at the beginning of the century, brought in very small returns from publishers. In 1625 the playwright, Alexandre Hardy, sold twelve of his works to a publisher for 180 *livres* (about £14). Five years later a minor playwright of the time received rather more—125 *livres* (just under £10) for two plays. Indeed from about 1630 onwards payments appear to have become less insignificant, probably because the theatre had become much more fashionable. In 1635 another playwright received nearly £10 (125 *livres*) for one play, and in the following year Rotrou obtained 750 *livres* (about £57) for four plays—an even better figure, but in 1637 he had to be content with 1500 *livres* (about £115) for ten plays. It is unfortunate that we have no precise figures concerning what either Corneille (who had a reputation amongst his contemporaries for striking a hard bargain) or later Racine managed to obtain from publishers for their plays. As for Molière, our information, though it is slightly less disappointing, is none the less incomplete. We know that he published his *Tartufe* in 1669 at his own expense, but with such a successful play which he had fought for five years to have performed, it is not surprising if he should have obtained 2000 *livres* (over £150) from a publisher for the second edition. That this sum was altogether exceptional is shown by the fact that Molière's widow received only 1500 *livres* (about £115) for seven of his plays—most of them short—which had not appeared during his life-time. Racine's son assures us that the amount of money which his father received from the publication of his plays from *La Thébaïde* to *Phèdre* was 'fort modique', and while there seems no doubt that in the course of our period such earnings did greatly improve, they continued to remain very modest, even for the successful plays of well-known authors.

For other types of literature—poetry, the novel and so on—we have unfortunately even less information. In 1654 Scarron signed a contract for the second part of his *Roman comique* for which he was to receive 1000 *livres* (about £75). Earlier he had received altogether exceptional terms when he sold eleven cantos of his *Virgile Travesti*, written in the burlesque style which enjoyed such phenomenal popularity about the time of the Fronde, for the enormous sum of 11,000 *livres* (over £800). It is true that it seems as if he drew the money in advance and therefore had no incentive to finish the work, for he did not write more than seven of these cantos. Contemporaries speak as if fashionable novelists like La Calprenède and Mlle de Scudéry earned large sums of money from the publication of their work, but we have no precise figures to justify these statements. Indeed, considering the phenomenal popularity which their novels enjoyed, it is surprising how small was the number of editions which they reached. Chapelain was regarded by a contemporary as exhibiting sordid avarice when he insisted on obtaining 100 free copies (some of them bound and printed on expensive paper) in addition to 3000 *livres* (about £230) for his epic poem, *La Pucelle*. La Fontaine is said by a contemporary to have received 1500 *livres* (over £100) for his *Psyché*—which would seem to have been a fairly normal price for a book of that type. No doubt, the earnings of writers from publishers varied greatly in our period, and could on occasion be quite high, but the general level seems to have been far from enabling even a successful writer to live on what he received from this source.

It must be remembered that in the eyes of most contemporaries there was something almost improper in introducing considerations of filthy lucre into literary questions. Boileau was merely restating in somewhat pompous verse what was the accepted attitude of the time when he wrote in the *Art Poétique*:

38. Medal of Jean Varin,
The emblem of Le Roi Soleil

39. The doors of the Salon de Vénus, Château de Versailles, showing the emblem of Le Roi Soleil

40. The bedroom of Louis XIV at Versailles

41. Salon de la Guerre, Château de Versailles

Travaillez pour la gloire, et qu'un sordide gain
Ne soit jamais l'objet d'un illustre écrivain.
Je sais qu'un noble esprit peut, sans honte et sans crime,
Tirer de son travail un tribut légitime [1];
Mais je ne puis souffrir ces auteurs renommés,
Qui, dégoûtés de gloire et d'argent affamés,
Mettent leur Apollon aux gages d'un libraire
Et font d'un art divin un métier mercenaire.

In the numerous literary controversies which were fought out with bitter violence throughout the seventeenth century, the accusation that a writer was trying to make money from his works was regarded as one of the most telling pieces of abuse at the disposal of his enemies. In the famous quarrel which developed in 1637 after the success of *Le Cid*, the charge was repeatedly brought against Corneille. His jealous rival, the playwright Mairet, compared his visits to Paris from Rouen where he was still living, with trading-expeditions:

> Vos caravanes de Rouen à Paris me font souvenir de ces premiers marchands qui passerent dans les Indes; d'où par le bonheur du temps autant que par la simplicité de quelques peuples, ils apportèrent de l'or, des pierreries et d'autres solides richesses, pour des sonnettes, des miroirs et de la quincaille qu'ils y laissèrent. Vous nous avez autrefois apporté la *Mélite*, la *Veuve*, la *Suivante*, la *Galerie du Pàlais* et de fraîche mémoire le *Cid*, qui d'abord [2] vous a valu l'argent et la noblesse, qui vous en restent avec ce grand tintamarre de réputation qui vous bruirait encore aux oreilles, sans vos vanités et le malheur de l'impression. (A. Gasté, *La Querelle du Cid*, p. 290.)

Twenty years later another contemporary refers to him as 'un grand avare' and declares: 'En vérité, il a plus d'avarice que d'ambition, et pourvu qu'il en tire bien de l'argent, il ne se tourmente guère du reste'. (Tallemant, *Historiettes*, vii. 125, 181.) And all this because Corneille strove—not very success-

[1] According to Louis Racine Boileau assured him that the last two lines were only inserted 'pour consoler mon père, qui avait retiré quelque profit de l'impression de ses tragédies. Le profit qu'il en retira fut fort modique; et il donna dans la suite *Esther* et *Athalie* au libraire, de la manière dont Boileau avait donné tous ses ouvrages'. (*Mémoires*, i. 229) Boileau was a bachelor with a modest private income.

[2] Immediately.

fully, as we shall see—to make a reasonable living out of his works.

If poverty was widespread among writers of the age, it was not because they earned less from publishers and actors than in the previous century. Publishers did generally pay something—at times fairly substantial sums—whereas in the past they generally paid authors nothing at all. Similarly it was only at the beginning of our period that a professional theatre emerged in France which offered payment to writers; before that, theatrical performances had been given by amateurs, and the authors of the plays which they performed, doubtless earned nothing whatever. It is true that at the beginning of our period the playwright's position was often one of abject dependence on the actors: he was a mere *poète à gages*—that is to say, he was hired by a company of actors to write so many plays a year for their theatre. The poet, Théophile de Viau, spent part of his wild youth as a *poète à gages*, while even Corneille's contemporary, Rotrou, began his career in this way; but the best-known example of a writer reduced to this humble status is the early seventeenth century playwright, Alexandre Hardy.

Thanks to a fortunate discovery of recent years, we now know something of Hardy's relations with the company of actors for whom he worked. He is known for his phenomenal output of plays—some 600 in the thirty years or so of his career as a playwright—and yet only thirty-four of these were published, so that the greater part of his production is lost. The reason for his failure to publish more of his plays is now clear. His agreement with the actors forbade him to publish his plays, since, once published, they could, by the custom of the time, be freely performed by any other company; and it was only reluctantly—and with plays which were already old—that they would give him permission to publish. Moreover, as we have seen, the rewards offered him by publishers were so small that there was little incentive to print his plays. Poorly as he was paid by the actors—various contemporaries bear witness to his poverty—they were certainly more generous than publishers. In contrast to the 180 *livres* which he received in 1625 from a publisher for twelve plays, we know that in the same year the actors at least gave him 100 *livres* (about £7) for one comedy. Thus Hardy was bound hand and foot to the actors, since it was only from their payments to him that he could manage to keep alive. It is true that, in 1627, wearying of this state of complete dependence, he deserted the company to which he had long been attached, and made an agreement on a royalty basis with another set of actors, who were then in Paris. This provided that, in return for writing six plays a year, Hardy was to receive a proportion of the takings of the actors. Unfortunately for him this company does not seem to have been successful, and was soon compelled to leave Paris: it is therefore doubtful whether the agreement did anything to improve his poverty-stricken state.

However, the younger generation of playwrights who began to write about 1630 (Corneille is, of course, the greatest of them), seem gradually to have secured more favourable terms from the actors; but it is not until Molière came back to Paris in 1658 and one of his actors, Lagrange, began shortly afterwards to keep his famous Register, that we begin to know anything definite about the earnings of playwrights from this source. Even then, we know nothing of the payments received by authors who wrote for the other two theatres, the Hôtel de Bourgogne and the Marais. We learn from Lagrange's Register that in the 1660's Molière's company twice paid the veteran Corneille 2000 *livres* (about £150) for a play—a sum which compares very favourably with the 100 *livres* which Hardy received some forty years earlier. It was by this time more common for a playwright to be paid a proportion of the receipts during the first run of his play, the amount varying according to the number of acts in it. Sometimes under this system writers drew quite considerable sums, reaching during the last two decades of the century at the Comédie Française (founded in 1680) figures around 3000 *livres* (about £240). Undoubtedly therefore, even from the scanty evidence at our disposal we can safely deduce that a playwright's earnings greatly improved in the course of the century.

Even so, playwriting could hardly be considered, even in

the second half of our period, to offer a satisfactory career. The trouble was that until the Revolution the profits derived by a playwright from the performance of his work were limited to those which he drew from its first run. Once his play was published (this was generally as soon as the first run of the play was over, and he could hope for nothing more from the actors), it was open to anyone, in Paris or the provinces, to perform it without payment to the author.

No doubt a successful play brought in day by day during its first run a sum of money which must have seemed large, especially to an impecunious author at the beginning of his career. If he was lucky enough to write a successful play (and not all the masterpieces of the age—Racine's *Britannicus* is an example—were well received by audiences), he would certainly earn more ready cash in the theatre than from any other form of writing at a time when publishers' payments were seldom large. But this flow of money dried up after 20 or at the most 30 performances, and since he had now earned as much as he could get out of his play, all that he could now do was to write another. Yet, however prolific he might be, and however successful, he discovered in the long run that, while the theatre might bring him fame, it could not offer him a livelihood.

The third source of income open to a writer in seventeenth century France was patronage. Indeed in earlier periods, before the coming of professional actors and of publishers, it had been his only source of income. In our period the writer continued to depend to a large extent on patrons, be they great noblemen, wealthy tax-farmers, the King's ministers, or even the King himself, if he could be brought to interest himself in literature and the needs of men of letters. This explains the presence at the beginning of almost any seventeenth century book one may pick up, of a dedication full of exaggerated praise for the virtues and noble qualities of the person to whom it is addressed. Occasionally, no doubt, this praise was disinterested and sincere, but very often the flattery was lavished in return for (or in expectation of) a substantial money gift. The best-known example of such interested eulogy in our period is the famous dedication which Corneille in 1643 prefixed to his tragedy, *Cinna*, when he offered the play to an upstart tax-farmer. Even his contemporaries who were accustomed to such insincere flattery, considered that Corneille had rather over-stepped the limits of good taste when he compared his patron to the Emperor Augustus:

> . . . Je dirai seulement un mot de ce que vous avez particulièrement de commun avec Auguste: c'est que cette générosité qui compose la meilleure partie de votre âme et règne sur l'autre, et qu'à juste titre on peut nommer l'âme de votre âme, puisqu'elle en fait mouvoir toutes les puissances; c'est, dis-je, que cette générosité, à l'exemple de ce grand empereur, prend plaisir à s'étendre sur les gens de lettres, en un temps où beaucoup pensent avoir trop récompensé leurs travaux quand ils les ont honorés d'une louange stérile. Et, certes, vous avez traité quelques-unes de nos muses avec tant de magnanimité, qu'en elles vous avez obligé toutes les autres, et qu'il n'en est point qui ne vous en doive un remerciement. Trouvez donc bon, Monsieur, que je m'acquitte de celui que je reconnais vous en devoir, par le présent que je vous fais de ce poème, que j'ai choisi comme le plus durable des miens, pour apprendre plus longtemps à ceux qui le liront que le généreux Monsieur de Montoron, par une libéralité inouïe en ce siècle, s'est rendu toutes les muses redevables, et que je prends tant de part aux bienfaits dont vous avez surpris quelques-unes d'elles, que je m'en dirai toute ma vie,
>
> Monsieur,
>
> Votre très humble et très obligé serviteur,
>
> CORNEILLE.

Perhaps Corneille thought that all this flattery was worth it since, according to a contemporary, his dedication was rewarded with a gift of 2000 *livres* (about £150), probably at least as much as he received from the actors and his publisher combined.

Although the history of literary patronage in seventeenth century France still remains to be written, parts of it have been studied in great detail and the rest can be sketched in fairly clear outline. Neither Henry IV nor Louis XIII showed any particular interest in men of letters. It is true that Henry had the poet Malherbe brought to his court, but he left it to the Duc de Bellegarde to provide him with a pension when he came. Later the poet received pecuniary encouragement from the Queen-Mother and even from Louis XIII. Yet the latter enjoyed a poor reputation as a patron, for Tallemant tells us that 'il raya après la mort du Cardinal [1] toutes les pensions des gens de lettres, en disant: "Nous n'avons plus affaire de cela"' (*Historiettes*, ii. 159 n.), while he adds the following picturesque anecdote about the King's anxiety when asked to accept the dedication of one of Corneille's plays:

> Depuis la mort du Cardinal, M. de Schomberg lui dit que Corneille voulait lui dédier la tragédie de *Polyeucte*. Cela lui fit peur, parce que Montoron avait donne deux cents pistoles à Corneille pour *Cinna*. 'Il n'est pas nécessaire, dit-il.—Ah! Sire, reprit M. de Schomberg, ce n'est point par intérêt.—Bien donc, dit-il, il me fera plaisir.' Ce fut à la reine qu'il la dédia, car le roi mourut entre deux.[2] (*Ibid.*, ii. 160.)

The lack of interest in men of letters shown by Henry IV and Louis XIII was all the more galling to them because in the second half of the sixteenth century the last Valois Kings, Charles IX and Henry III, had been extremely generous towards the writers of their reign. Ronsard had been provided with various comfortable sinecures in the Church, while his successor, Desportes, who lived long enough to be insulted by Malherbe, had almost been overwhelmed with similar posts and with pensions until he had an income which appeared fabulous to the writers of the next age. This is how Tallemant describes his rise to wealth:

> Il fit sa grande fortune durant la faveur de M. de Joyeuse, dont il était le conseil. Il eut quatre abbayes qui lui valurent plus de quarante mille livres de rente [i.e. over £3000]. M. de Joyeuse le mit si bien avec Henri III qu'il avait grande part aux affaires. Ce fut alors qu'il fit donner beaucoup de bien aux gens de lettres, et leur fit donner bon nombre de bénéfices.[3] (*Historiettes*, i. 59.)

[1] Richelieu. [2] In the meantime.

[3] Livings in the Church were, as we have seen (p. 92), often used to reward men of letters, even in our period.

One could fill a book with the jeremiads of seventeenth century poets on their fall from grace, and their comparisons between their wretched lot and the prosperity of their predecessors. In his *Excuse à Ariste* (1637) Corneille wrote, with sorrowful backward glances at this lost golden age:

> Le Parnasse, autrefois dans la France adoré,
> Faisait pour ses mignons un autre âge doré,
> Notre fortune enflait du prix de nos caprices,
> Et c'était une blanque à de bons bénéfices [1]:
> Mais elle est épuisée, et les vers à présent
> Aux meilleurs du métier n'apportent que du vent . . .

The poet, Maynard, is even more explicit in his references to the departed Valois Kings and their generous patronage of men of letters:

> Apollon, que ton cœur s'ouvre
> A des regrets infinis:
> Ceux qui t'appelaient au Louvre
> Sont poussière à Saint-Denis.[2]
>
> Ma lyre a peu de pareilles;
> Mais le prince que je sers,
> Éloigne de ses oreilles
> Les charmes de mes concerts.
>
> Adieu, Cour; adieu, Fortune,
> Puisqu'un Orphée importune
> Le plus auguste des rois.
>
> Cet accident me convie
> A pleurer toute ma vie
> Sur la tombe des Valois.

The poetry of the first half of the century—particularly satire—is full of vivid pictures of the poverty which was the poet's lot. Take, for instance, the grotesque portrait of the

[1] 'A lottery with good prizes.'
[2] The burial-place of the Kings of France.

impecunious writer in one of the satires of Mathurin Régnier, written shortly after 1600:

> Aussi, lorsque l'on voit un homme par la rue
> Dont le rabat [1] est sale et la chausse rompue,
> Ses grègues [2] aux [3] genoux, au coude son pourpoint,
> Qui soit de pauvre mine et qui soit mal en point,[4]
> Sans demander son nom, on le peut reconnaître;
> Car si ce n'est un poète, au moins il le veut être.
>
> (*Satire* II.)

One of the most moving accounts of the poverty of a writer to be found in the memoirs of the period is that of Pierre Du Ryer, a contemporary of Corneille, who gradually gave up writing for the stage and tried to earn a living by translating —then as now ill-paid hackwork:

> M. Du Ryer traduisait les auteurs à la hâte pour tirer promptement du libraire Sommaville une médiocre récompense, qui l'aidait à subsister avec sa pauvre famille dans un petit village auprès de Paris. Un beau jour d'été nous allâmes plusieurs ensemble lui rendre visite. Il nous reçut avec joie, nous parla de ses desseins, et nous fit voir ses ouvrages; mais ce qui nous toucha, c'est que, ne craignant pas de nous laisser voir sa pauvreté, il voulut donner la collation.[5] Nous nous rangeâmes dessous un arbre, on étendit une nappe sur l'herbe, sa femme apporta du lait, et lui des cerises, de l'eau fraîche et du pain bis. Quoique ce repas nous semblât très bon, nous ne pûmes dire adieu à cet excellent homme sans pleurer de le voir si maltraité de la fortune, surtout dans sa vieillesse, et accablé d'infirmités. (Vigneul-Marville, *Mélanges*, i. 203-4.)

Yet not all writers of the first half of the century were reduced to such a poverty-stricken existence. If neither Henry IV nor his successor showed generosity towards them, men of letters did not entirely lack patrons. Wealthy tax-farmers, as Corneille found with Montoron, were often prepared to show an interest in men of letters and to hand over to them some morsels of their rapidly acquired fortunes.

[1] Bands. [2] Breeches. [3] Out at. [4] In a bad way. [5] A light meal.

Moreover, many a great nobleman considered it part of the duties of his station to have attached to his household one or more men of letters to whom, in addition to rewards for flattering dedications, he would offer free meals and sometimes lodging. However in the unsettled state of the country in the opening decades of the century the great nobleman's interest in men of letters was not always purely aesthetic. In the rivalries and intrigues which went on, a good writer could serve as a kind of publicity-agent for his master, by replying to the attacks of his enemies and launching a counter-offensive. The poet, Théophile de Viau, was mixed up in this fashion in the political struggles which went on during the troubled period between the death of Henry IV and the coming to power of Richelieu in 1624.

Of all the literary patrons of the first half of the century the Cardinal was by far the most outstanding. In the midst of his multifarious activities, he found time to take an interest in literature, especially Drama, and he came to the aid of struggling writers with all manner of gifts and pensions. It is significant that during the 1630's, when Richelieu was taking an active interest in Drama and dramatists, the output of new plays was greater than in any other decade of the century. The considerable decline on the number of new plays produced in the decade after his death was no doubt partly due to the disorders of the Fronde: but the death of Richelieu and the failure of any new patron to take his place were responsible in some degree for the abandonment of the theatre by certain writers of Corneille's generation. Payments from actors and publishers still remained small, and an additional source of income was necessary if playwrights were to make any sort of a living: 'N'était que Monseigneur le Cardinal se délasse parfois en l'honnête divertissement de la comédie,[1] et que Son Éminence me fait l'honneur de me gratifier de ses bienfaits', wrote Tristan in the preface to one of his plays in 1639, 'j'appliquerais peu mon loisir sur les ouvrages de théâtre'. There is no question that Richelieu's death was a severe blow to the dramatists of Corneille's generation. They above all

[1] Theatre.

people must have echoed the sentiments expressed so irreverently in Benserade's famous epitaph:

> Ci-gît par la morbleu
> Le Cardinal de Richelieu,
> Et ce qui cause mon ennui
> Ma pension avec lui.

Richelieu's generosity towards all kinds of men of letters had helped to make the career relatively lucrative and the dire effects of his death on their position are vividly depicted in the following lines, written some ten years later:

> Les pauvres courtisans des Muses
> Sont aujourd'hui traités de buses,[1]
> Qu'autrefois défunt Richelieu,
> Qu'ils ont traité de demi-dieu,
> Traitait de la façon qu'Auguste,
> Prince aussi généreux que juste,
> A traité les hommes savants
> Dont les vers sont encore vivants . . .
> Les beaux vers et la belle prose
> Valent aujourd'hui peu de chose.
> Se voir en auteur érigé
> Est un sinistre préjugé
> Pour la fortune d'un pauvre homme . . .
>
> (Scarron, *A Monseigneur Rosteau*, Epître Chagrine.)

If no minister at once took Richelieu's place as a generous patron of men of letters, it is not, however, true that they were completely deprived of all support. The Chancellor, Séguier, who succeeded him as Patron of the Académie Française, showed some interest in men of letters, and so did even Mazarin, although during the period of the Fronde he was bitterly attacked for his avarice in such matters. Although the total amount of the pensions and gifts which he bestowed on writers, was not perhaps in keeping with the enormous wealth which he amassed during his term of office, he did go to the trouble of making arrangements in his will for the pensions to be paid during the rest of the lifetime of the recipients. Corneille, who

[1] Fools, dolts.

dedicated his tragedy, *La Mort de Pompée*, to Mazarin, wrote a poem of thanks in the usual exalted style suitable for such occasions:

C'est toi, grand cardinal, âme au-dessus de l'homme,
Rare don qu'à la France ont fait le ciel et Rome,
C'est toi, dis-je, ô héros, ô cœur vraiment romain,
Dont Rome en ma faveur vient d'emprunter la main.
Mon bonheur n'a point eu de douteuse apparence;
Tes dons ont devancé même mon espérance;
Et ton cœur généreux m'a surpris d'un bienfait,
Qui ne m'a pas coûté seulement un souhait . . .
Qui donne comme toi donne plus d'une fois . . .

Not all writers were as fortunate in their dealings with Mazarin as Corneille. Though he was more successful in his requests for aid from the Queen-Mother, Anne of Austria, the poet Scarron had a bitter disappointment in his approaches to Mazarin, as we see from the following sonnet which, for all its comic style, reveals bitter resentment:

Après que d'un style bouffon,
Pur et net de pédanteries,
J'eus bâti mon pauvre *Typhon*
De cent mille coyonneries [1]:

Avide d'or comme un griffon,
D'or, d'argent ou de pierreries,
Je le couvris, non d'un chiffon,
Mais de chiffres et d'armoiries.[2]

Mon livre étant ainsi paré
Et richement élaboré,[3]
J'en régalai le mauvais riche;

Mais, ô malheureux Scarronnet!
Il n'en fut jamais un si chiche.
Déchire ton chien de sonnet.

[1] Jests, foolish sayings.
[2] It was customary to have a book handsomely bound and adorned with the patron's arms and initials.
[3] Decked out.

In the 1650's, however, appeared a new and extremely generous patron, the *Surintendant des Finances*, Nicolas Fouquet, to whom not only Scarron, but also Mlle de Scudéry, La Fontaine and Corneille owed much. Indeed, it was through Fouquet's intervention that Corneille came out of his retirement and embarked on a new career as playwright which opened with his *Œdipe* (1659). Unfortunately this supply of manna failed suddenly with the arrest and trial of Fouquet in 1661.

It was now that the young Louis XIV began to take an interest in literature and in men of letters. Colbert drew up lists of poets, playwrights, scholars, scientists—foreigners as well as Frenchmen—who qualified for the receipt of the King's bounty. The King himself was personally acquainted with the men of letters who brought distinction to his reign: he knew Molière, partly through his role as actor and court-entertainer, but he also rewarded the writer with a pension. In 1677 he was to make Racine and Boileau *historiographes du Roi*. Yet perhaps too much has been made of the undoubted interest which Louis showed in literature. The terms in which historians since Voltaire have spoken of his munificence, seem somewhat exaggerated when we look at the cold facts of the case. It was perhaps inevitable that in giving pensions to the men of letters of his time Louis and his minister, Colbert, should have failed to discriminate between the really great writers of the reign and the second-rate and the totally forgotten: any scheme of patronage runs that risk. Thus we search in vain for the name of La Fontaine among the recipients of the royal bounty, while in the 1660's men like Molière and Racine received pensions which in no way distinguished them from third-rate writers. Indeed, they often received less than men who are now forgotten.

Less excusable is the fact that Louis's pensions to men of letters were given, not out of a disinterested desire to help men of letters, or with the more interested, but none the less reasonable intention of making the reign illustrious through its great writers, but simply to encourage the production of propaganda writings which would boost the name of 'Louis le

Grand' at home and abroad. In his letters to the foreign recipients Colbert's agent, Chapelain, makes it abundantly clear that the continuation of these pensions depends entirely on the provision of suitable eulogies of the King which will serve to advance Louis's fame. At home the fortunate writers who received these gifts were also expected to contribute their quota of praise.

Moreover, these pensions which were first paid with great *éclat* in 1663, had a relatively short life. The cost of Louis's wars and the heavy expenditure on buildings like Versailles soon reduced the amount of money available for pensions to men of letters almost to nothing. There is an ironical account of the rapidity with which Louis's generosity dried up in the following lines written by a contemporary who had been among the recipients:

> Tout ce qui se trouva d'hommes distingués pour l'éloquence, la poésie, les mécaniques [1] et les autres sciences, tant dans le royaume que dans les pays étrangers, reçurent des gratifications, les uns de 1000 écus, les autres de 2000 livres, les autres de 500 écus, d'autres de 1200 livres, quelques-uns de 1000 livres, et les moindres de 600 livres. Il alla de ces pensions en Italie, en Allemagne, en Danemark, en Suède, et aux dernières extrémités du Nord; elles y allaient par lettres de change, et à l'égard de celles qui se distribuaient à Paris, elles se portèrent la première année chez tous les gratifiés par le commis du trésorier des bâtiments,[2] dans des bourses de soie et d'or les plus propres [3] du monde; la seconde année dans des bourses de cuir, et comme toutes choses ne peuvent pas demeurer au même état et vont naturellement en diminuant, les années suivantes il fallut les aller recevoir soi-même chez le trésorier, en monnaie ordinaire, et les années commencèrent à avoir quinze ou seize mois. Quand on déclara la guerre à l'Espagne,[4] une grande partie de ces pensions s'amortirent . . . (Charles Perrault, *Mémoires*, pp. 48-9.)

Ten years after these pensions had been inaugurated with a great flourish of trumpets, only a handful of people were still receiving them. Among the favoured few were Racine and

[1] Mechanical arts.

[2] The pensions were paid out by one of Colbert's departments, the *Surintendance des Bâtiments*.

[3] Elegant.

[4] In 1667.

Quinault, the author of the *libretti* for Lulli's operas; Boileau finally joined this select band in 1676, but after 1673 Corneille received nothing for nine years, until shortly before his death in 1684. Even earlier than that he had, like other people, suffered delays in the payment of his pension, a situation which produced the following lines generally attributed to him:

> Au Roi, sur le retardement du paiement de sa pension.
>
> Grand Roi, dont nous voyons la générosité
> Montrer pour le Parnasse un excès de bonté
> Que n'ont jamais eu tous les autres,
> Puissiez-vous dans cent ans donner encore des lois,
> Et puissent tous vos ans être de quinze mois
> Comme vos commis [1] font les nôtres!
>
> (*Œuvres*, x. 185.)

It is clear that Louis's generosity to men of letters only lasted for a short number of years in the 1660's and early 1670's, and that while he continued to show favour to such writers as Racine, Boileau and Quinault at least until the 1690's, in his later years the piety which made him avoid such profane entertainments as the theatre, and the increasing disorder of the royal finances finally wiped out any royal patronage of literature. Indeed, if one may venture a minor heresy, it would seem that in the following century during the reigns of Louis XV and Louis XVI the State did much more for men of letters than was ever attempted by Louis XIV in his long personal reign.

The patronage of great noblemen and wealthy tax-farmers continued, of course, in the second half of the century. In a contemporary satire we are given an amusing picture of the needy poet's hopes of profit from a volume of his verses:

> Il espérait tirer cent écus du libraire
> Et vendre cent louis l'épître liminaire,[2]
> Prenant pour protecteur quelque orgueilleux faquin
> Qui payerait chèrement l'or et le maroquin.[3]
>
> (Furetière, *Les Poètes*, Satire V.)

[1] Officials.
[2] Dedication.
[3] The gilt arms and morocco leather-binding.

It is true that these hopes were often disappointed, but none the less writers continued to lavish infinite care on their dedications, as we see from the following satirical account of a playwright who has just composed a new tragedy; it is taken from Lesage's *Diable boiteux*, written in the opening years of the eighteenth century:

> Il a dessein de la dédier, et il y a six heures qu'il travaille à l'épître dédicatoire; il en est à la dernière phrase en ce moment. On peut dire que c'est un chef-d'œuvre que cette dédicace: toutes les vertus morales et politiques, toutes les louanges que l'on peut donner à un homme illustre par ses ancêtres et par lui-même, n'y sont point épargnées; jamais auteur n'a tant prodigué l'encens.—A qui prétend-il adresser cet éloge? reprit l'écolier.—Il n'en sait rien encore, répliqua le diable; il a laissé le nom en blanc. Il cherche quelque riche seigneur qui soit plus libéral que ceux à qui il a déjà dédié d'autres livres; mais les gens qui paient les épîtres dédicatoires sont bien rares aujourd'hui . . . (Chap. 3.)

Even so there were still patrons to come to the aid of many men of letters in their need. La Fontaine led a comfortable, if not particularly dignified existence as the hanger-on of princes of the blood, of great noblemen and particularly of wealthy *financiers*; indeed it was in the house of a wealthy *parvenu* that he spent the closing years of his life. For some time Corneille had 'la table et le couvert' in the Paris mansion of the Duc de Guise. A famous patron of men of letters, the Duc de Saint-Aignan to whom Racine dedicated his first tragedy, gave an obscure playwright 100 *louis* for the dedication of a play, even though, owing to his impecunious state, he had to give him 20 *louis* in cash and pay off the remainder of the gift in monthly instalments!

We may conclude from all these details on the economic position of the writer in seventeenth century France that it was at best a precarious one. The income to be derived from publishers, and also from the actors in the case of playwrights, was generally small and, even when not altogether unsatisfactory, of short duration. Patronage was an equally uncertain source of income since it could end suddenly through such accidents as death, or disgrace, or economic stringency. Some writers, it is true, were fortunate enough to be able to exploit their literary reputation to obtain well-paid sinecures. Racine is the foremost example of this. Thanks to the favour of Louis XIV, who made him one of his *historiographes*, he was able to cease writing for the theatre and to embark on a career at court which made it possible for him to spend the latter part of his life in security and comfort. But his older rival, Corneille, even if he did not die in poverty, drew only meagre rewards from his long and on the whole successful career: although in his life-time he was 'le grand Corneille', he was certainly much less prosperous than Racine in his later years. No doubt Molière's career in Paris from 1658 to his untimely death brought him a very comfortable living, but that was primarily because he was an actor and at that time this was a much more lucrative profession than that of playwright. Writers who are almost forgotten today also managed to achieve a comfortable existence through the good fortune of finding wealthy patrons, from the King downwards, and yet affluence in a writer was altogether exceptional, as we see from the following epitaph of Benserade who owed his position to the great success of his ballets:

> Ce bel esprit eut trois talents divers,
> Qui trouveront l'avenir peu crédule.
> De plaisanter les grands il ne fit point scrupule
> Sans qu'ils le prissent de travers.
> Il fut vieux et galant, sans être ridicule,
> Et s'enrichit à composer des vers.
>
> (Pellisson et d'Olivet, *Histoire de l'Académie Française*, ii. 250 n.)

As usual, it is in the *Caractères* of La Bruyère that we find the most vivid picture of the position of the writer in our period:

> Rien ne découvre mieux dans quelle disposition sont les hommes à l'égard des sciences et des belles-lettres, et de quelle utilité ils les croient dans la république,[1] que le prix qu'ils y ont mis,[2] et l'idée qu'ils se forment de ceux qui ont pris le parti de les cultiver. Il n'y a point d'art si mécanique ni de si vile condition, où les

[1] State. [2] 'The value they have placed upon them.'

42. Galerie des Glaces, Château de Versailles

43. *Pérelle*, Vue du Château de Versailles du côté du jardin

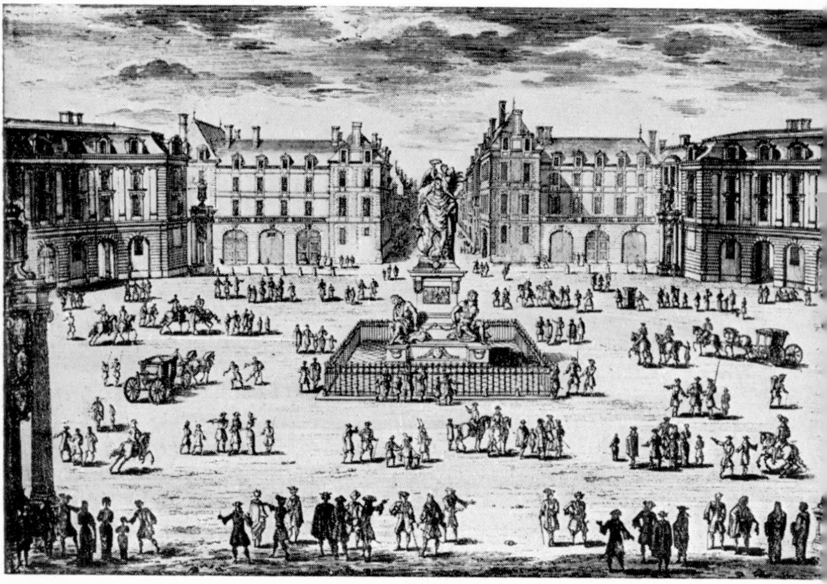

44. *Pérelle*, La Place des Victoires, Paris

avantages ne soient plus sûrs, plus prompts et plus solides. Le comédien, couché dans son carrosse, jette de la boue au visage de *Corneille*, qui est à pied. Chez plusieurs, savant et pédant sont synonymes. (xii. 17.)

It was not as if the poor financial rewards that awaited the writer, unless he had the good fortune to find a generous patron, were compensated by the respect paid to his calling. On the contrary, partly owing to the very poverty of the writer, but mainly because of the social structure of seventeenth century France which made the aristocracy despise anyone beneath them in rank, men of letters were looked down upon as mere bourgeois hangers-on. In the 1630's a poet could declare that at court 'poète, chantre,[1] baladin,[2] caimand,[3] bouffon et parasite, pour ne rien dire de pis, y sont synonymes et n'y passent que pour un' (Chapelain, *Lettres*, i. 18). Forty years later a nobleman could speak sneeringly of the plebeian sentiments which Racine gave the characters of his tragedies, and express the fear that he would introduce them into his history of the reign of Louis XIV, 'étant donné que l'auteur était un homme du peuple' (Visconti, *Mémoires*, p. 245). If noblemen took to writing, they did their best to make it clear that they were not impecunious plebeians trying to turn an honest penny, but officers and gentlemen for whom writing was merely an amusement. Hence the flamboyant declarations of Georges de Scudéry in his prefaces, for instance his answer to those noblemen who held that writing was 'un métier indigne d'un gentilhomme':

La poésie me tient lieu de divertissement agréable, et non pas d'occupation sérieuse. Si je rime, ce n'est qu'alors que je ne sais que faire, et n'ai pour but en ce travail que le seul désir de me contenter; car, bien loin d'être mercenaire, l'imprimeur et les comédiens témoigneront que je ne leur ai pas vendu ce qu'ils ne me pouvaient payer. (Preface to *Ligdamon et Lidias*, 1631.)

Yet a dozen years later, when Scudéry was about to be appointed Governor of a fortress at Marseilles, it was objected 'qu'il était de dangereuse conséquence de donner ce gouvernement

[1] *Chanteur.* [2] Ballet-dancer. [3] *Quémand*(*eur*) = beggar.

à un poète qui avait fait des poésies pour l'Hôtel de Bourgogne et qui y avait mis son nom' (Tallemant, *Historiettes*, vii. 37). It was by no means the general rule in our period for a writer to put his name on the title page of a book, even if there were no dangerous thoughts in it, since to put one's name to one's writings was to label oneself as a professional writer, and that was too much for many people's pride.

In such an aristocratic society the writer himself would blush for his profession. There is an amusing passage in a novel of the second half of the century, the hero of which describes how he was accosted by a courtier who asked him a question about his last book:

> Ce compliment me fit rougir, et jugeant . . . que j'étais découvert pour auteur, je répondis à ce courtisan qu'il me faisait plus de tort qu'il ne pensait, puisque j'étais avec des personnes qui me regardaient comme un cavalier [1] fort important, et non pas comme un excrément du Parnasse. (Préchac, *Voyage de Fontainebleau*, p. 21.)

Racine himself had no illusion about the interest which great noblemen took in him at court. He told one of his sons:

> Ne croyez pas que ce soient mes vers qui m'attirent toutes ces caresses [2] . . . Sans fatiguer les gens du monde [3] du récit de mes ouvrages, dont je ne leur parle jamais, je me contente de leur tenir des propos amusants, et de les entretenir de choses qui leur plaisent. Mon talent avec eux n'est pas de leur faire sentir que j'ai de l'esprit, mais de leur apprendre qu'ils en ont. (Louis Racine, *Mémoires* i. 295-6.)

His success in this direction, as well as the prevailing aristocratic attitude towards the man of letters, is vividly summed up in Saint-Simon's verdict on Racine the courtier: 'Rien du poète dans son commerce, et tout de l'honnête homme'.[4]

If the name of the d'Urfé family lives today, it is through the famous pastoral novel, *l'Astrée*, published by Honoré d'Urfé in the opening decades of the seventeenth century. Yet fifty years later it was a matter of shame, and not of pride, for

[1] Nobleman. [2] Attentions. [3] People of high society. [4] See p. 225.

members of his family that their ancestor should have written a book:

> En France, en effet, on n'estime que les titres de guerre; ceux des lettres et de toute autre profession sont méprisés et l'on considère comme vil l'homme de qualité qui sait écrire; je sais que les seigneurs d'Urfé ont honte que leur aïeul Honoré d'Urfé ait écrit le poème [sic] de *l'Astrée*. (Visconti, *Mémoires*, pp. 225-6.)

It is true that by the second half of the century this disdainful attitude was not universal. The growth of interest in literature in aristocratic circles was fostered by the *salons*, and several noblemen, such as Mme de Sévigné's cousin, Bussy-Rabutin, sat side by side with ordinary writers in the Académie Française. In his memoirs Bussy speaks thus of his election and of the hostile attitude of many noblemen to literature:

> Jusqu'ici la plupart des sots de qualité, qui ont été en grand nombre, auraient bien voulu persuader, s'ils avaient pu, que c'était déroger à noblesse [1] que d'avoir de l'esprit; mais la mode de l'ignorance à la cour s'en va tantôt passer, et le cas que fait le roi des habiles gens achèvera de polir toute la noblesse de son royaume. (ii. 217.)

Some noblemen published books; but even when a nobleman actually went to that length, he generally abstained from putting his name on the title-page. Moreover, contemporaries felt that there was a gulf between the nobleman writing for his own amusement and the plebeian professional writer who sought to make a living with his pen, witness the comments of a great lady in the 1660's on the style of the *Maximes* of M. le Duc de La Rochefoucauld: 'Ces modes de parler me plaisent, parce que cela distingue bien un honnête homme [2] qui écrit pour son plaisir et comme il parle, d'avec les gens qui en font métier.' (Victor Cousin, *Madame de Sablé*, p. 154.)

This gulf between the nobleman and the professional writer is best illustrated by the aristocratic attitude to any alleged offence received from these plebeian fellows. A writer who happened to annoy a nobleman ran a serious risk of being

[1] 'Perform an action unworthy of one's rank.' [2] See p. 225.

beaten up by servants and paid thugs, as Voltaire was to discover to his cost in the following century. In the 1660's Chapelain reminded Boileau that a quarrel between men of letters and one between a writer and a nobleman were two very different things: 'Les poètes ne se vengent qu'à coup de plumes et qu'avec des pointes d'épigrammes. Les ducs et pairs et les marquis le font à coup d'étrivières, et les bastonnades ne leur coûtent qu'à commander. On a vu depuis peu couper des nez; on pourrait bien voir dans peu des oreilles coupées.' (*Lettre au cynique Despréaux* in E. Magne, *Bibliographie de Boileau*, ii. 144.) The reference to noses is to an episode during the Fronde where a nobleman who had been insulted by an obscure pamphleteer, had the offender seized by his servants who

> Coupèrent à coups de ciseau
> Son très infortuné naseau,
> Ce qui fait qu'après cet outrage
> On peut dire de son ouvrage:
> 'Ce sont des discours mal tournés
> D'un auteur qui n'a point de nez.'
> (Loret, *Muse historique*, 23 July 1651.)

Even a cultured nobleman like Count Bussy-Rabutin, *de l'Académie Française*, lost all sense of proportion when he thought that a mere bourgeois writer like Boileau was on the point of forgetting the distance which separated them. In 1673 he wrote from his exile in the provinces to a friend in Paris:

> Il a passé en ce pays un ami de Despréaux,[1] qui a dit à une personne de qui je l'ai su, que Despréaux avait appris que je parlais avec mépris de son *Épître au Roi* sur la campagne de Hollande, et qu'il était résolu de s'en venger dans une pièce [2] qu'il faisait. J'ai de la peine à croire qu'un homme comme lui soit assez fou pour perdre le respect qu'il me doit et pour s'exposer aux suites d'une pareille affaire. Cependant, comme il peut être enflé du succès de ses satires impunies, qu'il pourrait bien ne pas savoir la différence qu'il y a de moi aux gens dont il a parlé, ou croire que mon absence [3] donne lieu de tout entreprendre, j'ai

[1] The name used by Boileau to distinguish him from his brothers.
[2] Poem.
[3] Bussy had been exiled from the court.

> cru qu'il était de la prudence d'un homme sage d'essayer à détourner les choses qui lui pourraient donner du chagrin et le porter à des extrémités.
>
> Je vous avouerai donc, mon révérend père, que vous me ferez plaisir de m'épargner la peine des violences, à quoi pareille insolence me pousserait infailliblement. J'ai toujours estimé l'action de Vardes qui, sachant qu'un homme comme Despréaux avait écrit quelque chose contre lui, lui fit couper le nez. (*Correspondance*, ii. 240-1.)

Fortunately for Boileau the affair was smoothed over, but he was involved in further trouble in the controversy which broke out over Racine's *Phèdre* in 1677. The two poets were accused of having written a sonnet full of the most violent insults for a great nobleman and his sister who were hostile to Racine's play. Bussy-Rabutin, writing from the provinces, was shocked to the core by such insolence: 'Jamais il n'y eut rien de si insolent que ce sonnet: deux auteurs reprochent à un officier de la couronne [1] qu'il n'est ni courtisan, ni guerrier, ni chrétien. . . . Et bien que ces injures fussent des vérités, elles devaient attirer mille coups d'étrivières à des gens comme ceux-là.' (*Correspondance*, iii. 208.) It is not generally believed today that Racine and Boileau were responsible for the offending sonnet, but it seems reasonably certain that they were for a time in danger of being beaten up. Indeed, some contemporaries alleged that Boileau did not escape this fate. A poem of the time begins:

> Dans un coin de Paris, Boileau, tremblant et blême,
> Fut hier bien frotté, quoiqu'il n'en dise rien. . . .
>
> (E. Magne, *Bibliographie*, ii. 212.)

and twenty years later another writer said of him:

> Son dos même endurci est fait aux bastonnades . . .

Here the wish was perhaps father to the thought, but a satirist like Boileau was undoubtedly in some danger of incurring the punishment which awaited men of letters who forgot the distance which separated them from their betters.

[1] Holder of a high post at court.

It was only slowly, in the course of the following century, that the social status of men of letters changed. Gradually, as the Revolution came nearer and writers were seen to control that new power in the state, public opinion, they came to be treated as equals by the members of the aristocratic society in which they moved. Indeed, foreign travellers noticed that even in the caste-ridden society of eighteenth century France, the writer was accorded a position of pre-eminence. Nothing illustrates this more vividly than the career of Voltaire—in the 1720's beaten up by the hired bullies of a nobleman to whom he had given offence, and fifty years later, at the age of eighty-four, returning to Paris to receive honours and popular applause of the kind hitherto reserved for royal personages.

Very different was the position of the writer a century earlier. Unless he had private means or a comfortable job, he seldom rose above hardship and even poverty. Welcomed into polite society, he yet remained a kind of inferior being, to be tolerated and even encouraged for his wit, but subjected to brutal ill-treatment if he forgot his place. If royal favour raised him to a higher position in society, as when Racine and Boileau were appointed *historiographes du Roi*, courtiers would sneer behind their backs at their bourgeois ways, and they themselves would speak with gratitude of the King's bounty which had raised them above the status of mere writers. Such, paradoxically enough, was the lowly position of the writer in one of the greatest ages of French literature.

To appreciate the difference between the attitude of the community to literature in the twentieth century and that which prevailed in the seventeenth, we must constantly bear in mind the social changes which have taken place since that time. If in the last hundred years or so universal primary education has reduced illiteracy to almost negligible proportions, three centuries ago in a country like France millions of people never learned to read or write. An examination of marriage registers shows that very often a man was unable to sign his name and was compelled to put a cross in its place; with women this happened still more frequently, as their education was even more neglected. It is impossible to say how large a proportion of men and women in seventeenth century France were illiterate, as we have no statistics about the numbers who received some form of education. In many places primary education of a kind existed for the children of the poor, and although the State did nothing for them, the Church took a certain interest in teaching them to read and write if only because such rudiments were necessary as a basis for religious instruction. Yet, although it is possible to paint a glowing picture of the efforts made by the Church in the seventeenth century to bring at least some education even to the poorest, there is no doubt that there were millions of illiterates of both sexes.

Even in a society where universal education has virtually stamped out illiteracy, there remain inevitably many levels of taste and literary appreciation. At the present time it is customary in certain circles to look back with longing to the good old days when culture was a monopoly of a small social group, and to lament the degradation of taste brought about by mass education. This is to ignore the obvious fact that, even allowing for the increase in population which has taken place in the last two or three centuries, there are in modern society infinitely more people with enough education to appreciate all forms of the arts than at any time in the past. If in the seventeenth century the French aristocracy gradually acquired an interest in literature and came to exercise an influence upon its development, this was a slow process, starting from low and brutish beginnings.

That greater refinement in manners, language and general behaviour was much needed by the nobles of the period is clear enough to anyone who is acquainted with the memoirs and other documents of the time. Indeed, despite the refining influence exercised by the social life of seventeenth century Paris, what astonishes the modern reader is how crude the manners of the aristocracy still remained even at the end of the century. Nowhere is this more clearly seen than in the manuals of etiquette of the time, even those of the second half of the century when an undoubted improvement in these matters had already taken place. Take, for instance, the

Nouveau traité de la civilité qui se pratique en France parmi les honnêtes gens, published by Antoine de Courtin in 1671, which had reached its thirteenth edition in 1700 and was apparently still needed. Often its injunctions in the matter of behaviour are staggeringly rudimentary, some of them indeed to the point of being unquotable. Among other pearls we find such injunctions on one's behaviour in the presence of a great nobleman as the following:

> Il faut éviter de bâiller, de se moucher et de cracher; et si on y est obligé, là et en d'autres lieux que l'on tient proprement,[1] il faut le faire dans son mouchoir, en se détournant le visage et se couvrant de sa main gauche, et ne point regarder après son mouchoir.
>
> A propos de mouchoir on doit dire qu'il n'est pas honnête[2] de l'offrir à quelqu'un pour quelque chose, quand même il serait tout blanc, si on ne vous y oblige absolument . . .
>
> Si on est assis près du feu, il faut bien se donner de garde[3] de cracher dans le feu, sur les tisons, ni contre la cheminée. (pp. 57-8.)

The section on table manners is a joy to read. Here are some of the choicest extracts:

> Quand on mange, il ne faut pas manger vite ni goulûment, quelque faim que l'on ait, de peur de s'engouer[4]; il faut en mangeant joindre les lèvres pour ne pas laper[5] comme les bêtes.
>
> Il ne faut pas manger le potage au plat,[6] mais en mettre proprement sur son assiette; et s'il était trop chaud, il est indécent de souffler à chaque cuillerée; il faut attendre qu'il soit refroidi.
>
> Il faut tailler ses morceaux petits pour ne se point faire des poches aux joues comme des singes.
>
> Il ne faut pas non plus ronger les os, ni les casser ou secouer pour en avoir la moelle. Il faut en couper la viande sur son assiette, et puis la porter à la bouche avec la fourchette.
>
> Je dis avec la fourchette, car il est, pour le dire encore une fois, très indécent de toucher à quelque chose de gras, à quelque sauce, à quelque sirop etc., avec les doigts; outre que cela vous

[1] In an elegant state.
[2] Polite.
[3] *Prendre garde de.*
[4] Choke oneself.
[5] Lap up food.
[6] Soup-tureen.

oblige à deux ou trois autres indécences. L'un est d'essuyer fréquemment vos mains à votre serviette et de la salir comme un torchon de cuisine, en sorte qu'elle fait mal au cœur à ceux qui la voient porter à la bouche, pour vous essuyer. L'autre est de les essuyer à votre pain, ce qui est encore très malpropre; et la troisième, de vous lécher les doigts, ce qui est le comble de l'impropriété.

Il faut, quand on a les doigts gras, ou son couteau, ou sa fourchette etc., les essuyer à sa serviette, et jamais à la nappe ni à son pain. Et pour s'empêcher d'avoir les doigts gras, il ne faut point manger avec, mais avec sa fourchette, comme nous avons déjà remarqué.

Il est incivil de se curer les dents devant le monde, et de se les curer durant et après le repas avec un couteau ou avec une fourchette: c'est une chose tout à fait malhonnête et dégoûtante.

Il faut observer aussi que c'est une chose très malhonnête, quand on est à la table d'une personne que l'on veut honorer, de serrer du fruit ou autre chose dans sa poche ou dans une serviette, pour l'emporter. Et c'est une grande incivilité de présenter du fruit ou quelque autre chose dont on aurait déjà mangé. (*Ibid.*, pp. 128-40.)

Yet though these elementary instructions indicate an extraordinarily low standard of manners, it is clear from what the author has to say of changes in this sphere that earlier in the century the standard had been even lower:

Autrefois, par exemple, il était permis de cracher à terre devant des personnes de qualité, et il suffisait de mettre le pied dessus; à présent c'est une indécence.

Autrefois on pouvait bâiller, et c'était assez, pourvu que l'on ne parlât pas en bâillant; à présent une personne de qualité s'en choquerait.

Autrefois on pouvait tremper son pain dans la sauce, et il suffisait, pourvu que l'on n'y eût pas encore mordu; maintenant ce serait une espèce de rusticité.

Autrefois on pouvait tirer de sa bouche ce que l'on ne pouvait pas manger et le jeter à terre, pourvu que cela se fît adroitement; et maintenant ce serait une grande saleté et ainsi de plusieurs autres. (*Ibid.*, pp. 346-7.)

Volumes could be written on this subject, but these few extracts

suffice to give one some notion of how much the *honnêtes gens* of seventeenth century France stood in need of refinement.

At the beginning of our period the court of Henry IV was profoundly affected by the years of strife through which France had passed in the Wars of Religion. The language of King and courtiers was more suited to a camp than to a palace. However great his qualities as King, Henry was incapable of setting an example of refinement and intellectual interests, for he himself was notorious for the crudeness of his speech and the roughness of his manners. Moreover, the intellectual attainments of noblemen were, and indeed in many cases remained throughout the century, extremely low. Like the King, they despised all learning; education was fit only for pedants of the lower orders or at best a smattering might be excusable in a younger son destined for the Church. It was beneath a nobleman's dignity to study anything but the art of war. What he learned in a few years at school before going to an *Académie* to receive the training necessary for a future soldier, was unworthy of being remembered. A smattering of mathematics which would be useful for a military career, together with fencing, riding and dancing, were the accomplishments which the young nobleman picked up before he went into the army at the age of sixteen or seventeen. The contempt of the aristocracy for even the most elementary forms of knowledge is well brought out in a letter written in the 1650's by a well-known poet, the Marquis de Racan:

> Il y a céans un gentilhomme qui me touche de fort près, qui, après avoir été sept ans au collège, s'est défait de son latin comme d'un habit indécent à un cavalier,[1] et a cru que c'était assez imiter la valeur, la bonne conduite [2] et la gentillesse des maréchaux de Toiras, d'Effiat et de feu Chantal [3] que d'imiter leur mauvaise orthographe. (*Œuvres complètes*, i. 341.)

The strength of the nobleman's prejudice against education is seen in a most amusing contemporary account of an argument on this subject. One nobleman praises learning, and in support of his case quotes various examples, beginning with the

[1] Nobleman. [2] Military skill. [3] Generals of the first part of the century.

great general and prince of the blood, Condé; b[...] brutally interrupted by a nobleman of the old school [...] the other side of the question in a most vigorous and comic manner:

> A commencer par Monsieur le Prince, il alla jusqu'à César, de César au grand Alexandre, et l'affaire eût été plus loin si le commandeur ne l'eût interrompu avec tant d'impétuosité qu'il fut contraint de se taire. 'Vous nous en contez bien, dit-il, avec votre César et votre Alexandre. Je ne sais s'ils étaient savants ou ignorants; il ne m'importe guère; mais je sais que de mon temps on ne faisait étudier les gentilshommes que pour être d'Église; encore se contentaient-ils le plus souvent du latin de leur bréviaire. Ceux qu'on destinait à la cour ou à l'armée, allaient honnêtement [1] à l'académie. Ils apprenaient à monter à cheval, à danser, à faire des armes, à jouer du luth, à voltiger, un peu de mathématiques, et c'était tout. Vous aviez en France mille beaux gens-d'armes, galants hommes. C'est ainsi que se formaient les Thermes [2] et les Bellegardes.[3] Du latin! De mon temps du latin! Un gentilhomme en eût été déshonoré. Je connais les grandes qualités de Monsieur le Prince, et suis son serviteur; mais je vous dirai que le dernier connétable de Montmorency [4] a su maintenir son crédit dans les provinces et sa considération à la cour, sans savoir lire. Peu de latin, vous dis-je, et de "bon français".' (Saint-Évremond, *Œuvres*, ii. 81.)

If the ingrained aristocratic prejudice against learning in time lost something of its force, it must not be imagined that the education of the average seventeenth century French nobleman was ever carried very far. A glance at a book published in 1661, at the beginning of the personal reign of Louis XIV, will show that in these more enlightened times the educational standards demanded of a nobleman, if an advance on the illiteracy of earlier generations, still remained quite modest. The author of this work, a nobleman, seeks a mean between ignorance and learning. On the one hand, he argues, too much learning would hinder rather than help a nobleman in his career: 'A le bien prendre, à quoi sert cette grande science à un homme de guerre, qu'à le rendre pauvre, en

[1] 'As was fitting.'
[2] d. 1646.
[3] A sixteenth century general.
[4] d. 1614.

l'empêchant de s'appliquer à sa fortune? Quelle utilité tirera-t-il de la philosophie d'Aristote et de Platon, ou de la *Rhétorique* de Quintilien?' But, he goes on, ignorance is another extreme to be avoided:

> Ce n'est pas que je sois du sentiment d'un de nos ducs et pairs qui croyait qu'un gentilhomme offensait sa noblesse quand il parlait latin. J'approuve non seulement qu'il [le] sache, mais de plus j'estime qu'il est très difficile qu'il puisse prétendre à la qualité d'un fort honnête homme,[1] s'il n'a aucune connaissance des bonnes lettres.[2]

Hence, so far as his military training permits, the nobleman is advised to acquire a modest stock of knowledge:

> J'approuve fort qu'il étudie jusqu'à l'âge de seize ou dix-sept ans; aussi bien jusque-là n'est-il encore propre à rien; mais quand il aura tiré du collège ce qu'un bon écolier en peut apprendre, qu'il partage son temps, et qu'il en soit bon ménager,[3] en le donnant aux exercices qui lui sont propres, et aux sciences qui lui sont nécessaires; qu'il apprenne à se servir de ses armes et de son cheval, qu'il sache la géométrie, les fortifications, la géographie, l'histoire latine et française, qu'il apprenne le dessin, et, s'il se peut, qu'il ajoute à la langue latine l'allemande, l'italienne et l'espagnole.

This is no doubt the ideal. In practice, the accomplishments demanded of a nobleman by the author of this manual are not very great. What he requires is, above all, a store of knowledge sufficient to equip him for an ordinary conversation among men of his class on such subjects as war, hunting and horses. Beyond that he suggests a certain minimum of general knowledge which will prevent him from making gross blunders: 'Ne serait-il pas ridicule de mettre Nuremberg en Italie et Florence en Allemagne, de dire . . . que Jules César et Charlemagne ont été bons amis, et qu'Alexandre le Grand fut bien malheureux de mourir sans confession?' (J. de Callières, *La Fortune des Gens de Qualité et des Gentilshommes particuliers*, pp. 215-24.)

Times had changed since the days when literature had been

[1] See p. 225. [2] Classical literature. [3] 'Let him make good use of it.'

enveloped in the aristocratic contempt for all forms of learning, for the author of this manual requires of a nobleman a certain acquaintance with literature: 'Je voudrais aussi qu'il eût appris les poètes anciens et modernes, qu'il sût faire des vers en notre langue, pourvu que cette étude fût son divertissement, et non pas sa passion.' (p. 227.)

How the nobleman was gradually brought to take an interest in intellectual and literary matters will be seen in the next chapter. Our present purpose is to study the audience to which the writers of our period addressed themselves. It is generally agreed that it was an aristocratic audience. Given the high degree of illiteracy and the restricted educational opportunities which existed in seventeenth century France, it was inevitable that literature should be addressed to a much smaller circle of readers than in the twentieth century. There is no question that numerically the audience of the great writers of the age was an *élite*. This is clearly shown by the smallness of editions of books and by the small number of times even the most successful works were reprinted. As far as the theatre was concerned, at least in the last two decades of the century, after the foundation of the *Comédie Française*, we have even more concrete evidence. An examination of the receipts of that theatre shows that, in a city of some half a million inhabitants, which was in addition frequented by many visitors from the provinces and from abroad, the Comédie Française could attract to most new plays only something like 15,000 spectators. Once that number had attended the theatre, even quite a successful new play had to be taken off because there were no longer enough spectators to keep it on.

If it is clear enough that the theatre audience and even the wider reading public of the time, were a small *élite*, it is less easy to justify the expression 'aristocratic' generally applied to them, in its full social sense, as denoting at least a majority of people with blue blood. Even today it is not possible to state exactly what sections of the community purchase and read specific books, except where learned, medical, theological and similar works are concerned: it is, of course, even more difficult to do so for the seventeenth century. Nor did all the authors of the period oblige by putting down on paper their views as to what sections of the community they were writing for. It is, however, clear that, living in an aristocratic society, they wrote for the upper strata of that society—from the King and court down to the more cultured sections of the middle classes. Occasionally writers of the time state quite explicitly their intentions in this respect. Unlike the poets of the Pléiade in the previous century who at least aspired to appeal to the learned, poets like Malherbe and Racan aimed their works at the world of the court. Malherbe declared that 'il n'apprêtait pas les viandes [1] pour les cuisiniers', that is, that in his translations he was not writing for scholars, or as Racan puts it: 'Il se souciait fort peu d'être loué des gens de lettres qui entendaient les livres qu'il avait traduits, pourvu qu'il le fût des gens de la cour.' And Racan himself states that his own aim as a poet was to produce verses which would be read 'dans le cabinet du Roi et dans les ruelles [2] plutôt que dans sa chambre ou dans celles des autres savants en poésie' (Racan, *Œuvres complètes*, i. 276). From beginning to end of the century writers proclaim both in public and in private that, to be successful, one's books must appeal to the court and especially to the ladies. 'C'est la moindre chose que de plaire aux savants', wrote one, 'Il faut plaire à la cour. Il faut être du goût des dames pour réussir'. Another warns the learned that his eclogues may not be in the manner of the Ancients, but that he has written them to conform to the taste of 'les dames et les gens de la cour'. For La Bruyère the court is 'le centre du bon goût et de la politesse'. It is true that many seventeenth century readers must have been remote from the world of the court, either because they lived far from Paris or because socially they came far beneath such exalted circles. It is also true that to the court one must add members of the upper classes in Paris who were on the fringe of the court. Together they formed what Boileau and other writers of the time call 'la Cour et la Ville'. Even so it is clear that the seventeenth century writer had in mind as his audience the upper classes of society. Boileau's aim, he tells us, was to

[1] Foods.

[2] *Salons* (see p. 222).

please 'ce qu'ont d'esprits plus fins et la Ville et la Cour' (*Épître* XI).

In the theatre things were perhaps somewhat more complicated. Here we are much better informed about the audience since out of scattered remarks in a host of contemporary writings it is possible to piece together a fairly clear picture of the audience of the period. It is true that the history of the French theatre in the first two or three decades of the seventeenth century is peculiarly obscure. At a time when the English theatre produced the plays of Shakespeare and when in Spain Lope de Vega was at the height of his powers, not a single masterpiece was performed on the French stage. While London had as many as five theatres, Paris had only one, and even so it was not until 1629 that any company was able to establish itself permanently there. Until then there was a succession of companies—mostly French, but occasionally also Italian, or even English at the very beginning of the century—none of which managed to secure enough support to last out longer than a short period.

The striking thing about the plays of this early part of the century—be they comedies, tragedies, tragi-comedies, or pastoral plays—is their aesthetic and moral crudity. From this it is easy—all too easy—to deduce that the audience which frequented the theatre was a plebeian one, lacking the refining influence of the upper classes of society and especially that of respectable women. Attractive as this conclusion may be, it is not altogether borne out by the facts. The theatre was undoubtedly a much less fashionable entertainment than it was to become by about 1630; the plays produced were of little literary worth and were often extremely crude, even obscene, in their subject-matter and language. Even so it is impossible to get away from such contemporary documents as the following extract from a diary under the date of January 1607:

> Le vendredi 26e de ce mois fut jouée à l'Hôtel de Bourgogne à Paris une plaisante farce à laquelle assistèrent le roi, la reine, et la plupart des princes, seigneurs et dames de la cour. (L'Estoile, *Mémoires-Journaux*, viii. 271.)

Thus not only did the King and the great noblemen of the Court make a special visit to the Hôtel de Bourgogne—then the only Paris theatre—but they were accompanied by many ladies, from the Queen downwards—and all to see a farce! Another interesting source of information is the Journal of the doctor of the young Dauphin, later Louis XIII. From this we learn that in 1604, when he was a child of three, Louis was present at a performance given by English actors at Fontainebleau, and that before his father's assassination in 1610, he went several times to the Hôtel de Bourgogne to see the Italian actors perform, as well as seeing them at Fontainebleau, probably in the company of his parents. Some years after he ascended the throne, between January 1613 and February 1614, he was present at over a hundred theatrical performances roughly half of which were by French actors and half by Italian. A few years later when his mother, Marie de Médicis, was driven into exile at Blois, she whiled away the time by seeing performances given by two of the famous farce-actors of the period, Gros Guillaume, a great favourite at the Hôtel de Bourgogne, and Tabarin, who performed in the Place Dauphine in Paris in order to attract a crowd round the booth of a quack-doctor!

Even if we grant that the theatre was not as popular in the upper ranks of society in the first decades of the century as it was later to become, it is quite clear that the royal family and the court did occasionally go to theatrical performances, whether in the royal palaces or at the Hôtel de Bourgogne. If the plays they saw were, from an aesthetic and moral point of view, extremely crude, then that is natural enough, as the taste of the court and the aristocracy was crude enough.

In the ten years between 1625 and 1635 a great change came over the Parisian theatre. The drama became much more fashionable. Not only was a permanent company set up at the Hôtel de Bourgogne, but shortly afterwards a second company —aided partly by the early plays of Corneille—was able to establish itself in the capital at the Théâtre du Marais. A younger generation of playwrights succeeded Alexandre Hardy, and supported by the patronage of various great noblemen and

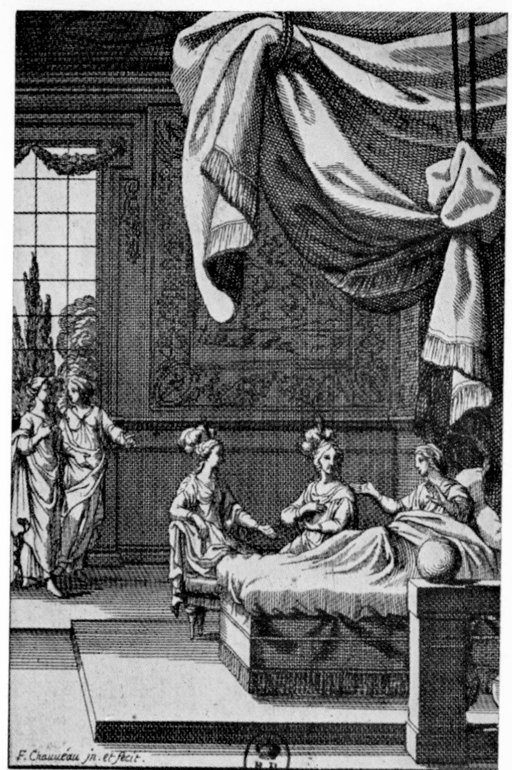

F. Chauveau, A lady receiving her guests, from the engraving for La Calprenède's *Pharamond*

J. Lepautre, Spectators on the stage

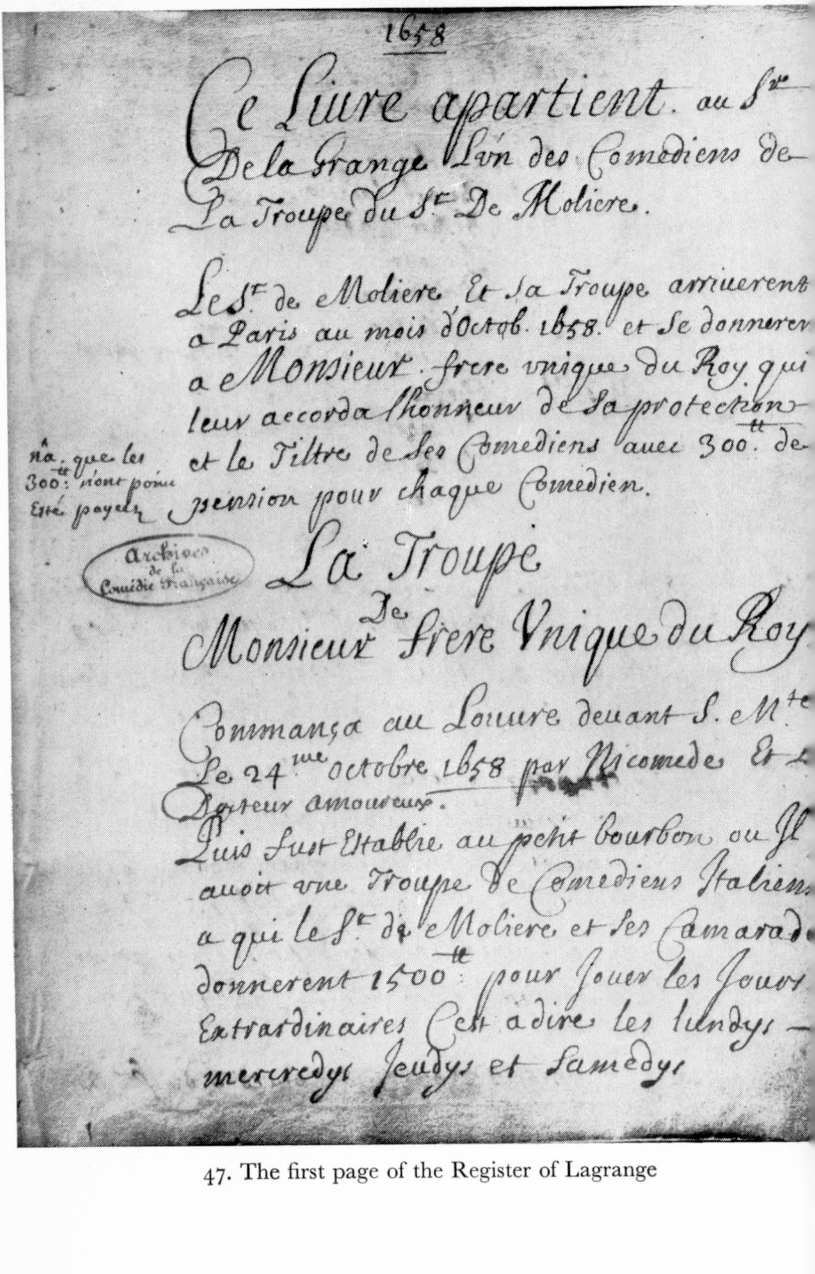

1658

Ce Liure apartient au Sr De la Grange l'un des Comediens de La Troupe du Sr De Moliere.

Le Sr de Moliere Et sa Troupe arriuerent a Paris au mois d'Octob. 1658. et se donnerent a Monsieur frere vnique du Roy qui leur accorda l'honneur de sa protection et le Tiltre de ses Comediens auec 300.tt de pension pour chaque Comedien.

nâ que les 300.tt n'ont point Esté payez

La Troupe

de Monsieur Frere Vnique du Roy

Commança au Louure deuant S. Mte Le 24me octobre 1658 par Nicomede Et le Docteur amoureux.

Puis fust Establie au petit bourbon ou Il auoit vne Troupe de Comediens Italiens a qui le Sr de Moliere et ses Camarades donnerent 1500.tt pour Jouer les Jours Extraordinaires C'est a dire les lundys mercredys Jeudys et samedys

47. The first page of the Register of Lagrange

especially Richelieu, raised French drama to a new level. It is clear that, both from the moral and the aesthetic point of view, plays composed during the rest of the century were written for a more refined and sophisticated audience than in the first two or three decades of our period. In fact, it is generally claimed that the audience of Corneille, Molière and Racine was an aristocratic audience.

This is naturally true of the first spectators to see a great many of Molière's plays, in particular his *comédies-ballets* such as *Le Bourgeois Gentilhomme*, as they received their first performance at the court of Louis XIV. Even Racine's *Iphigénie* was first given there. But what of the audience which frequented the different Paris theatres of the period—the Hôtel de Bourgogne, the Marais, Molière's theatre (from 1658 to his death in 1673), and then finally the Comédie Française, founded in 1680? It is obvious that the price of theatre tickets—varying from the cheap *parterre* (or pit) to the very expensive boxes or seats on the stage—presupposed differences, at least in purse, between the various sections of the audience.

The *parterre* which was reserved for men, contained an unruly crowd, compelled to stand for hours on end, often jammed together like sardines, if the play was a popular one. Its occupants, who perhaps accounted for half the total audience, had a powerful influence on the fate of a new play. Its success or failure depended very largely on the reactions of this crowd of men squashed together in a confined space, and ready to bring the house down with applause or cat-calls as the spirit moved them. This explains the frequent flattery of the *parterre* in the comedies of the period. The example was set by Molière himself in his *Critique de l'École des Femmes*. In this play a foolish Marquis who observes that the *parterre* has laughed at Molière's *École des Femmes*, exclaims: 'Je ne veux point d'autre chose pour témoigner qu'elle ne vaut rien', and Molière's mouthpiece is made to praise this section of the audience in a long speech which concludes thus:

> Apprends, marquis, je te prie, et les autres aussi, que le bon sens n'a point de place déterminée à la comédie [1]; que la différence

[1] Theatre.

> du demi-louis d'or et de la pièce de quinze sols [1] ne fait rien du tout au bon goût; que debout et assis, on y peut donner un mauvais jugement; et qu'enfin, à le prendre en général, je me fierais assez à l'approbation du parterre, par la raison qu'entre ceux qui le composent, il y en a plusieurs [2] qui sont capables de juger d'une pièce selon les règles, et que les autres en jugent par la bonne façon d'en juger . . . (Sc. 6).

What sort of people frequented the *parterre* of the seventeenth century Paris theatre? It would probably be wrong to think of the occupants of the *parterre* as being as plebeian as Shakespeare's groundlings. It is true that there are occasional references in the literature of the time (there is one in the *Critique de l'École des Femmes*) to the presence in the theatre of such lowborn fellows as lackeys. Yet in a general way the occupants of the *parterre* were of much higher social status, certainly very far from plebeian. There was a large proportion of bourgeois—merchants, professional men, teachers and quite a number of writers or aspiring writers—and even a sprinkling of army officers (most of them noblemen) whose presence is revealed by official documents concerning rows in the theatre, when they refused to pay for admission, or were drunk, or both. There was no absolutely clear-cut line of demarcation between the spectators in the *parterre* and those in the more expensive parts of the theatre, such as the boxes and the seats on the stage. If noblemen would occasionally frequent the *parterre*, a bourgeois who went there when he was on his own, would hire one of the cheaper boxes if he took his wife and family. On the other hand, the boxes, especially the dearer ones, were normally the preserve of the aristocracy, particularly the ladies of the court, for that was the only part of the theatre suited to their rank. There they could receive their male friends and, if they felt so disposed, gossip to their heart's content, with only an occasional glance at what was happening on the stage. Until the middle of the eighteenth century the sides of the stage were occupied by seats, again reserved for men, where the fops of the aristocracy disported themselves in the manner

[1] I.e. the difference between the price of the dearest seats and that of a ticket to the *parterre*.

[2] Probably in the sense of 'many'.

so vividly described, not without a certain amount of comic exaggeration, by a character in one of Molière's slighter comedies, *Les Fâcheux*:

J'étais sur le théâtre [1] en humeur d'écouter
La pièce, qu'à plusieurs [2] j'avais ouï vanter;
Les acteurs commençaient, chacun prêtait silence,
Lorsque, d'un air bruyant et plein d'extravagance,
Un homme à grands canons [3] est entré brusquement
En criant: 'Holà! ho! un siège promptement!'
Et, de son grand fracas surprenant l'assemblée,
Dans le plus bel endroit a la pièce troublée . . .
Tandis que là-dessus je haussai les épaules,
Les acteurs ont voulu continuer leurs rôles;
Mais l'homme pour s'asseoir a fait nouveau fracas,
Et traversant encor le théâtre à grands pas,
Bien que dans les côtés il pût être à son aise,
Au milieu du devant il a planté sa chaise,
Et, de son large dos morguant les spectateurs,
Aux trois quarts du parterre a caché les acteurs.
Un bruit s'est élevé, dont un autre eût eu honte;
Mais lui, ferme et constant, n'en a fait aucun compte,
Et se serait tenu comme il s'était posé,
Si, pour mon infortune, il ne m'eût avisé.
'Ah! marquis! m'a-t-il dit, prenant près de moi place,
Comment te portes-tu? Souffre que je t'embrasse.'
Au visage sur l'heure un rouge m'est monté,
Que l'on me vît connu d'un pareil éventé . . .
Il m'a fait d'abord [4] cent question frivoles,
Plus haut que les acteurs élevant ses paroles.
Chacun le maudissait: et moi, pour l'arrêter:
'Je serais, ai-je dit, bien aise d'écouter.
—Tu n'as point vu ceci, marquis? Ah! Dieu me damne!
Je le trouve assez drôle, et je n'y suis pas âne;
Je sais par quelles lois un ouvrage est parfait,
Et Corneille me vient lire tout ce qu'il fait.'
Là-dessus de la pièce il m'a fait un sommaire,
Scène à scène averti de ce qui s'allait faire;
Et jusques à des vers qu'il en savait par cœur,

[1] Stage.
[2] By many.
[3] Ornaments worn on legs of breeches.
[4] At once.

> Il me les récitait tout haut avant l'acteur.
> J'avais beau m'en défendre, il a poussé sa chance,
> Et s'est devers la fin levé longtemps d'avance;
> Car les gens du bel air,[1] pour agir galamment,
> Se gardent bien surtout d'ouïr le dénouement . . .
> (Act i., Sc. 1.)

It is a pity that neither Molière nor any other writer of the period has left behind so vivid, even if caricatural, picture of the behaviour of the other sections of the seventeenth century Paris theatre audience.

It is clear from what has been said that the expression 'aristocratic audience' is somewhat misleading when applied to the theatre of the time. If the dearer seats—the boxes and the stage—were occupied by people of noble birth and the upper classes generally, the *parterre*, which was as important for its numbers as for its influence on the fate of new plays, was frequented for the most part by people of a somewhat lower social stratum. Thus the spectators in a Paris theatre in the seventeenth century did not come only from the upper classes, even though, at any rate for the greater part of our period, plebeian elements were almost excluded from it. Not infrequently there was an open clash between the taste of the aristocratic or at least upper class occupants of the boxes and the seats on the stage, and that of the more bourgeois *parterre*. It is significant that in the *Critique de l'École des Femmes* Molière was careful to balance his praise of the taste and discrimination of the *parterre* with similar flattery of the Court.

> Sachez, si vous plaît, monsieur Lysidas, que les courtisans ont d'aussi bons yeux que d'autres; qu'on peut être habile avec un point de Venise et des plumes, aussi bien qu'avec une perruque courte et un petit rabat uni [2]; que la grande épreuve de toutes vos comédies,[3] c'est le jugement de la cour; que c'est son goût qu'il faut étudier pour trouver l'art de réussir . . . (Sc. 7.)

Since the spectators who attended theatrical performances at court were much more aristocratic than the more mixed

[1] 'The best people.'
[2] I.e. in the costume of a courtier as well as in that of a bourgeois writer.
[3] Plays.

audiences in the Paris theatres, there were right down to the Revolution numerous clashes between the taste of the court and the taste of Paris. A play might succeed before one audience and be a failure with the other, while a comparison of the reception given, say, to the comedies of Molière in Paris and at court shows that plays most popular with a more mixed audience often enjoyed less success when given before the King, or *vice versa.*

When we have shown that the audience before which the plays of Corneille, Racine and Molière were performed was certainly not uniformly aristocratic, we still have not entirely disposed of the question. If we may assume that the *parterre,* largely bourgeois in composition, had a great influence on the fate of a new play, because its members composed approximately half the audience, it must not be forgotten that the author by no means neglected the tastes of his more aristocratic spectators, and particularly that of the ladies who were so important, as we shall see, in the literary life of seventeenth century Paris. An interesting sign of the influence of this numerically smaller, but socially highly important section of the audience is to be seen in the choice of characters in the little comedies of the time written to attack or to defend new plays. The model of the genre, Molière's *Critique de l'École des Femmes,* brings on the stage a selection of social types which was to be copied fairly closely by his successors in this field. We are shown in this play, in addition to the playwright, jealous of the success of the comedy, an intelligent nobleman who acts as Molière's mouthpiece, a foolish Marquis ('Elle est détestable, parce qu'elle est détestable'), and three ladies—one of them bitterly opposed to the play, and the other two favourable to it—but all three of them belonging very obviously to the aristocracy. This preponderance of the aristocracy in the play shows clearly that, despite his flattery of the *parterre,* Molière considered that it was above all to the upper classes of society that he must appeal. If he shows two of the members of the aristocracy to be foolish people, the other three, who are, of course, on his side, are depicted as the embodiment of reason and commonsense.

In the aristocratic society of the time in which the King and his court and the best society of Paris towered above the rest of mortals, it was inevitable that the writer should aim first to appeal to their taste. No doubt, just as the theatre audience in our period included a high proportion of bourgeois, so the books turned out from the printing presses of seventeenth century France found their way into a wide variety of hands. They were certainly not read only by the upper classes of the time; they no doubt also reached middle and lower middle class households, and indeed penetrated to people of all classes who happened to be able to read—to lackeys and servant-maids as well as to princes and duchesses. But the fact remains that they were written primarily to appeal to a more restricted public, to those sections of society which moved in the orbit of the court of the French Kings in or near Paris. That restricted society left an indelible mark on the language as well as the literature of seventeenth century France.

CHAPTER VIII

LANGUAGE AND LITERATURE

THE history of French language and literature in our period is closely bound up with social and political developments. After the Wars of Religion, with the setting up of a centralized absolutist monarchy, the court settled permanently in the Paris region, and gave up the wandering existence from château to château which it had led in the past. An aristocracy deprived of all political functions in the provinces flocked to the capital, which had become the centre of court and social life. With their abundant leisure—for even during wartime those who served in the army, normally returned to the capital in winter—noblemen gradually developed a certain interest in intellectual and artistic matters. Literature and language alike now passed under the control of a narrow circle established in the capital, that of the cultured section of the upper classes and the writers who conformed to their tastes. The rest of France fell into contempt; *provincial* became a synonym for backward, ignorant and uncultured. It is amusing to see the sympathy which the poet, the Marquis de Racan, lavished on a lady, who had the misfortune to have to leave Paris for the provinces and suffer from the ignorance and lack of breeding of the natives:

> Plus je pense au sujet qui vous retient à la campagne et plus je trouve de raisons qui vous obligent à revenir voir Paris, hors duquel il n'y a point de salut pour les belles, ni pour les honnêtes gens. Ni le soin de conserver une maison ou une seigneurie, ni les tendresses d'amitié [1] que monsieur votre père vous témoigne, ne sont point raisons qui vous doivent faire préférer le séjour des bêtes à celui des dieux. Certes, madame, les larmes me viennent aux yeux toutes les fois que je pense qu'il faille qu'un esprit fait comme le vôtre soit réduit à entretenir des gens qui n'ont jamais vu le Louvre qu'en peinture, et qui parlent du Cours [2] et des

[1] Affection.

[2] Cours-la-Reine, a fashionable meeting place.

Tuileries comme nous parlerions de la situation de Goa ou des promenoirs du roi de Narcingue. Peut-être qu'à l'instant même que vous recevrez cette lettre, quelqu'un est en peine de savoir de vous combien M. le Grand [1] a des coudées de haut au-dessus de la taille ordinaire des autres hommes, ou quelque autre s'imagine qu'un roman est l'histoire des Romains. (*Œuvres complètes*, i. 315.)

It was inevitable that a literature written to appeal, in the first instance at least, to the upper classes of society, to 'la Cour et la Ville', should concern itself mainly with characters of high rank, and that certain sections of society should seldom appear in the literature of the age, or if they did, should generally be portrayed unfavourably. In the literature of the age one can, of course, occasionally find pictures of the peasants who formed the overwhelming majority of the population, but these are generally famous just because they are so exceptional. One remembers the vivid paragraph in which La Bruyère shows sympathy with their hard lot, and one can find a number of fables of La Fontaine in which peasants make their appearance. Yet, even if occasionally his characters are real peasants of the seventeenth century and not merely figures inherited from writers like Aesop, they occupy only a modest place in the fables as a whole. In *Le bûcheron et la mort* he gives us in two or three lines a vivid picture of the sufferings of the poorer type of peasant, yet, neither in this fable nor in the more original poem, *Le Jardinier et son seigneur*, which has as its basis the nobleman's *droit de chasse*, does one find any trace of a protest against the condition of the peasants, even though the poet does show some sympathy with them. In general, the peasant was relegated to the lower forms of literature, such as satire or comedy. Molière himself, like one or two of his predecessors and several other playwrights of the second half of the century, introduces peasant characters into his plays, but they are generally represented as rather laughable creatures, sometimes stupid, sometimes endowed with a certain rustic cunning, and, of course, speaking a barbarous dialect. Moreover, peasants, when introduced into comedy, tend to

[1] An abbreviation of 'le grand Écuyer'.

appear in farces and generally as mere episodic characters. Even La Bruyère, despite his sympathy with the hard lot of the peasants, did not wish to see them on the stage except in farce: 'Le paysan ou l'ivrogne fournit quelques scènes à un farceur; il n'entre qu'à peine dans le vrai comique: comment pourrait-il faire le fond ou l'action principale de la comédie?' (*Caractères*, i. 52.)

A less restricted place was given to the middle classes in seventeenth century French literature. Yet many of the bourgeois characters in the literature of the time—one thinks, for instance, of the wealthy middle class households portrayed by Molière in such comedies as *Tartufe* or *Les Femmes Savantes*—belong very definitely to the upper classes of society, and are in fact on the fringe of the aristocracy. If we leave aside such characters drawn from the upper ranks of the *bourgeoisie*, we see that, despite their middle class origins, contemporary writers do not attempt to depict in a favourable light the representatives of their own class. In the following century writers were to exalt the importance of the middle classes in society and to demand the creation of a new dramatic genre —the *drame*—which would deal sympathetically with the problems and aspirations of people drawn from the middle ranks of society. For the seventeenth century dramatist it was axiomatic that tragedy confined itself to portraying the misfortunes of kings and princes, while lesser mortals were to be made fun of in comedy. Molière, it is true, created a mild stir by bringing on the stage in a number of his comedies foolish, young *marquis* of the court of Louis XIV, but in general he showed the warmest regard for the taste of the court, which he stoutly defends in the words put into the mouth of Clitandre in the *Femmes Savantes*:

> Vous en voulez beaucoup à cette pauvre cour,
> Et son malheur est grand de voir que chaque jour
> Vous autres beaux esprits vous déclamiez contre elle,
> Que de tous vos chagrins vous lui fassiez querelle,
> Et, sur son méchant goût lui faisant son procès,
> N'accusiez que lui seul de vos méchants succès.[1]

[1] *Succès* had the sense of 'issue, outcome', hence 'méchant succès' = 'failure'.

> Permettez-moi, Monsieur Trissotin, de vous dire
> Avec tout le respect que votre nom m'inspire,
> Que vous feriez fort bien, vos confrères et vous,
> De parler de la cour d'un ton un peu plus doux;
> Qu'à le bien prendre, au fond, elle n'est pas si bête
> Que vous autres messieurs vous vous mettez en tête;
> Qu'elle a du sens commun pour se connaître à tout,
> Que chez elle on se peut former quelque bon goût;
> Et que l'esprit du monde [1] y vaut, sans flatterie,
> Tout le savoir obscur de la pédanterie.
>
> (Act iv., Sc. 3.)

Molière fully accepts the rigid hierarchy of social classes which existed in the France of Louis XIV. To him a peasant like George Dandin or a wealthy bourgeois like M. Jourdain who strive to rise out of their social class into the aristocracy are fit subjects for comedy; in neither case had he any more sympathy with his characters than had the court audience before which both plays were first performed.

In general the bourgeois writers of the time, with their eye on the aristocratic tastes of their audience, do not show much sympathy with the outlook of their middle class characters. In *Le Roman bourgeois* (1666) Furetière's aim is to depict, not the heroic exploits to be found in the aristocratic novel, but middle class life in the Paris of his time—to portray 'ces bonnes gens de médiocre [2] condition, qui vont tout doucement leur grand chemin'. But though himself of fairly modest bourgeois origins, he does not show any sympathy with the middle class characters whom he depicts. He constantly compares their manners and behaviour with those of the aristocracy in order to pour contempt upon them. How clumsy and ridiculous love amongst the middle classes appears to him, when compared with the ease and charm of the aristocracy in these matters! A young *bourgeoise*, he declares, is so afraid of never marrying that she rushes off to church the first man who has shown the slightest interest in her:

> C'est la cause de cette grande différence qui est entre les gens de la cour et la bourgeoisie: car la noblesse, faisant une profession

[1] High society.

Ordinary.

ouverte de galanterie, et s'accoutumant à voir les dames dès la plus tendre jeunesse, se forme certaine habitude de civilité et de politesse qui dure toute la vie. Au lieu que les gens du commun ne peuvent jamais attraper cet art de plaire qui ne s'apprend qu'auprès des dames, et qu'après être touché de quelque belle passion. Ils ne font jamais l'amour qu'en passant et dans une posture forcée, n'ayant autre but que de se mettre vitement en ménage. Il ne faut pas s'étonner après cela si le reste de leur vie ils ont une humeur rustique et bourrue qui est à charge à leur famille et odieuse à tous ceux qui les fréquentent. (p. 39.)

Thus, despite his bourgeois origins, Furetière adopts unquestioningly the standards and outlook of the aristocratic section of his public, including their pitying contempt for his bourgeois characters. A few pages later he depicts a young *bourgeoise* whom he describes as not unintelligent, but adds: 'C'est dommage qu'elle n'avait pas été nourrie [1] à la cour ou chez des gens de qualité, car elle eût été guérie de plusieurs grimaces et affectations bourgeoises qui faisaient tort à son bel esprit, et qui faisaient bien deviner le lieu où elle avait été élevée.' (p. 50). In practice, if the great middle class writers of the age brought to literature certain eminently bourgeois qualities, the fact remains that the taste of the age was predominantly aristocratic, as we see from the advice given to the young poet by one of the characters in Furetière's novel:

Je tiens que la plus nécessaire qualité à un poète pour se mettre en réputation, c'est de hanter la cour ou d'y avoir été nourri; car un poète bourgeois, ou vivant bourgeoisement, y est peu considéré. Je voudrais qu'il eût accès dans toutes les ruelles, réduits et académies illustres [2]; qu'il eût un Mécénas de grande qualité qui le protégeât, et qui fît valoir ses ouvrages, jusques là qu'on fût obligé d'en dire du bien malgré soi, et pour faire sa cour. (p. 139.)

The literature of the period, in contrast to that of the sixteenth and eighteenth centuries, was, too, essentially *conformiste*; it accepted as wholly natural both the social and political institutions of the time and the dominant religious outlook. It is true that in the somewhat unsettled period of the first half of the century, there was a certain air of freedom

[1] Brought up. [2] *Ruelles, réduits, académies,* all stand for *salons* (see p. 222).

abroad, especially in the period between the death of Henry IV and the emergence of Richelieu, and in the troubled years which culminated in the Fronde. One thinks, for instance, of the free thought (*libertinage*) of Théophile de Viau and his group around 1620, or of the attacks on absolutism which appeared during the Fronde. Yet free thought, whether in a political or a religious sense, was confined to a tiny minority and it was driven entirely underground when Louis XIV made himself master of France. Even in the first half of the century a great writer like Corneille, despite the fact that the themes of many of his plays reflect the unrest of the time, remained faithful to the orthodox political outlook. This is even more true of the writers of the great period of the reign of Louis XIV. It may be argued that neither Molière nor La Fontaine were pillars of religious orthodoxy, but they kept any subversive ideas they may have held, so well covered up that even today critics are divided on the question. In political matters all the great writers of the Classical Age were sincerely, even enthusiastically orthodox. Their writings are full of the conventional praise which was lavished so abundantly on Louis at the height of his reign. In the 1660's Boileau addresses the young King thus:

> Jeune et vaillant héros, dont la haute sagesse
> N'est point le fruit tardif d'une lente vieillesse,
> Et qui seul, sans ministre, à l'exemple des Dieux,
> Soutiens tout par toi-même, vois tout par tes yeux,
> Grand Roi . . . (*Discours au Roi.*)

In the fifth act of *Tartufe* Molière brings on an officer of the watch to arrest Tartufe and to spout line after line in praise of the King:

> Nous vivons sous un prince ennemi de la fraude,
> Un prince dont les yeux se font jour dans les cœurs,
> Et que ne peut tromper tout l'art des imposteurs.
> D'un fin discernement sa grande âme pourvue
> Sur les choses toujours jette une droite vue;
> Chez elle jamais rien ne surprend trop d'accès,
> Et sa ferme raison ne tombe en nul excès . . .
>
> (Act v., Sc. 7.)

One of the most extravagant examples of the adulation offered to the *Roi Soleil* is to be found in the words of Racine, speaking in 1678, the year of the Treaty of Nimeguen, in the French Academy of which Louis was patron: 'Tous les mots de la langue, toutes les syllabes nous paraissent précieuses, parce que nous les regardons comme autant d'instruments qui doivent servir à la gloire de notre auguste protecteur'. (*Œuvres*, iv. 356.) It is true that the authorities did all they could at this period of the century to encourage orthodoxy in writers. The publication of dangerous literature was not only hampered by a vigilant censorship and severe punishment of all attempts to evade it; in addition, the number of printers and publishers in Paris was reduced by about half, while in the provinces many towns were allowed only one printer. It was thus easier for the government to keep an eye on the printing presses and to track down seditious publications. By these means criticism of the regime, if not entirely banished, was driven underground, at least in the opening decades of the personal reign of Louis XIV.

Even so, it would be a mistake to attribute the religious and political orthodoxy of the writers of the Classical Age merely to this repressive action. Absurdly exaggerated as the praise which they lavished on the King may seem to us today, there is no reason to doubt its sincerity. It was only when disillusionment with absolutism grew towards the end of the reign and swelled in the eighteenth century into the movement of ideas which led finally to the social and political upheaval of the Revolution, that there began that estrangement between men of letters and absolute monarchy which was to characterize the following age in French literature.

If in the seventeenth century the aristocracy exercised a great influence on the development of French culture, it was, as we have seen, scarcely fitted for this role at the beginning of our period. Coarse speech and manners and a complete contempt for all intellectual and literary pursuits were characteristic of most French noblemen at a time when the country had just emerged from the Wars of Religion. For the first half of the century periods of political disorder, especially during the minorities of Louis XIII and Louis XIV, continued to provide an outlet for their energies; but with the collapse of the Fronde and the beginning of the personal reign of Louis XIV, all political activity was finally denied them. For the thousands of noblemen and their womenfolk whom a brilliant court attracted to Paris and the royal residences in the neighbourhood, this vacuum was filled by the development of social life which in its turn led them towards literature.

At the beginning of the century the court of Henry IV, with King and noblemen equally crude and ignorant, cannot be said to have exercised much influence on literary taste. The movement which was to lead the aristocracy in this direction came, not from the court, but the *salons*, which brought together men and women of high birth and a sprinkling of writers and wits. With our period begins the domination of society (*le monde*) over literature which was to last until the Revolution of 1789.

Strictly speaking, the term *salon* is an anachronism; the word most commonly used in the seventeenth century was *ruelle*. One of the meanings of the word given by the Dictionary of the Academy is 'l'espace qu'on laisse entre un des côtés du lit et la muraille', and as it was customary for a seventeenth century lady to receive her guests sitting on her bed, the word *ruelle*, standing for the space occupied by her visitors, gradually came to be applied to what the Dictionary describes as 'les assemblées qui se font chez les dames pour des conversations d'esprit'.

Of the innumerable *salons* which sprang up in Paris in the seventeenth century and which continued in an uninterrupted stream down to 1789, the most famous was the Hôtel de Rambouillet which opened its doors to the aristocracy and to writers and wits about 1608 and flourished until the time of the Fronde. The Paris mansion of the Marquis de Rambouillet had been newly built, like many another big house erected at this time to lodge the great noble families who had come to Paris to be near the court. In the famous *Chambre bleue* the Marquise de Rambouillet, half Italian in origin, attempted to enjoy the pleasures of social life which she was unable to obtain at the court of Henry IV. *Salons* like the Hôtel de Rambouillet exercised a great influence on the taste of the French aristocracy, and brought about a much-needed refinement of manners, taste and language. Yet it would be a mistake to imagine that a *salon* like the Hôtel de Rambouillet was a very highbrow institution. The tastes of the noblemen whom Mme de Rambouillet wished to attract to her house were as yet often far from polished; they would not have been attracted by the prospect of literary and philosophical debates. Moreover, for all her smattering of learning and her ideals of refinement, the Marquise was fond of fun and even of rather boisterous practical jokes. She therefore organized her *salon* in a way which was likely to attract, and not to repel, the aristocracy of the period.

No doubt the opportunity for feminine society offered by the Hôtel de Rambouillet had its attractions for contemporary noblemen: a satirist of the time describes the Hôtel as

> la retraite
> De la plupart des coquettes.

Whatever the truth of this allegation, there is no doubt about Mme de Rambouillet's love of practical jokes, witness the one which she played on the poet and wit, Vincent Voiture, who himself, as we shall see, greatly enjoyed this form of amusement:

> Il avait fait un sonnet dont il était assez content; il le donna à Mme de Rambouillet, qui le fit imprimer avec toutes les précautions de chiffre et d'autre chose, et puis le fit coudre adroitement dans un recueil de vers imprimé il y avait assez longtemps. Voiture trouva ce livre, que l'on avait laissé exprès ouvert à cet endroit-là; il lut plusieurs fois ce sonnet; il dit le sien tout bas pour voir s'il n'y avait point quelque différence. Enfin cela le brouilla tellement qu'il crut avoir lu ce sonnet autrefois, et qu'au lieu de le produire, il n'avait fait que s'en ressouvenir; on le désabusa enfin, quand on eut assez ri. (Tallemant, *Historiettes*, iii. 37-8.)

Voiture was quite capable of getting his own back on Mme de Rambouillet:

> Ayant trouvé deux meneurs d'ours, dans la rue Saint-Thomas, avec leurs bêtes emmuselées, il les fait entrer tout doucement

dans une chambre où Mme de Rambouillet lisait, le dos tourné aux paravents. Ces animaux grimpent sur les paravents; elle entend du bruit, se tourne et voit deux museaux d'ours sur sa tête. N'était-ce pas pour guérir de la fièvre si elle l'eût eue? (*Ibid.*, iii. 37.)

On another occasion Mme de Rambouillet egged on Voiture to play a trick on a young nobleman of their circle, the Comte de Guiche. The latter had one day told Voiture, a confirmed bachelor, that the rumour was going round that he was married, and asked him jokingly if the news was true. To punish him for this, Voiture decided to pull the Count's leg in return. He called at the Count's house after midnight and caused him to be wakened as the matter was urgent. The following dialogue then ensued:

Eh bien! qu'y a-t-il? dit le comte en se frottant les yeux.

Monsieur, répond très sérieusement Voiture, vous me fîtes l'honneur de me demander, il y a quelque temps, si j'étais marié, je viens vous dire que je le suis.

Ah, peste! s'écria le comte. Quelle méchanceté de m'empêcher ainsi de dormir!

Monsieur, reprit Voiture, je ne pouvais pas, à moins d'être un ingrat, être plus longtemps marié sans vous le venir dire, après la bonté que vous avez eue de vous informer de mes petites affaires. (*Ibid.*, iii. 37.)

The best-known of the practical jokes played on the Comte de Guiche by the guests of Mme de Rambouillet was, if anything, even less subtle. Here is the same author's version of the story:

On lui fit encore une malice à Rambouillet. Un soir qu'il avait mangé force champignons, on gagna son valet de chambre qui donna tous les pourpoints des habits que son maître avait apportés. On les étrécit promptement. Le matin, Chaudebonne le va voir comme il s'habillait; mais quand il voulut mettre son pourpoint, il le trouva trop étroit de quatre grands doigts. 'Ce pourpoint-là est bien étroit, dit-il à son valet de chambre, donnez-moi celui de l'habit que je mis hier.' Il ne le trouva pas plus large que l'autre. 'Essayons-les tous', dit-il; mais tous lui étaient également étroits. 'Qu'est-ceci?' ajouta-t-il, 'Suis-je

48. *A. Bosse*, Le théâtre de Tabarin

49. Frontispiece of *La Comédie des Comédiens* by Georges de Scudéry (1635)

50. *J. Lepautre, Le Malade Imaginaire* performed at Versailles in 1674

> enflé? serait-ce d'avoir trop mangé de champignons?' 'Cela pourrait bien être, dit Chaudebonne, vous en mangeâtes hier au soir à crever.' Tous ceux qui le virent lui en dirent autant, et voyez ce que c'est que l'imagination: il avait, comme vous pouvez penser, le teint tout aussi bon [1] que la veille; cependant il y découvrait, ce lui semblait, je ne sais quoi de livide. La messe sonne, c'était un dimanche; il fut contraint d'y aller en robe de chambre. La messe dite, il commence à s'inquiéter de cette prétendue enflure, et il disait en riant du bout des dents: 'Ce serait pourtant une belle fin que de mourir à vingt-et-un ans pour avoir mangé des champignons!' Comme on vit que cela allait trop avant,[2] Chaudebonne dit qu'en attendant qu'on pût avoir du contrepoison, il était d'avis qu'on fît une recette [3] dont il se souvenait. Il se mit aussitôt à l'écrire, et la donna au comte. Il y avait: *Recipe* [4] *de bons ciseaux, et décous ton pourpoint.* (*Ibid.*, ii. 309-10.)

These are some examples of the rather boisterous fun in which Mme de Rambouillet and her guests indulged. It is well to remember that the tastes of the aristocracy in this period of the century were by no means overweighted in favour of the purely intellectual, and that the *habitués* of the Hôtel de Rambouillet enjoyed there the pleasures both of crude jokes and flirtation. Yet it is hardly necessary to add that there was another side to the activities of the Hôtel which give it a place in the literary history of seventeenth century France.

The first important influence which the *salons* exercised on those who frequented them, was in the direction of greater refinement of manners and taste. From the emergence of the *salons* dates the predominance of women in French social life, and their emancipation from a semi-feudal subjection to a position, not merely of equality, but even of supremacy over men. It was in the *salons* that the new ideal of the gentleman, the *honnête homme*, was formed; the rough-mannered warrior was replaced by the gentleman, distinguished for his refinement, good taste, and politeness towards the ladies. Needless to say, the *honnête homme* was a thoroughly aristocratic ideal;

[1] Healthy. [2] *Trop loin.* [3] Prescription.
[4] Latin for 'take', and once used as a heading for prescriptions (hence our word 'recipe').

P

in the literature of the time—Furetière's *Roman bourgeois* is a good example—the nobleman, polished and refined by the *salons* through contact with the fair sex, is contrasted with the clumsy and dull bourgeois.

Naturally the term *honnête homme* is one which defies exact analysis. Even those contemporaries who attempted to define the term, found it easier to say what an *honnête homme* was not than what he was, as, for instance, in the following summary of a discussion in a *salon* on the meaning of the word *galant* (which in the phrase *galant homme* had approximately the same meaning as *honnête homme*):

> J'ai vu autrefois agiter cette question parmi des gens de la cour et des plus galants de l'un et de l'autre sexe, qui avaient bien de la peine à le définir. Les uns soutenaient que c'est ce *je ne sais quoi*, qui diffère peu de la *bonne grâce*; les autres que ce n'était pas assez du *je ne sais quoi*, ni de la *bonne grâce*, qui sont des choses purement naturelles, mais qu'il fallait que l'un et l'autre fût accompagné d'un certain air qu'on prend à la cour, et qui ne s'acquiert qu'à force de hanter [1] les grands et les dames. D'autres disaient que ces choses extérieures ne suffisaient pas, et que ce mot de *galant* avait bien une plus grande étendue, dans laquelle il embrassait plusieurs qualités ensemble: qu'en un mot, c'était *un composé où il entrait du je ne sais quoi ou de la bonne grâce, de l'air de la cour, de l'esprit, du jugement, de la civilité, de la courtoisie et de la gaieté, le tout sans contrainte, sans affectation et sans vice.* (Vaugelas, *Remarques sur la langue française*, pp. 476-7.)

Though the author admits that this definition is not fully adequate, it brings out the essential fact that the *honnête homme* owed his reputation less to his moral, than to his social virtues—refinement, ease, polish, wit and so forth. The same point is stressed in another famous definition of the *honnête homme*, made somewhat later in the century by the Chevalier de Méré:

> Il me semble que dans le dessein de se rendre honnête homme et d'en acquérir la réputation, le plus important consiste à connaître en toutes les choses les meilleurs moyens de plaire et de les savoir pratiquer. Car ce n'est [pas] seulement pour être

[1] Frequent.

agréable qu'il faut souhaiter d'être honnête homme, et qui en veut acquérir l'estime, doit principalement songer à se faire aimer. En effet, on ne loue que bien sèchement ce qu'on n'aime pas, quelque bonne opinion qu'on en puisse avoir; et puis le mérite qui nous est cher, nous paraît d'un tout autre prix que celui que nous haïssons. Je trouve qu'il sied bien de se montrer d'une humeur douce, enjouée et même plaisante, autant que l'occasion, le génie et la bienséance le peuvent permettre; cette façon de procéder ouvre des entrées que l'air grave et sérieux ne donne pas, et fait bien souvent qu'on s'émancipe au-dessus de sa volée [1] et de bonne grâce.

D'ailleurs on adresse volontiers ce qu'on dit d'agréable à des gens d'un accès facile et gai; au lieu qu'on n'aborde que par contrainte une mine sombre et enfoncée; surtout il faut être hardi en effet sous une apparence modeste et oser presque tout ce qui doit réussir, sans craindre les événements.[2] Le cœur n'est pas moins nécessaire que l'esprit pour être d'un commerce agréable, et je ne crois pas qu'on puisse rencontrer un homme qui n'ait quelque défaut dans l'un ou dans l'autre. Mais il y a de certains défauts dont l'honnêteté me semble toujours exempte, et je trouve qu'il est bon de les remarquer afin de la connaître plus aisément, car outre qu'elle ne les a jamais, on les voit quasi partout où elle n'est point: comme l'injustice, la vanité, l'avarice, l'ingratitude, la bassesse, le mauvais goût, ne pas être épuré,[3] l'air grossier et peu noble, l'air qui sent le Palais,[4] la bourgeoisie, la province et les affaires, la façon de procéder qui s'attache trop aux coutumes et qui ne voit rien de meilleur; dire des choses trop communes, des équivoques, des quolibets, et tout ce qui vient d'un esprit mal fait, estimer plus la fortune que le mérite, se vouloir mettre en honneur par de faux moyens et de lâches flatteries, être dur et sans complaisance, préférer en tout ses intérêts à ceux de ses meilleurs amis, être fourbe ou menteur, chercher des apparences plutôt que la vérité, prendre mal son temps et ses mesures, être dupe et se connaître mal en gens, être sujet à s'encanailler et même avec les gens de la plus haute volée, souffrir sans ressentiment l'injustice et les avanies, n'en pas garantir les faibles quand on le peut, et se mettre toujours du parti des plus forts, mais principalement n'avoir pas je ne sais quoi de noble et d'exquis qui élève un honnête homme au-dessus

[1] Rank. [2] Outcome. [3] 'Possessing a noble and disinterested outlook.' [4] Palais de Justice (law courts).

d'un autre honnête homme. Il faut tant de rares qualités pour se rendre parfaitement honnête homme, qu'il est plus aisé de dire les choses qu'il faut fuir, que celles qu'on doit suivre, et je crois qu'en évitant ces défauts et quelques autres, l'on peut faire de grands progrès dans l'honnêteté. (*Lettres*, i. 55-8.)

In this definition more stress is laid on the necessity of possessing certain moral virtues, but it will have been noticed that these are merely qualities without which it would be impossible for a nobleman to create a pleasing impression in polite society. Indeed, the sterner moralists of the time noted with concern this attitude, as we see from the following criticism of *honnêteté*:

Pourvu qu'on soit civil et agréable en compagnie, que l'on aime les plaisirs, que l'on sache vivre avec cette politesse que la routine du monde [1] apprend, que l'on ait quelque habitude [2] chez les grands, on passe aisément pour honnête homme: il n'en faut pas d'avantage dans l'usage du siècle [3] pour faire donner ce nom et cette qualité à celui qui est peut-être fort libertin et qui n'a peut-être ni cœur ni honneur. Chez les dames, pourvu qu'un homme soit fort respectueux, qu'il sache et débite des nouvelles, qu'il soit toujours prêt de donner la comédie [4] ou d'aller à la promenade, et que son équipage soit en bon état, c'est un fort galant et fort honnête homme. . . . A parler sincèrement, c'est peu de chose que d'être honnête homme selon le monde. (Abbé Goussault, *Réflexions sur les défauts ordinaires des hommes*, pp. 267-72.)

The occupation of the *salons* which principally contributed to the formation of the *honnête homme* was, of course, conversation, partly with poets and wits, but above all with the ladies who exercised a much needed refining influence on both the manners and language of the noblemen. For those men and women who had been formed in the *salons* conversation was the greatest pleasure in life. Its importance in the polite société of the time is well summed up in the words of Mlle de Scudéry in her novel, *Clélie*, which so clearly mirrors the outlook of the *salons* of the age: 'La conversation est le lien de la société des hommes, le plus grand plaisir des honnêtes gens, et

[1] Polite society.
[2] Acquaintance.
[3] World.
[4] Plays in general.

le moyen le plus ordinaire d'introduire, non seulement la politesse dans le monde, mais encore la morale la plus pure et l'amour de la gloire et de la vertu.' Naturally the themes of the conversations at the Hôtel de Rambouillet did not always attain such a lofty ideal; no doubt gossip and scandal, as well as the latest news, furnished a good part of the material. Yet at the same time some place was found for a discussion of literary questions. Plays were read or even performed, and literature gave rise to discussions which, far from being learned or pedantic, were both light and intelligent. As the poet and critic Chapelain wrote: 'Vous ne sauriez avoir de curiosité pour aucune chose qui le mérite davantage que l'hôtel de Rambouillet. On n'y parle point savamment, mais on y parle raisonnablement, et il n'y a lieu au monde où il y ait plus de bon sens et moins de pédanterie.' (*Lettres*, i. 212.)

The general level of taste among the members of the Hôtel is perhaps best reflected in the light verse which they adored, and which provided them with an amusing pastime. It was in this type of verse that Vincent Voiture excelled. The son of a well-to-do wine merchant, he had made the acquaintance of a nobleman who frequented the Hôtel de Rambouillet, and who, struck by his talents, had said to him: 'Vous êtes un trop galant homme pour demeurer dans la bourgeoisie; il faut que je vous en tire.' Introduced into the circle of Mme de Rambouillet, Voiture had made himself indispensable by his wit and skill in conversation, as well as in light verse. It was entirely to his wit and charm that this vain, coquettish little man owed his place among the lords and ladies who frequented the Hôtel de Rambouillet.

Love was the chief theme of the type of poetry in which Voiture shone. In most of his verse he expresses highly artificial sentiments in equally artificial language. Yet, however insipid they may appear today, his poems charmed his contemporaries by their grace and wit. They show too a great ingenuity in the variety of verse-forms used. For instance, Voiture revived the mediaeval *rondeau*, a poem of three stanzas of 5, 3 and 5 lines on two rhymes, in which the first half of the first line is repeated as a refrain at the end of the second and third verses. Here is the celebrated *rondeau* in which Voiture wittily laid down the rules for this type of poem:

Ma foi, c'est fait de moi, car Isabeau
M'a conjuré de lui faire un rondeau.
Cela me met en une peine extrême.
Quoi! treize vers, huit en *eau*, cinq en *eme*!
Je lui ferais aussi tôt un bateau!

En voilà cinq pourtant en un monceau.
Faisons-en huit en invoquant Brodeau,[1]
Et puis mettons, par quelque stratagème:
Ma foi, c'est fait.

Si je pouvais encore de mon cerveau
Tirer cinq vers, l'ouvrage serait beau;
Mais cependant je suis dedans [2] l'onzième,
Et ci [3] je crois que je fais le douzième;
En voilà treize ajustés au niveau.
Ma foi, c'est fait.

The use of the refrain gives a neat and witty ending to the poem, as for instance, in a *rondeau* on the conventional love-theme:

Le soleil ne voit ici-bas
Rien qui se compare aux appas
Dont Philis nos sens ensorcelle.
Son air n'est pas d'une mortelle,
Sa bouche, ses mains, ni ses bras.

Ses beaux yeux causent cent trépas:
Ils éclairent tous les climats;
Et portent en chaque prunelle
Le soleil.

Tout son corps est fait par compas.
La grâce accompagne ses pas.
Enfin, Vénus n'est pas si belle,
Et n'a pas si bien faites qu'elle
Les beautés qui ne voient pas
Le soleil.

[1] A dictionary of rhymes. [2] *Dans*. [3] *Ici*.

Occasionally Voiture used the *rondeau* for satirical ends, as in his poem against Chapelain, a rival at the Hôtel who had dared to poach on his preserves by writing a poem of this kind entitled 'Contre M. Voiture au nom d'une dame à qui il avait donné quinze jours pour faire un rondeau'. Voiture retorted by treating his impudent rival with lofty contempt:

A vous ouïr, Chapelain, chapeler,
J'ai bien jugé que vouliez quereller;
Et que de plus vous êtes téméraire,
Quand vous osez un si grand adversaire,
Sans plus de force, au combat appeler.

Lorsque sa plume au ciel le fait voler,
Qu'avec les Dieux il ose se mêler:
Penseriez-vous qu'il se voulût distraire
A vous ouïr?

Ne prétendez ainsi vous signaler:
Vous ne sauriez ses efforts égaler.
Croyez-moi donc, laissez le dire et faire,
Et quand il parle, apprenez à vous taire.
Car par justice à lui convient parler,
A vous ouïr.

It was, however, chiefly for his love poetry that Voiture was distinguished. His most celebrated effort in this direction was the *Sonnet à Uranie*, one of his earliest pieces of poetry:

Il faut finir mes jours en l'amour d'Uranie!
L'absence ni le temps ne m'en sauraient guérir,
Et je ne vois plus rien qui me pût secourir,
Ni qui sût rappeler ma liberté bannie.

Dès longtemps je connais sa rigueur infinie!
Mais, pensant aux beautés pour qui je dois périr,
Je bénis mon martyre et, content de mourir,
Je n'ose murmurer contre sa tyrannie.

Quelquefois ma raison, par de faibles discours,
M'invite à la révolte et me promet secours.
Mais, lorsqu'à mon besoin je me veux servir d'elle,

Après beaucoup de peine et d'efforts impuissants,
Elle dit qu'Uranie est seule aimable et belle,
Et m'y rengage plus que ne font tous mes sens.

After Voiture's death in 1648 a great controversy arose at the Hôtel de Rambouillet as to the merits of this sonnet and Benserade's *Sonnet de Job*. Rival parties of *Jobistes* and *Uranistes* were formed among the lords and ladies and the writers who frequented the Hôtel. The victorious party was, it is said, the *Uranistes*, headed by Condé's sister, the Duchesse de Longueville. To the modern reader Voiture's *Sonnet à Uranie* would not appear to have any marked superiority over the rather tortured wit of Benserade's *Sonnet de Job*:

Job, de mille tourments atteint,
Vous rendra sa douleur connue,
Et raisonnablement il craint
Que vous n'en soyez point émue.

Vous verrez sa misère nue:
Il s'est lui-même ici dépeint.
Accoutumez-vous à la vue
D'un homme qui souffre et se plaint.

Bien qu'il eût d'extrêmes souffrances,
On voit aller des patiences
Plus loin que le sien n'alla.

S'il souffrit des maux incroyables,
Il s'en plaignit, il en parla;
J'en connais de plus misérables.

The vogue of *rondeaux* launched by Voiture was quickly superseded by another fashion, that for riddles in verse (*énigmes*), which continued every now and again to become the rage right down to 1789. The ladies of the Hôtel were kept busy for a few weeks guessing riddles which were often remarkable for their obscurity. The following is a typical example:

Souvent on me ravit, mais toujours je demeure
Sans passer dans les mains de celui qui me prend.
Je suis le plus petit, mais je suis le plus grand,
Et l'on ne peut me voir qu'aussitôt je ne meure.

It would require a great deal of ingenuity to discover that the answer to this riddle was 'le cœur'. More amusing examples of *énigmes* are to be found amongst those produced in another *salon* slightly later in the century. The following example is distinguished both for a greater simplicity and a very graceful suggestiveness, arising out of the use of a feminine word as the answer to the riddle:

De quelque éclat que je puisse briller,
Souvent le plus galant pâlit à me voir nue,
Alexandre se plut à me déshabiller,
Darius eût voulu ne m'avoir jamais vue.

The word is 'une épée'.

Undoubtedly some of these amusements in verse are rather childish; even the more sophisticated sonnets and *rondeaux*, despite their grace and wit, have no claim to count as literature. Nevertheless these occupations, and the discussions to which they gave rise, provided the aristocrats who frequented the Hôtel de Rambouillet and similar *salons* with an introduction to questions of literature and language. Among the more serious topics of conversation, points of language played an important part, and here again we find Voiture at work. Round about the year 1638 there was a discussion on the form of the word *muscadin*: was it to be spelt and pronounced *muscadin* or *muscardin*? As usual, instead of treating the problem in a dull and pedantic spirit, Voiture once more distinguished himself by his witty solution to the question. He wrote a little poem, ridiculing the form *muscardin* by rhyming it with words like *paladin* and *citadin* to which he added a wholly superfluous *r*:

Au siècle des vieux pal*a*rdins,
Soit courtisans, soit cit*a*rdins,
Femmes de cour ou cit*a*rdines,
Prononçaient toujours musc*a*rdins,
Et bal*a*rdins et bal*a*rdines;
Même l'on dit qu'en ce temps-là
Chacun disait rose musc*a*rde;
J'en dirais bien plus que cela,

Mais, par ma foi, je suis malarde.
Et même, en ce moment, voilà
Que l'on m'apporte une panarde.

(Pellisson et d'Olivet, *Histoire de l'Académie Française*, i. 119.)

Finally the controversy was decided in favour of *muscadin*.

Some idea of the discussions on linguistic questions at the Hôtel may be derived from a letter which Voiture wrote during a stay in the provinces to Julie d'Angennes, the eldest daughter of Mme de Rambouillet, on hearing from her that there was a movement on foot to ban the conjunction *car*. This is one of the most famous passages among the letters and poems published after Voiture's death which were long admired both in France and abroad as models of wit and good style:

> *CAR* étant d'une si grande considération dans notre langue, j'approuve extrêmement le ressentiment que vous avez du tort qu'on lui veut faire: et je ne puis bien espérer de l'Académie [1] dont vous me parlez, voyant qu'elle se veut établir par une si grande violence. En un temps où la Fortune joue des tragédies par tous les endroits de l'Europe, je ne vois rien si digne de pitié que quand je vois que l'on est prêt de chasser et de faire le procès à un mot qui a si utilement servi cette monarchie, et qui dans toutes les brouilleries du royaume s'est toujours montré bon Français.
>
> Pour moi, je ne puis comprendre quelles raisons ils pourront alléguer contre une diction qui marche toujours à la tête de la raison, et qui n'a point d'autre charge que de l'introduire. Je ne sais pour quel intérêt ils tâchent d'ôter à *Car* ce qui lui appartient, pour le donner à *Pour ce que* [2]: ni pourquoi ils veulent dire avec trois mots ce qu'ils peuvent dire avec trois lettres. Ce qui est le plus à craindre, Mademoiselle, c'est qu'après cette injustice on en entreprendra d'autres. On ne fera point de difficulté d'attaquer *Mais*, je ne sais si *Si* demeurera en sûreté. De sorte qu'après nous avoir ôté toutes les paroles qui lient les autres, les beaux esprits nous voudront réduire au langage des anges; ou, si cela ne se peut, ils nous obligeront au moins à ne parler que par signes.
>
> Certes, j'avoue qu'il est vrai ce que vous dites, qu'on ne peut

[1] The *Académie Française*, founded in 1635.
[2] Now replaced by *parce que*.

mieux connaître par aucun exemple l'incertitude des choses humaines. Qui m'eût dit,[1] il y a quelques années, que j'eusse dû vivre plus longtemps que *Car*, j'eusse cru qu'il m'eût promis une vie plus longue que celle des Patriarches. Cependant il se trouve qu'après avoir vécu onze cents ans plein de force et de crédit, après avoir été employé dans les plus importants traités, et assisté toujours honorablement dans le Conseil de nos Rois, il tombe tout d'un coup en disgrâce, et est menacé d'une fin violente. Je n'attends plus que l'heure d'entendre en l'air des voix lamentables qui diront, Le grand *Car* est mort; et les trépas du grand Cam [2] ni du grand Pan ne semblerait pas si important, ni si étrange.

Je sais que si l'on consulte là-dessus un des plus beaux esprits de notre siècle, et que j'aime extrêmement, il dira qu'il faut condamner cette nouveauté; qu'il faut user du *Car* de nos pères, aussi bien que de leur terre et de leur soleil; que l'on ne doit point chasser un mot qui a été dans la bouche de Charlemagne et de Saint Louis. Mais c'est vous principalement, Mademoiselle, qui êtes obligée d'en prendre la protection. Puisque la grande force, et la plus parfaite beauté de notre langue, est en la vôtre, vous y devez avoir une souveraine puissance, et faire vivre ou mourir les paroles comme il vous plaît. Aussi crois-je que vous avez déjà sauvé celle-ci du hasard qu'elle courait, et qu'en l'enfermant dans votre lettre vous l'avez mise comme dans un asile et dans un lieu de gloire, où le temps ni l'envie ne al sauraient toucher. (*Œuvres*, pp. 180-1.)

It is interesting to note how Voiture places *car* under the protection of Julie d'Angennes; in the *salons* it was increasingly the women who were the arbiters of taste. The interest which the Hôtel de Rambouillet, like other *salons* of the century, showed in questions of language was no accident; it has, as we shall see, a very great importance for the history of both language and literature in seventeenth century France.

Conversation, the discussion of questions of language and literature, the writing of such forms of society verse as *rondeaux*, *chansons*, sonnets, *madrigaux*, epigrams, *énigmes* and the like, does not exhaust the list of occupations of seventeenth century *salons*. In the 1650's came the fashion of the portrait, which

[1] 'Si on m'avait dit.' [2] King of Tartary.

was probably inaugurated by the success of the portraits in the novels of Mlle de Scudéry, *Le Grand Cyrus* (*1649-53*) and *Clélie* (*1654-1660*) which, under the guise of depicting life in pre-Christian times, one in the East and the other in Rome, offered a vivid picture of the occupations of polite society in seventeenth century Paris. The new fashion swept the *salons*. The portrait took two forms; it could be a self-portrait such as the well-known one by La Rochefoucauld, or, more commonly, it was a portrait of another person. An interesting example of this second type is to be found in the portrait of Mme de Sévigné composed in 1659 by her friend, Mme de La Fayette, the author of the *Princesse de Clèves*, who writes, be it noted, as if she were an unknown man describing her friend:

> Tous ceux qui se mêlent de peindre les belles, se tuent de les embellir pour leur plaire, et n'oseraient leur dire un seul mot de leurs défauts. Pour moi, Madame, grâce au privilège d'*inconnu* dont je jouis auprès de vous, je m'en vais vous peindre bien hardiment, et vous dire vos vérités bien à mon aise, sans crainte de m'attirer votre colère. Je suis au désespoir de n'en avoir que d'agréables à vous conter; car ce me serait un grand plaisir si, après vous avoir reproché mille défauts, je me voyais cet hiver aussi bien reçu de vous que mille gens qui n'ont fait toute leur vie que vous importuner de louanges. Je ne veux point vous en accabler, ni m'amuser à vous dire que votre taille est admirable, que votre teint a une beauté et une fleur qui assure que vous n'avez que vingt ans; que votre bouche, vos dents et vos cheveux sont incomparables; je ne veux point vous dire toutes ces choses, votre miroir vous le dit assez; mais comme vous ne vous amusez pas à lui parler, il ne peut vous dire combien vous êtes aimable, quand vous parlez, et c'est ce que je veux vous apprendre. Sachez donc, Madame, si par hasard vous ne le savez pas, que votre esprit pare et embellit si fort votre personne qu'il n'y en a point sur la terre de si charmante, lorsque vous êtes animée dans une conversation dont la contrainte est bannie. Tout ce que vous dites a un tel charme, et vous sied si bien, que vos paroles attirent les ris et les grâces autour de vous; et le brillant de votre esprit donne un si grand éclat à votre teint et à vos yeux que, quoiqu'il semble que l'esprit ne dût toucher que les oreilles, il est pourtant certain que le vôtre

éblouit les yeux, et que, quand on vous écoute, on ne voit plus qu'il manque quelque chose à la régularité de vos traits, et l'on vous cède la beauté du monde la plus achevée. Vous pouvez juger que si je vous suis inconnu, vous ne m'êtes pas inconnue, et qu'il faut que j'aie eu plus d'une fois l'honneur de vous voir et de vous entendre, pour avoir démêlé ce qui fait en vous cet agrément, dont tout le monde est surpris. Mais je veux encore vous faire voir, Madame, que je ne connais pas moins les qualités solides qui sont en vous, que je fais les agréables, dont on est touché. Votre âme est grande, noble, propre à dispenser des trésors, et incapable de s'abaisser aux soins d'en amasser. Vous êtes sensible à la gloire et à l'ambition, et vous ne l'êtes pas moins aux plaisirs: vous paraissez née pour eux, et il semble qu'ils soient faits pour vous; votre présence augmente les divertissements, et les divertissements augmentent votre beauté, lorsqu'ils vous environnent. Enfin, la joie est l'état véritable de votre âme, et le chagrin vous est plus contraire qu'à qui que ce soit. Vous êtes naturellement tendre et passionnée; mais, à la honte de notre sexe, cette tendresse vous a été inutile, et vous l'avez renfermée dans le vôtre, en la donnant à madame de La Fayette. Ha! Madame, s'il y avait quelqu'un au monde assez heureux pour que vous ne l'eussiez pas trouvé indigne du trésor dont elle jouit, et qu'il n'eût pas tout mis en usage pour le posséder, il mériterait de souffrir seul toutes les disgrâces [1] à quoi l'amour peut soumettre tous ceux qui vivent sous son empire. Quel bonheur d'être le maître d'un cœur comme le vôtre, dont les sentiments fussent expliqués par cet esprit galant que les dieux vous ont donné! Votre cœur, Madame, est sans doute un bien qui ne se peut mériter; jamais il n'y en eut un si généreux, si bien fait et si fidèle. Il y a des gens qui vous soupçonnent de ne le montrer pas toujours tel qu'il est; mais, au contraire, vous êtes si accoutumée à n'y rien sentir qui ne vous soit honorable, que même vous y laissez voir quelquefois ce que la prudence vous obligerait de cacher. Vous êtes la plus civile et la plus obligeante personne qui ait jamais été; et par un air libre et doux, qui est dans toutes vos actions, les plus simples compliments de bienséance paraissent en votre bouche des protestations d'amitié; et tous les gens qui sortent d'auprès de vous, s'en vont persuadés de votre estime et de votre bienveillance, sans qu'ils puissent dire à eux-mêmes quelle marque vous leur avez donnée de l'une ou de

[1] Torments.

l'autre. Enfin, vous avez reçu des grâces du ciel qui n'ont jamais été données qu'à vous, et le monde vous est obligé de lui être venu montrer mille agréables qualités, qui jusqu'ici lui avaient été inconnues. Je ne veux point m'embarquer à vous les dépeindre toutes, car je romprais le dessein que j'ai fait de ne vous accabler pas de louanges; et de plus, Madame, pour vous en donner qui fussent 'dignes de vous, et dignes de paraître, il faudrait être votre amant, et je n'ai pas l'honneur de l'être'[1]. (Mme de Sévigné, *Lettres*, i. 321-3.)

No doubt, even in the hands of a great writer, the portrait had a considerable amount of artificiality and, since the sitter looked for praise, often lacked sincerity. There is no question that the portraits inserted by La Bruyère in his *Caractères* some thirty years later were vastly superior to the products of this parlour-game, both for their psychological penetration and for their vivid description of costume, gesture and other external details. Yet this vogue of the portrait gave the people who frequented the *salons* training in the study and analysis of character, and so helped to prepare them to appreciate the great masterpieces of the age.

Another fashion which developed about this time and had perhaps an even greater influence in the same direction was that for *questions d'amour*—that is, the discussion of subtle points of psychology, particularly as they affected the passion of love. The pseudo-Roman characters of Mlle de Scudéry's *Clélie* debate with great subtlety and keenness questions like these:

Pourquoi la plupart des belles sont avares des louanges, et même souvent fort injustes.

Si l'amour est une passion plus illustre que l'ambition.

Si l'amour peut subsister durant une absence qu'on sait qui ne doit jamais finir, et si avec la certitude de ne devoir jamais revoir la personne qu'on aimerait, l'amour pourrait demeurer constante dans le cœur d'un amant et d'une maîtresse.

S'il y a plus d'amour à ne pouvoir s'empêcher de dire qu'on aime, ou à ne le dire point, parce que le respect en empêche.

Si une femme qu'un homme cesserait d'aimer, doit être plus irritée qu'une autre qui ne pourrait se faire aimer par un homme qu'elle aimerait.

[1] These last words are a quotation from a contemporary work.

Qui est le plus malheureux, d'un amant qui reçoit mille faveurs de sa maîtresse et qui en est jaloux, et d'un qui n'en obtient rien et qui n'a point de jalousie?

If contemporary works of literature offered models of such conversations on subtle points of love, some of the questions actually treated with great ingenuity in the *salons* of the time have come down to us, for instance:

Pourquoi l'Amour [1] est peint les yeux bandés, nu et enfant.

Lequel est moins avantageux pour la gloire d'un amant, ou qu'il change le premier, ou qu'on le change.

Si un véritable amant peut être gai et se réjouir pendant l'absence de sa maîtresse.

The vogue of *questions d'amour* reached such proportions that Louis XIV himself ordered the poet Quinault to compose answers in verse to five questions proposed by a lady of the court:

1. Savoir si la présence de ce que l'on aime cause plus de joie que les marques de son indifférence ne donnent de peine.
2. De l'embarras où se trouve une personne quand son cœur tient un parti, et sa raison un autre.
3. Si l'on doit haïr quelqu'un de ce qu'il nous plaît trop, quand nous ne pouvons lui plaire.
4. S'il est plus doux d'aimer une personne dont le cœur est préoccupé, qu'une autre dont le cœur est insensible.
5. Si le mérite d'être aimé doit récompenser le chagrin de ne l'être pas.

As a sample here is the answer of Quinault to the first of these questions:

C'est un tourment d'aimer, sans être aimé de même,
Mais pour un bel objet,[2] quand l'amour est extrême,
Quels que soient ses regards, ils sont toujours charmants;
Et, si l'on s'en rapporte à tous les vrais amants,
C'est un plaisir si doux de voir ce que l'on aime
Qu'il doit faire oublier les plus cruels tourments.

(Mme de la Suze et Pellisson, *Recueil de pièces galantes*, iv. 137-40.)

[1] Cupid. [2] Woman.

Once again, this vogue of *questions d'amour* had in it something of a mere parlour-game, and yet this interest in subtle psychological problems no doubt contributed to calling forth and preparing the public to appreciate the penetrating analysis of the passions which we find in the writings of La Rochefoucauld (his *Maximes* were after all first submitted to a *salon*), Mme de La Fayette and especially Racine.

No doubt the *salons* often stood for artificiality, for excessive refinement of feeling and language—in a word for preciosity. The first recorded use of the word *précieuses* in our period is to be found in a letter of 1654: 'Il y a une nature de filles et de femmes à Paris que l'on appelle précieuses . . . '. Some historians of literature argue that since the word is not recorded in this sense before that date, the phenomenon did not exist earlier, but this is an untenable position. Preciosity is part and parcel of the whole movement of refinement set in motion by the *salons* of the period, and was no doubt as old as that movement. Again, far from preciosity having received its death-blow from Molière and Boileau, it lived on victoriously for many a decade.

Preciosity cannot easily be imprisoned in any simple formula, and the more one studies such contemporary documents on the subject as have come down to us, the more complex it appears. Yet for our purpose it may be defined as an attitude both to life and to matters of literature and language, which reflects the increased refinement brought about by the *salons* and particularly by women. The *précieuses* revolted against the sordid realities of contemporary marriage, which was seldom based on mutual affection, but much more frequently on family interests of rank and money, and was therefore arranged, not by the individuals concerned, but by their parents and other relatives. The unhappiness which this conception of marriage brought about in real life, seems to have led occasionally to a revolt against marriage as an institution which turned women into the slaves of men; but much more commonly the *précieuses*—and here Mlle de Scudéry was their chief spokesman—sought refuge in what they called 'une belle amitié', that is to say a Platonic attachment between man and woman out-

disoit, *pendant le temps que vous ferez cela.* Le principal but de cette remarque est de faire entendre, qu'il ne faut jamais dire *cependant que*, mais *pendant que.* Ceux qui sçauent la pureté de la langue, n'y manquent jamais, & si quelques Autheurs modernes, quoy que d'ailleurs excellens, ne l'obseruent pas, ils s'en doiuent corriger, parce que c'est du consentement general de tous nos Maistres, que l'on en vse ainsi.

A present.

IE sçay bien que tout Paris le dit, & que la plus part de nos meilleurs Escriuains en vsent; mais je sçay aussi que cette façon de parler n'est point de la Cour, & j'ay veu quelquefois de nos Courtisans, & hommes, & femmes, qui l'ayant rencontré dans vn liure, d'ailleurs tres-elegant, en ont soudain quitté la lecture, comme faisans par là vn mauuais jugement du langage de l'Autheur. On dit *à cette heure, maintenant, aujourd'huy, en ce temps, presentement.*

A qui mieux mieux.

CEtte locution est vieille, & basse, & n'est plus en vsage parmy les bons Autheurs, & encore moins *à qui mieux*, comme l'escriuent quelques-vns, ne disant

mieux

51. A page from the *Remarques sur la langue française* of Vaugelas (1647)

52. *Nicolas de Largillière*, The French Royal Family (This picture, painted *c.* 1710, shows Louis XIV with his son, grandson and great-grandson, all of whom died before him)

side marriage. Speaking more generally, it may also be said that for the *Précieuses* love in one form or another was the chief interest in life, and this preoccupation with love is reflected in every branch of seventeenth century French literature, not only in the vast outpouring of society verse, but also in drama and the novel.

Preciosity also stood for refinement in matters of language. The *précieuses* sought to eliminate everything that was coarse, vulgar and plebeian in language, and aimed at elegance and distinction, at being different from the common herd. Of course, they sometimes carried refinement in these matters to somewhat ridiculous lengths, as when they condemned words which contained syllables with unfortunate meanings and associations. This gave Molière an opportunity for an amusing passage in his *Femmes Savantes*, where he makes one of his blue-stockings say:

> Mais le plus beau projet de notre académie,
> Une entreprise noble, et dont je suis ravie,
> Un dessein plein de gloire, et qui sera vanté
> Chez tous les beaux esprits de la postérité,
> C'est le retranchement de ces syllabes sales
> Qui dans les plus beaux mots produisent des scandales,
> Ces jouets éternels des sots de tous les temps,
> Ces fades lieux communs de nos méchants plaisants,
> Ces sources d'un amas d'équivoques infâmes,
> Dont on vient faire insulte à la pudeur des femmes.
>
> (Act iii., Sc. 2.)

However, the charge brought against the *précieuses* by several contemporaries that in their search for distinction, for a language different from that of the common herd, they created new words, has been shown to be false; their ingenuity was exercised rather on new combinations of words. Some of those attributed to them by contemporaries were ridiculous and rapidly died out; yet others lived on, and have become so much part-and-parcel of the language that they seem quite natural to us. To the *précieuses* we appear to owe such expressions as *faire figure dans le monde*, *perdre son sérieux*, *il a la taille tout à fait élégante*, and the like.

Finally the *précieuses* were very interested in literature, both as readers and as writers. The literature which emerged from the *salons*—tremendous quantities of society verse and other ephemeral writings, together with many novels of the time (especially those of Mlle de Scudéry)—was not for the most part of any great aesthetic value. Again, the taste of these circles was often superficial and influenced by a strong coterie spirit, summarized in the naïve remark of Armande in the *Femmes Savantes*:

> Nul n'aura de l'esprit hors nous et nos amis.
> (Act iii., Sc. 2.)

No doubt here, and in the following passage from Molière's *Précieuses ridicules* on the advantages of frequenting the *salons* for those who want to be 'in the know' in literary matters, there is a decided element of comic exaggeration, but none the less both throw light on the literary interests of the *précieuses*:

> On apprend par là chaque jour les petites nouvelles galantes, les jolis commerces de prose et de vers. On sait à point nommé: 'Un tel a composé la plus jolie pièce du monde sur un tel sujet; une telle a fait des paroles sur un tel air; celui-ci a fait un madrigal sur une jouissance; celui-là a composé des stances sur une infidélité: monsieur un tel écrivit hier au soir un sizain à mademoiselle une telle, dont elle a envoyé la réponse ce matin sur les huit heures; un tel auteur a fait un tel dessein; celui-là en est à la troisième partie de son roman; cet autre met ses ouvrages sous la presse.' C'est là ce qui vous fait valoir dans les compagnies, et si l'on ignore ces choses, je ne donnerais pas un clou de tout l'esprit qu'on peut avoir. (Sc. 9.)

No doubt an author extracting comic effects from a satire of a contemporary fashion is not to be taken literally, especially when he puts these words into the mouth of a stupid little provincial hussy; yet these lines do give a vivid picture of the element of snobbery and superficiality which entered into the appreciation of literature in *précieux* circles.

Preciosity was merely an extreme form of the general movement of refinement which developed through the *salons* in our period. Far from having been killed off by the Classical writers of the 1660's, the movement continued victoriously on its way to the very end of the century. The different forms of society verse continued to be turned out in almost incredible profusion: now one form was all the rage and now another. If the portrait enjoyed less popularity, the production of maxims and the concoction of *questions d'amour* were still as fashionable occupations as before. The literature of the time—the works of the really great writers—was not untouched by the influence of the *salons*. Molière may have made fun of the occupations of the literary *salons* in the *Précieuses Ridicules* and the *Femmes Savantes*, but his own plays were not unaffected by the conventional jargon which the *salons* had created for the poetic expression of love. Clitandre in the *Femmes Savantes* in his speech to Armande manages to cram the maximum amount of this *précieux* love jargon into the following lines:

> Vos attraits m'avaient pris, et mes tendres soupirs
> Vous ont assez prouvé l'ardeur de mes désirs;
> Mon cœur vous consacrait une flamme immortelle;
> Mais vos yeux n'ont pas cru leur conquête assez belle.
> J'ai souffert sous leur joug cent mépris différents,
> Ils régnaient sur mon âme en superbes tyrans,
> Et je me suis cherché, lassé de tant de peines,
> Des vainqueurs plus humains et de moins rudes chaînes . . .
>
> (Act i., Sc. 2.)

Equally typical examples of this conventional jargon can be found in the tragedies of Racine, for instance in the words which he puts into the mouth of the brutal Pyrrhus addressing Andromaque:

> Je souffre tous les maux que j'ai faits devant Troie:
> Vaincu, chargé de fers, de regrets consumé,
> Brûlé de plus de feux [1] que je n'en allumai,
> Tant de soins, tant de pleurs, tant d'ardeurs inquiètes . . .
> Hélas! fus-je jamais si cruel que vous l'êtes?
>
> (Act i., Sc. 4.)

Moreover, as we shall see in a moment, the influence of the taste of the *salons* on the works of the great Classical writers,

[1] Meaning 'love' and the 'fires' started by Pyrrhus at Troy.

goes further and deeper than in a few scattered examples of *précieux* love jargon.

Now that we have sketched in rapidly the background against which the French language as well as the literature of the age developed, it is time to examine the different ways in which they were influenced by that background. First, we may take the history of the French language in our period, for here the influence of the social and political environment is too strikingly obvious to be questioned.

In the sixteenth century, the age of the Renaissance, French writers had striven to enrich their language in order to make it the equal of the classical tongues. The result was to enlarge the vocabulary to an unprecedented degree. Not only were borrowings made from Greek and Latin; it was also a period in which the literary and intellectual life of France had not yet become centralized, along with the monarchy, in Paris. In their daily lives all the different classes of the community were drawn closely together; thus terms taken from agriculture and from all trades and occupations were used by all classes of society, and therefore in literature. Men of letters were not yet all concentrated in Paris, and in their writings could still make use of provincial and dialect words and expressions without giving offence to their readers. The literary language was thus rich even to the point of incoherence.

All this was changed in the seventeenth century. Like literature, the French language came under the control of a narrow circle, established in Paris, the centre of the court and social life. The literary world of Paris which consisted of the few thousand people who frequented the *salons* and the writers who sought to gain their favour, began a systematic attempt to endow the French language, as it had developed in the sixteenth century, with the qualities of clarity and precision. The great name associated with this movement is that of François Malherbe (1555-1628) who came to the court from the provinces in 1605, and in the last twenty years or so of his life exercised an increasing influence both on language and literature. With him begins the linguistic reform which led both to a great impoverishment of the vocabulary of the literary language and of the speech of educated people, and to an immense gain in clarity and precision. If Malherbe's influence was in one sense restrictive, his reforms in language as in poetry helped to contribute to the magnificent achievements of French literature in the seventeenth century.

From Malherbe's time dates the principle that the court, and in a slightly wider sense polite society, is the arbiter of language. Naturally this new principle was not adopted without opposition. Several writers ridiculed the pretentions of an aristocracy, at once ignorant and ruled by fashion, to set itself up as a judge in these matters. In 1625 a contemporary vigorously denounced the whole idea:

> Et à quel tribunal est-ce que l'on traîne la pauvre éloquence pour être jugée? Comme si les courtisans (gens pour la plupart sans littérature,[1] et qui tiendraient à honte le titre de savants) étaient établis pour donner le cours aux phrases aussi bien qu'aux fraises[2] . . .; à la cour rien n'est de longue durée, et il en est des mots comme des airs; quand ils ont été chantés quelque temps, ils importunent autant qu'ils ont plu. (Bishop Camus, *Issue aux Censeurs*, pp. 596-7.)

However such protests were of no avail, and soon the principle that the only good usage in matters of language was that of the court and polite society, went unchallenged.

This principle is established with all possible force in the most famous work on the French language to appear in the seventeenth century, the *Remarques sur la langue française* published in 1647 by Vaugelas, a nobleman who had spent most of his life in the *salons* observing and discussing points of language. Good usage is defined in the preface to this work as 'la façon de parler de la plus saine partie de la cour, conformément à la façon d'écrire de la plus saine partie des auteurs du temps'. By the former Vaugelas meant the more cultured section of the men and women of the aristocracy who frequented Paris and the court, to whom he added 'plusieurs personnes de la ville où le prince réside, qui par la communication qu'elles ont avec les gens de la cour participent à sa

[1] Learning, especially in the Classical literatures. [2] Ruffs.

politesse' (p. 482). The authority of polite society—of 'la cour et la ville'—in all matters of language is axiomatic for Vaugelas. Thus by about the middle of the seventeenth century a clear line of demarcation had been drawn between the language of the mass of the people and the language of polite society and literature. For more than a century the language of the common people disappeared from all the higher forms of literature—from tragedy, and all serious types of poetry and prose—and the aristocratic, literary language, reinforced by its adoption in the works of the great writers of the Classical Age, reigned supreme.

This domination of the court and polite society over the French language is made clear in a text-book, published in London in 1639 by a certain Delamothe, entitled *The French Alphabet.* Although the author, no doubt owing to his residence abroad, is somewhat behind the times in attributing to the *Parlements* and Universities an influence in matters of language which they no longer possessed, the following piece of dialogue makes it clear what restricted sections of the community foreigners had to frequent if they wanted to learn to speak and pronounce French correctly:

> S'ils n'ont ou fréquenté la cour, ou hanté la noblesse, ou appris de quelque homme de lettres, il leur est impossible ni de bien prononcer, ni de bien parler . . . —Et quoi, ne peut-on pas aussi bien apprendre du commun peuple que des gentilshommes?—Non, il n'y a ni province, ni ville, ni place [1] en France où l'on parle le vrai et parfait français, tel qu'on le lit par les livres, excepté parmi les courtisans, entre les gentilshommes, dames et demoiselles, et généralement parmi ceux qui font profession des lettres, comme aux cours de Parlements et Universités, qui seuls se sont réservé la naïveté [2] de la langue française. (p. 95.)

The true situation—the supremacy of the court in the matter of language—is made even clearer in the introduction to the 1650 edition of Cotgrave's French-English Dictionary:

> Touching the modern French that is now spoken at the King's Court, in the Courts of Parliament and in the Universities of

[1] Fortress, fortified town. [2] Natural state.

France, there hath been lately a great competition which was the best, but by the learnedest and most indifferent [1] persons it was adjudged that the style of the King's Court was the smoothest and most elegant, because the other two did smell, the one of Pedantery, the other of wrangling and Chicanery; and the late Prince of Condé,[2] with the Duke of Orleans that now is,[3] were used to have a Censor in their houses, that if any of their family [4] spoak any word that savourd of the Palace [5] or the Schools hee should incur an amercement.[6]

Good usage, declared Vaugelas in the preface to the *Remarques sur la langue française*, is that of an élite, bad usage that of the mass of the population: 'Le mauvais se forme du plus grand nombre de personnes, qui presque en toutes choses n'est pas le meilleur; et le bon, au contraire, est composé, non pas de la pluralité, mais de l'élite des voix.' The court, polite society, 'est comme un magasin d'où notre langue tire quantité de beaux termes pour exprimer nos pensées'. It is true that this aristocratic standpoint is tempered by the concession that the authority of the best writers is important, and that in some cases it can be decisive. Yet so great is the power attributed by Vaugelas to polite society that he declares that even with technical terms which would appear quite outside its province, it is the usage of society which must prevail. If sailors say *naviguer* and the court *naviger*, it is the latter form which is correct. Except in the lower forms of literature, such as comedy, satire and the burlesque, the writer must be guided by the rules of good usage, that is the usage of polite society. Even in ordinary conversation one must avoid bad usage: 'car il ne faut pas oublier cette maxime que jamais les honnêtes gens ne doivent en parlant user d'un mot bas ou d'une phrase basse, si ce n'est par raillerie' (p. 123). In the spoken, as in the written language, one must constantly aim at purity and clarity of style and expression.

The success of Vaugelas's *Remarques sur la langue française* as of the oral teaching of Malherbe twenty or thirty years earlier

[1] Impartial.
[2] The father of the great general.
[3] Gaston d'Orléans.
[4] Household.
[5] Palais de Justice (law-courts).
[6] Fine.

was due to both men's theories being in line with the general development of the French language in the seventeenth century. No better proof of the authority which Vaugelas's principles enjoyed could be provided than the fact that during his retirement from playwriting between 1652 and 1659 Corneille revised his plays of an earlier period to bring them into line with the principles set forth in the *Remarques*. Readers of Molière will remember how in 1672 he pokes gentle fun at the authority of this work when he makes the angry Chrysale exclaim:

> Je vis de bonne soupe et non de beau langage.
> Vaugelas n'apprend point à bien faire un potage . . .
> (*Les Femmes Savantes*, Act ii., Sc. 7.)

after the maid, Martine, has been dismissed by his blue-stocking of a wife for a terrible crime:

> Elle a, d'une insolence à nulle autre pareille,
> Après trente leçons, insulté mon oreille
> Par l'impropriété d'un mot sauvage et bas,
> Qu'en termes décisifs condamne Vaugelas.

What classes of words were then proscribed by Vaugelas and, earlier in the century, by Malherbe? In their pride in the increased refinement which they brought to the French language, the *salons* and the theorists would have nothing to do with old words or with words which were becoming archaic, especially since it was in the language of the common people or in the dialects of the provinces that old words still lingered on. A theorist of the second half of the century could see no difference between trying to keep alive an old word and the equally reprehensible endeavour to invent a new one: 'Je ne vois pas de différence entre faire un mot, et en renouveler un qui ne se dit plus, et qui est à notre égard comme s'il n'avait jamais été' (Bouhours, *Doutes sur la langue française*, p. 13). Thus by the second half of our period, French writers of the Renaissance were looked upon as using an ancient and incomprehensible tongue: witness the account given by Racine's son of the occasion when his father proposed to read to Louis XIV a passage from Amyot's translation of Plutarch, published just over a hundred years earlier:

> Mon père proposa une des *Vies* de Plutarque. 'C'est du gaulois',[1] répondit le Roi. Mon père répliqua qu'il tâcherait en lisant de changer les tours de phrase trop anciens, et de substituer les mots en usage aux mots vieillis depuis Amyot. Le Roi consentit à cette lecture; et celui qui eut l'honneur de la faire devant lui, sut si bien changer, en lisant, tout ce qui pouvait, à cause du vieux langage, choquer l'oreille de son auditeur, que le Roi écouta avec plaisir. (Louis Racine, *Mémoires*, i. 291.)

Thus only when the language of a sixteenth century writer like Amyot was modernized, could it be made acceptable to the King. Indeed, so great was the prejudice against old words and old style in general that by the end of the century even such reformers as Malherbe were already being criticized by the theorists for using archaic terms in their writings.

The progress of the ideas of refinement and propriety in the *salons*, especially through the influence of women in these matters, led to the banishment from the language of another category of words—those which were improper or capable of improper meanings or associations. The chaste ears of the ladies had to be spared. We have seen how Molière poked fun at their susceptibilities in the *Femmes Savantes* when he shows his blue-stockings anxious to ban 'les syllabes sales' from the language. In the *Critique de l'École des Femmes* he introduces a *précieuse* who indignantly asks: 'Peut-on, ayant de la vertu, trouver de l'agrément dans une pièce qui tient sans cesse la pudeur en alarme, et salit à tout moment l'imagination? . . . Je mets en fait qu'une honnête femme ne la saurait voir sans confusion, tant j'y ai découvert d'ordures et de saletés'. (Sc. 3). The whole question of the prudish susceptibilities of writers and theorists in matters of language in our period is rather puzzling for the modern reader, since even in the second half of the century when refinement was often being carried to extreme limits, one occasionally encounters in the literature of the time extraordinary lapses from the most elementary pro-

1 'On dit d'un vieux mot, d'une vieille façon de parler, que *C'est du gaulois* (*Dictionnaire de l'Académie*, 1694).

priety. Again, we find men whose lives were far from pure, exhibiting the most rigid and subtle prudery in questions of language. One of the favourite words of Malherbe in his marginal comments in his copy of the poems of Desportes is the word *sale*, and yet we know that, despite his prudery when he was dealing with the language of a literary work, he was in his private life extremely coarse. The principle, however, was undoubtedly accepted in the course of the century that there was no room either in literature or in the speech of polite society for words with indecent meanings or even for words capable of an improper interpretation. A theorist of the second half of the century claimed that the 'chastity' of the French language was one of its greatest merits:

> Quoique nos mœurs ne soient peut-être pas plus pures que celles de nos voisins, notre langue est beaucoup plus chaste que les leurs, à prendre ce mot dans sa propre signification. Elle rejette non seulement toutes les expressions qui blessent la pudeur, et qui salissent tant soit peu l'imagination, mais encore celles qui peuvent être mal interprétées. Sa pureté va jusques au scrupule, comme celle des personnes qui ont la conscience fort tendre, et auxquelles l'ombre même du mal fait horreur; de sorte qu'un mot cesse d'être du bel usage et devient barbare parmi nous, dès qu'on lui peut donner un mauvais sens. (Bouhours, *Entretiens d'Ariste et d'Eugène*, p. 65.)

The theorists, reflecting the outlook of the *salons*, were equally hostile to all words which were too realistic to suit the refined tastes of the ladies. *Cracher* and *vomir*, for instance, had to disappear from the language of polite society as of literature. Of the phrase *vomir des injures* Vaugelas says: 'A la cour ce mot est fort mal reçu, particulièrement des dames, à qui un si sale objet est insupportable' (*Remarques*, p. 127). Corneille had to replace the word *gueule* in the line from one of his early plays:

> Vomissant mille traits par sa *gueule* enflammée,

and to put in its place the more refined *gorge*, though he kept *vomissant* despite the ladies' grimaces at the word. *Poitrine* too came under the ban for a period, although even such a purist

as Vaugelas felt this was carrying refinement too far. Yet the tyranny of usage compelled him to condemn the word:

> *Poitrine* est condamné dans la prose comme dans les vers pour une raison aussi injuste que ridicule, parce, disent-ils, que l'on dit *poitrine de veau*: car par cette même raison il s'ensuivrait qu'il faudrait condamner tous les mots des choses qui sont communes aux hommes et aux bêtes, et que l'on ne pourrait pas dire la tête d'un homme, à cause que l'on dit *une tête de veau* . . . Néanmoins ces raisons-là, très impertinentes [1] pour supprimer un mot, ne laissent pas d'en empêcher l'usage, et l'usage du mot cessant, le mot vient à s'abolir peu à peu, parce que l'usage est comme l'âme et la vie des mots. (*Remarques*, p. 60.)

Thus, despite the coarseness and crudity of the manners and morals of many courtiers even in the second half of the century, it was universally accepted, indeed demanded, that realistic words should be banished from polite speech as from at least such higher forms of literature as tragedy.

If the ban on the categories of words which we have so far considered—provincial and dialect words, archaic words, improper and realistic words—can easily be traced to the prejudices and susceptibilities of the men and women who made up the polite society of Paris, the social reasons for the ban on the next group of words are even clearer. The aristocrats who frequented the *salons* would naturally have an aversion for words which, while neither improper nor realistic, were bourgeois and plebeian and therefore, in the language of the time, *bas*. An interesting example of the difference between bourgeois speech and that of the aristocracy is furnished by a late seventeenth century manual on questions of language (it is an aristocratic lady who is speaking; the offending words are italicized in the original):

> Vous savez, ajouta-t-elle, que les bourgeois parlent tout autrement que nous. Il n'y a pas longtemps qu'il en vint un chez moi. Il me dit qu'il était venu plusieurs fois pour avoir *le bien* [2] de me voir, et qu'il y avait longtemps qu'il était mon serviteur *bien humble*; car il aurait cru trop s'abaisser de dire qu'il était venu

[1] Ridiculous. [2] Pleasure.

pour avoir l'honneur de me voir, et qu'il était mon très humble serviteur; et comme il était marié depuis peu, 'Je vous amènerai', me dit-il, 'Madame Gobineau', en me parlant de sa femme, 'pour vous *rendre ses civilités*; j'ai aussi *un mien* beau-frère avocat *en Parlement*, nommé M. Grifonnet, qui a bien envie d'avoir *l'avantage de vous connaître*. Vous trouverez *qu'il a esprit*, et *qu'il sent bien son bien*. Aussi est-il souvent *en cour* et avec *les gens de cour*'; et après m'avoir tenu d'autres discours de cette sorte qui sentaient son bourgeois à pleine bouche, il sortit en disant qu'il avait pour moi *bien de la considération* et qu'il était mon *obéissant valet*. (François de Callières, *Des mots à la mode*, pp. 46-7.)

The comments of a nobleman present at this discussion are extremely illuminating:

Je demeure d'accord avec vous que beaucoup de gens de la ville ont de très méchantes façons de parler qui leur sont particulières, comme sont celles que vous avez fort bien remarquées; que c'est parler ridiculement que de dire *le bien* de vous voir, *l'avantage* de vous connaître. Il faut toujours dire *l'honneur* de vous voir, ou *vous voir* tout simplement. Il en est de même de votre serviteur *bien humble*; il faut dire votre *très humble serviteur*, et on ne doit jamais, au lieu de cette expression, se servir du terme de *valet*, qui ne convient qu'à ceux qui le sont effectivement, à moins qu'on ne s'en serve comme d'un terme de raillerie, car il est trop bas pour se l'appliquer autrement. *Un mien* beau-frère *qui a esprit* et *qui sent son bien*, sont trois façons de parler populaires et bourgeoises. La dernière est un peu plus en usage que les deux premières; elle est de la bonne bourgeoisie de Paris, et elle s'étend même jusqu'à des demi-courtisans. *Être en cour*, et avec *des gens de cour*, sont encore deux façons de parler bourgeoises. Il faut dire en ce sens-là, *être à la cour* et *avec des gens de la cour*; et au lieu de dire *le bien* de vous connaître, quand on parle à une dame, il ne suffit pas de dire *l'honneur de vous connaître*; il faut changer la phrase et dire *l'honneur d'être connu de vous*. *Vous rendre ses civilités* est une autre façon de parler bourgeoise qui ne doit jamais être employée en aucune occasion; il faut dire *vous rendre ses devoirs*, *vous rendre ses respects*, ou *vous rendre visite*. C'est aussi une sottise sans excuse à ce bourgeois de vous dire qu'il a pour vous *bien de la considération* pour éviter le terme de *respect* qui est toujours bienséant à un homme en parlant à une dame. (*Ibid.*, pp. 50-1.)

Nowhere is this aristocratic prejudice against the use of bourgeois or plebeian terms, whether in speech or in writing, better illustrated than in the following passage from a writer of the period.

> Les plus belles expressions deviennent basses, quand elles sont profanées par l'usage de la populace, qui les applique à des choses basses. L'application qu'elle en fait, attache à ces expressions une certaine idée de bassesse, qui fait qu'on ne peut pas s'en servir sans souiller, pour ainsi dire, les choses qui en sont revêtues. Ceux qui écrivent poliment évitent avec soin ces expressions. Les personnes de qualité et les savants tâchent de s'élever au-dessus de la populace, et n'emploient jamais ces expressions qu'elle gâte par le mauvais usage qu'elle en fait. (Morvan de Bellegarde, *Réflexions sur l'élégance et la politesse du style*, pp. 136-7.)

It must be remembered that the ban on bourgeois and plebeian words included all technical terms, those of the sciences as well as of trades and professions. Only words which were not *bas*—were neither bourgeois nor plebeian—could be used in polite society.

This gradual elimination of whole categories of words from the language of polite society is clearly illustrated in the Dictionary of the French Academy which at long last made its appearance in 1694. Founded sixty years earlier by Richelieu, the Academy had from the beginning taken seriously its role as custodian of the purity of the French language. Its aim, as defined by one of its members, was to

> nettoyer la langue des ordures qu'elle avait contractées ou dans la bouche du peuple, ou dans la foule du Palais [1] et dans les impuretés de la chicane, ou par les mauvais usages des courtisans ignorants, ou par l'abus de ceux qui disent bien dans les chaires ce qu'il faut dire, mais autrement qu'il ne faut. (Pellisson, *Histoire de l'Académie Française*, i. 23.)

In order to regulate the development of the French language it was proposed that the Academy should produce a dictionary and a grammar. Of the work accomplished by the Academy

[1] Palais de Justice (law-courts).

in the early years of its existence little is known, but we do know that it frequently concerned itself with linguistic and grammatical questions. Thus it intervened in the dispute about the form of the word *muscadin* in which Voiture had distinguished himself, and decided the question in the same way. From the beginning a start was made on the dictionary, and for a time Vaugelas was entrusted with the work. However, progress in this direction was extremely slow and it was not until 1694 that the two folio volumes of the dictionary at last saw the light of day. It was then presented to the King with solemn ceremony and all the usual flattery: the spokesman of the Academy harangued the King in the following terms:

> Pourrions-nous, Sire, n'avoir pas réussi? Nous avions pour gage de succès le zèle attentif qu'inspire l'ambition de vous satisfaire, et la gloire de vous obéir. Il nous est donc permis de nous flatter que notre ouvrage explique les termes, développe les beautés, découvre les délicatesses que vous doit une langue qui se perfectionne autant de fois que vous la parlez, ou qu'elle parle de vous.

To which His Majesty was graciously pleased to reply:

> Messieurs, voici un ouvrage attendu depuis longtemps. Puisque tant d'habiles gens y ont travaillé, je ne doute point qu'il ne soit très beau et fort utile pour la langue. Je le reçois agréablement; je le lirai à mes heures de loisir, et je tâcherai d'en profiter. (*Mercure*, Aug. 1694.)

The Dictionary set the seal of the authority of the Academy on this elimination from the language of whole classes of words scorned by polite society and therefore also by men of letters. The preface is quite clear on this point:

> L'Académie a jugé qu'on ne devait pas y mettre les vieux mots, ni les termes des arts et des sciences qui entrent rarement dans le discours.[1] Elle s'est retranchée à la langue commune, telle qu'elle est dans le commerce ordinaire des honnêtes gens et telle que les orateurs et les poètes l'emploient, ce qui comprend tout ce qui peut servir à la noblesse et à l'élégance du discours.

[1] The written or spoken language.

Other categories of words besides archaic and technical words are also treated with caution by the dictionary:

> On a eu soin aussi de marquer ceux qui commencent à vieillir, et ceux qui ne sont pas du bel usage, et que l'on a qualifiés de bas et de style familier selon que l'on a jugé à propos. Quant aux termes d'emportement ou qui blessent la pudeur, on ne les a point admis dans le dictionnaire, parce que les honnêtes gens évitent de les employer dans leurs discours.[1]

It was thus a very selective dictionary which the Academy offered to Louis XIV, one which excluded whole categories of words and branded others with the mark 'bas' or 'style familier'.

The language as it had been moulded in the seventeenth century *salons* left the writers of the age a very restricted choice of words in which to express themselves. There was indeed in seventeenth century France a definite hierarchy of words, not quite so clear-cut as the rigid social hierarchy, but none the less obvious enough. At the top came words and expressions admitted by polite society; beneath them came those of the middle classes, those of the masses and finally those of 'la lie du peuple'. There was at the same time a literary hierarchy for words. The language of the comedies of Moliére, the satires of Boileau, the fables of La Fontaine shows little trace of the impoverishment suffered by the literary vocabulary of the age, because, as these were regarded as inferior forms of literature, writers were free to use bourgeois and plebeian terms drawn from the language of everyday life. Old words and even despised dialect words could be used quite freely by La Fontaine or Molière whenever they thought fit. But it was very different in the higher forms of literature for which, in the words of a contemporary critic, 'il faut des paroles qui n'aient rien de bas et de vulgaire, une diction noble et magnifique' (Rapin, *Réflexions sur l'éloquence*, ii. 109).

From the time of Malherbe it became an accepted doctrine among writers and critics that all the higher forms of literature —tragedy, the epic, the ode, and the more serious types of prose-writing—required a vocabulary different from that of

[1] Speech.

ordinary, everyday speech in the sense that it was purged of all common, realistic expressions. Not that—like the Pléiade in the previous century or the Symbolist poets of the nineteenth—Malherbe wanted a special language for poetry. On the contrary, in the famous *boutade* attributed to him by Racan he affirms that language must be comprehensible even to the most humble and illiterate: 'Quand on lui demandait son avis de quelque mot français, il renvoyait ordinairement aux crocheteurs du Port-au-Foin,[1] et disait que c'étaient ses maîtres pour le langage.' (Racan, *Œuvres complètes*, i. 274.) By this he did not mean to suggest that high society should speak or poets write 'Billingsgate'; but simply that the literary language should be comprehensible to all, and not simply to an intellectual or aesthetic clique.

In all the higher forms of literature the vocabulary at the writer's disposal was thus an extremely restricted one. In a tragedy of Corneille or Racine, in an ode of Boileau, in a funeral oration of Bossuet, even in a novel of Mme de La Fayette, the language is noble and elevated, limited to the words admitted by the *salons* and the Academy. This explains why all realistic words from everyday life are absent, from, say, a tragedy of Racine. Naturally, given the conventional setting of Classical tragedy with its exalted personages far removed from the crude realities of everyday life, the need for realistic words rarely arises. If occasionally Racine is daring enough to use the *mot propre*, he hastens to cover up his boldness by adding an ennobling epithet: for instance, *chiens* is used in *Athalie*, but they are *chiens dévorants*. In general, when the need for a word from everyday life does arise, he gets round the difficulty by means of an elegant periphrasis. Thus, in *Athalie* the cosmetics with which the heroine's mother, Jezebel, sought to hide the ravages of the years are described with an elevated vagueness:

> . . . Elle avait encore cet *éclat emprunté*
> Dont elle eut soin de peindre et d'orner son visage,
> Pour réparer des ans l'irréparable outrage.
>
> (Act ii., Sc. 5.)

[1] Porters of a Paris market.

53. *Sébastien Leclerc*, Démolition du Temple de Charenton (in 1685, after the Revocation of the Edict of Nantes)

54. *A Benoist*, Louis XIV

In *Britannicus* Junie, torn from her bed by Nero's guards, arrives before the Emperor, not in her hastily thrown on clothes, but

> . . . dans le *simple appareil*
> D'une beauté qu'on vient d'arracher au sommeil.
> (Act ii., Sc. 2.)

Yet, despite the extraordinarily restricted vocabulary at his disposal, Racine's genius created some of the greatest poetry in the French language.

Two centuries later, Victor Hugo who had played a prominent part in the breaking down of the Classical conventions in the matter of language, made an amusing and generally accurate comparison between the rigid social hierarchy in France before 1789 and the hierarchy amongst words, some *nobles* and suitable for the highest forms of literature, others *bas* or *familiers* and therefore relegated to such inferior forms as comedy or satire. When he began his career as a poet, he declares,

> . . . l'idiome,[1]
> Peuple et noblesse, était l'image du royaume;
> La poésie était la monarchie; un mot
> Était un duc et pair, ou n'était qu'un grimaud;
> Les syllabes pas plus que Paris et que Londre
> Ne se mêlaient; ainsi marchaient sans se confondre
> Piétons et cavaliers traversant le Pont-Neuf;
> La langue était l'état avant quatre-vingt-neuf;
> Les mots, bien ou mal nés, vivaient parqués en castes;
> Les uns, nobles, hantant les Phèdres, les Jocastes,
> Les Méropes,[2] ayant le décorum pour loi,
> Et montant à Versailles aux carrosses du Roi;
> Les autres, tas de gueux, drôles patibulaires,
> Habitant les patois; quelques-uns aux galères
> Dans l'argot; dévoués à tous les genres bas;
> Déchirés, en haillons, dans les halles, sans bas,
> Sans perruque; créés pour la prose et la farce;
> Populace du style au fond de l'ombre éparse;
> Vilains, rustres, croquants, que Vaugelas leur chef
> Dans le bagne Lexique avait marqué d'une F[3];

[1] Language. [2] Classical tragedies. [3] For 'familier'.

N'exprimant que la vie abjecte et familière,
Vils, dégradés, flétris, bourgeois, bons pour Molière.
(*Les Contemplations*: Réponse à un acte d'accusation.)

The whole effort of theorists and the *salons* in seventeenth century France was thus bent towards restricting the vocabulary of French in the interests of clarity, precision and aristocratic taste. They were firmly convinced that their efforts in this direction had brought nothing but gain to the language. A writer of the second half of the century could declare: 'C'est par ce retranchement qu'on l'a perfectionnée, et qu'on en a fait une langue également noble et délicate'. (Bouhours, *Entretiens d'Ariste et d'Eugène*, p. 76.) Now that the language had been improved out of all recognition, these theorists argued, it would remain for ever unaltered in this state of complete perfection. In this they were a trifle over-optimistic, not to say unhistorical, in their ambitions; and yet, despite the growing resistance to these restrictions in the eighteenth century, it required the Romantic revolution of the 1820's to throw off the shackles imposed on French literature, especially poetry, by the developments which had taken place in the French language in the seventeenth century. There was, of course, gain as well as loss in these changes. There is no question that the French language gained enormously in clarity and precision in our period, and that it acquired qualities which were to make it for long an international language. In literature proper the consequences of this impoverishment of the language were on the whole less happy. However that may be, there is no doubt that the influence of the polite society of seventeenth century Paris on the development of the French language was both profound and durable.

Discussion of this influence on language has inevitably led to a discussion of its effects on literature. These are, if definite enough, less easy to describe, and are indeed occasionally somewhat controversial. In such a subject there is no room for dogmatic statements; all that can be offered are a few suggestions. Lyric poetry, for instance, practically died out in seventeenth century France, and had to wait for its revival until the coming of the Romantics in the 1820's. If no great lyric poets appeared in France either in the seventeenth or the eighteenth century, then that is a phenomenon which no one can explain, since the emergence of men of genius in any branch of art is a matter of pure chance. Yet one may at least ask whether it is a mere coincidence that the two centuries of French literature which saw the decline and virtual disappearance of lyricism, were precisely the centuries in which that literature was dominated by the taste of high society in Paris. The language which it had moulded was too rigid and restricted to give free rein to lyric poetry. Above all, the personal emotions which are the essence of lyric poetry, were discouraged by the atmosphere of the *salons*. There one's deepest feelings, one's griefs and sorrows, hopes and despair, were out of place; to give expression to them would have been almost an act of social impropriety.

The question of the attitude of the seventeenth century to Nature is more complicated. In some of the poets of the first thirty or so years of our period, a certain feeling for Nature and especially for the pleasures of country life does appear, and though less common later in the century, there are traces of such interests both in the fables of La Fontaine and the letters of Mme de Sévigné. Careful investigation of the problem has shown that throughout the whole century many people enjoyed contact with Nature and the sights and sounds of country life, even though there was nothing in the least 'romantic' in their attitude to them. Indeed so staid a Parisian as Boileau found pleasure in the country, and in general neither writers nor the *habitués* of the *salons* were as cut off from Nature as they are often represented as being. After all, even Paris, by far the largest city in France, was still small in area, and people could and did enjoy exploring the surrounding countryside—then largely unspoilt—which was on their doorstep.

Yet, even granted all this, granted that the love of Nature displayed in a few fables of La Fontaine and a few sentences in the letters of Mme de Sévigné was by no means exceptional among their contemporaries, it does remain a fact that Nature plays practically no role in French poetry or any other form of literature in our period. That is not surprising, given the extent to which the literature of the seventeenth century was moulded by a tiny élite living an essentially urban existence in the *salons* of Paris or the antechambers of Versailles. The Chevalier de Méré proclaims in a letter to a friend that he does not mind being away from Paris and its social life since the countryside has attractions of its own for him:

> J'aime les chants des oiseaux dans les bocages, le murmure d'une eau vive et claire, et les cris des troupeaux dans une prairie. Tout cela me fait sentir une douceur naturelle et tranquille qu'on ne connaît point dans le tumulte et dans l'embarras de Paris.

Yet he admits that such pleasures make no appeal to his friend, nor for that matter to the men and women of Parisian high society:

> Mais dans ces lieux sauvages que pourrait-on remarquer que vous fussiez bien aise d'apprendre, vous qui n'avez dans l'esprit que le monde,[1] et qui n'écoutez de bon cœur que ce qu'on vous dit de la cour ou de l'armée? Pour moi qui suis un peu solitaire, et qui me plais beaucoup à rêver, les déserts [2], quand il fait beau, ne me déplaisent pas. Les assidus courtisans ne pensent qu'à leur fortune ou qu'à leurs amours. La différence des saisons leur est inconnue, et ce n'est pas le soleil qui fait pour eux les beaux jours. Il me semble aussi que les dames de ce pays-là,[3] celles même qui n'ont ni ambition, ni galanterie, ne se mettent pas en peine s'il pleut ou s'il grêle. C'est qu'on les élève dans ce monde artificiel, et qu'elles n'ont que bien peu de sentiment dans les choses qui n'en sont pas. De sorte qu'un habit d'une étoffe agréable, des rubans à la mode, un appartement bien meublé les touche plus sensiblement que le plus beau spectacle de la nature. (*Lettres*, i. 197-8.)

No doubt many people shared Saint-Évremond's lukewarm attitude towards Nature in literature:

> Un discours [4] où l'on ne parle que de bois, de rivières, de prés, de campagnes, de jardins, fait sur nous une impression bien languissante, à moins qu'il n'ait des agréments tout nouveaux; mais ce qui est de l'humanité, les penchants, les tendresses, les

[1] Society. [2] Lonely retreats. [3] i.e. the court. [4] Discourse, essay.

> affections, trouvent naturellement au fond de notre âme à se faire sentir : la même nature les produit et les reçoit ; ils passent aisément des hommes qu'on représente, en des hommes qui voient représenter. (*Œuvres*, iii. 236.)

This well-known passage does in fact bring out clearly where the chief interests of seventeenth century French writers and the great and unsurpassed originality of the literature they created lie—in the study of Man. Corneille and Racine in tragedy, Molière in comedy, La Fontaine in the fable, Mme de La Fayette in the novel, like the three great moralists of the age—Pascal, La Rochefoucauld, La Bruyère—brought to literature, among their other varied gifts, an amazing insight into human nature. Once again, one cannot explain why such great writers happened to emerge in this short period of years, nor why their genius should have taken this particular form ; but if they stood far above the general level of taste of their contemporaries, if there remains an unbridgeable gulf between their writings and the occupations of contemporary polite society, there is no question that their genius was assisted in its development by the atmosphere of their times. In the world of the *salons* there was a similar interest in attempting to unravel the complexities of human nature, one which revealed itself in such glorified parlour-games as the writing of portraits and the invention and discussion of the psychological problems in the very fashionable *questions d'amour*.

The influence of the contemporary audience and especially of the world of the *salons* on the great writers of the age is seen perhaps even more clearly in another way. The literature of the seventeenth century, as every schoolboy knows, was founded on Reason. Literary composition in general and each particular type of writing, be it tragedy, the epic, the ode, or even to some extent comedy, were regulated by a series of rigid rules, worked out in elaborate detail by critics who followed Aristotle and especially the learned commentators of the previous hundred years. Yet while they accepted the necessity and validity of such rules, the great writers of the age would refuse to deny themselves a certain margin of freedom. They would accept the rules, would defend their works against any charge that they violated the sacred rules, and yet for them there was, above all detailed rules, one general rule which superseded all others—to give pleasure to the reader or the spectator, to 'plaire'.

Defending his tragedy *Bérénice* against the criticism that its simplicity of action 'ne pouvait être selon les règles du théâtre', Racine tells us how he asked whether his critics had been bored by the play:

> On me dit qu'ils avouaient tous qu'elle n'ennuyait point, qu'elle les touchait même en plusieurs endroits, et qu'ils la verraient encore avec plaisir. Que veulent-ils davantage? Je les conjure d'avoir assez bonne opinion d'eux-mêmes pour ne pas croire qu'une pièce qui les touche et qui leur donne du plaisir puisse être absolument contre les règles. La principale règle est de plaire et de toucher: toutes les autres ne sont faites que pour parvenir à cette première. Mais toutes ces règles sont d'un long détail, dont je ne leur conseille pas de s'embarrasser: ils ont des occupations plus importantes. Qu'ils se reposent sur nous de la fatigue d'éclaircir les difficultés de la *Poétique* d'Aristote; qu'ils se réservent le plaisir de pleurer et d'être attendris . . .

We see here how, while stoutly affirming that his tragedy *does* conform to the rules, Racine appeals to the great mass of his audience, to people who are not, like professional critics and scholars, immersed in the details of these rules, and addresses to them the argument that the supreme test of his play is whether or not it has given them pleasure.

Similarly, Molière's spokesman in the *Critique de l'École des Femmes* declares that nothing would be easier than to prove that *L'École des Femmes* is as much in accordance with the rules as any play in existence, but to the poet Lysidas who declares that the comedy violates all the rules, he makes the eloquent retort:

> Vous êtes de plaisantes gens avec vos règles dont vous embarrassez les ignorants, et nous étourdissez tous les jours. Il semble, à vous ouïr parler, que ces règles de l'art soient les plus grands mystères du monde; et cependant ce ne sont que quelques observations aisées, que le bon sens a faites sur ce qui peut ôter le plaisir que l'on prend à ces sortes de poèmes; et le même bon

sens qui a fait autrefois ces observations, les fait aisément tous les jours, sans le secours d'Horace et d'Aristote.

Once again the appeal is directed, over the heads of the critics and scholars, to the general theatre-going public. That the rules have their place, Molière does not deny, but, he adds, 'je voudrais bien savoir si la grande règle de toutes les règles n'est pas de plaire, et si une pièce de théâtre qui a attrapé son but, n'a pas suivi un bon chemin'. (Sc. 7.) Once again the stress is all on the higher rule of giving pleasure—an aim summed up by Molière so far as comedy is concerned by the words used in the same scene, 'faire rire les honnêtes gens'—the cultured and polished members of society who are not, of course, professional critics or scholars.

The same insistence on the aim of poetry as giving pleasure is to be found in La Fontaine. The preface to the fables affirms that 'On ne considère en France que ce qui plaît; c'est la grande règle, et, pour ainsi dire, la seule.' In the preface to his *Contes* he declares in almost the same terms: 'Le principal point . . . est d'attacher le lecteur, de le réjouir, d'attirer malgré lui son attention, de lui plaire enfin.' Here we see La Fontaine getting further away from the strict interpretation of the rules than either Racine or even Molière. The fact that, in his fables and *Contes*, he was using literary genres for which there were, strictly speaking, no rules, allows him to be even more cavalier in his treatment of the critics and their obsession with strict precepts. Thus we find him pouring doubts on the very validity of the rules when he wrote, again in the preface to his *Contes*: 'Le secret de plaire ne consiste pas toujours en l'ajustement, ni même en la régularité[1]; il faut du piquant et de l'agréable, si l'on veut toucher'.

We see how in their different ways and with varying degrees of emphasis all three writers stress the notion that the aim of literature is to 'plaire', to give pleasure to the reader or spectator. Here they were in accord with the general spirit of the *salons* and of the polite society of their age. Méré, we have seen,[2] declared that the principal quality of the *honnête homme*

[1] 'Strict observance of the rules.'

[2] p. 226.

'consiste à connaître en toutes les choses les meilleurs moyens de plaire et de les savoir pratiquer'. Literary theorists might build up an elaborate series of rules to regulate literature in general and its individual branches; but, although they enjoyed a tremendous reputation and a tremendous influence—revealed by the sweeping changes which took place in literature as a whole after the first two or three decades of the century towards a close conformity with the rules they expounded and codified—their power must not be exaggerated. They were, after all, only a tiny minority, even among the small literary public of the age. Their influence was at least counterbalanced by the general taste of the time, a taste which, we have seen, was largely moulded by the court and the polite society of Paris. The members of this restricted circle were seldom scholars, either by training or outlook. Few of the aristocrats and even fewer of the ladies who frequented the *salons* were versed in the Classical tongues, without which no one in that age could have any claim to learning. Nor were they distressed by this lack of knowledge. On the contrary, any show of learning was regarded in the *salons* as mere pedantry, and in that polished society nothing could be more contemptible than a pedant. Clitandre's violent onslaught on 'le savoir obscur de la pédanterie' in the *Femmes Savantes* expresses admirably the attitude of the aristocratic members of society in that period towards learning, or as they would call it, pedantry:

> Il semble à trois gredins, dans leur petit cerveau,
> Que, pour être imprimés, et reliés en veau,
> Les voilà dans l'État d'importantes personnes;
> Qu'avec leur plume ils font les destins des couronnes;
> Qu'au moindre petit bruit de leurs productions
> Ils doivent voir chez eux voler les pensions;
> Que sur eux l'univers a la vue attachée;
> Que partout de leur nom la gloire est épanchée,
> Et qu'en science ils sont des prodiges fameux,
> Pour savoir ce qu'ont dit les autres avant eux,
> Pour avoir eu trente ans des yeux et des oreilles,
> Pour avoir employé neuf ou dix mille veilles

A se bien barbouiller de grec et de latin,
Et se charger l'esprit d'un ténébreux butin
De tous les vieux fatras qui traînent dans les livres:
Gens qui de leur savoir paraissent toujours ivres,
Riches, pour tout mérite, en babil importun,
Inhabiles à tout, vides de sens commun,
Et pleins d'un ridicule et d'une impertinence [1]
A décrier partout l'esprit et la science.

(Act iv., Sc. 3.)

A similar attitude is revealed in a letter of Mme de Sévigné to her cousin, Bussy-Rabutin, on the famous controversy of the 1680's which was aroused by Furetière's expulsion from the Academy for preparing a dictionary of his own. Furetière had dared to attack La Fontaine and the poet, Benserade, famous for his ballets. Mme de Sévigné dismisses him with indignant disdain as a mere pedant, outside the world of high society and the court, who has therefore no claim to literary taste:

Je trouve que l'auteur fait voir clairement qu'il n'est ni du monde,[2] ni de la cour, et que son goût est d'une pédanterie qu'on ne peut même pas espérer de corriger. Il y a de certaines choses qu'on n'entend jamais, quand on ne les entend pas d'abord[3]: on ne fait point entrer certains esprits durs et farouches dans le charme et dans la facilité des ballets de Benserade et des fables de La Fontaine; ils sont indignes de comprendre ces sortes de beautés, et sont condamnés au malheur de les improuver,[4] et d'être improuvés aussi des gens d'esprit . . . C'est le sentiment que j'aurai toujours pour un homme qui condamne le beau feu et les vers de Benserade dont le Roi et toute la cour a fait ses délices, et qui ne connaît pas le charme des fables de La Fontaine. Je ne m'en dédis point, il n'y a qu'à prier Dieu pour un tel homme, et qu'à souhaiter de n'avoir point de commerce avec lui. (14 May 1686.)

To people with such a contempt for pedantry, to judge literature by so-called rules, the creation of pedants and the standards of pedants, was unthinkable. For them the only approach to literature was the one recommended by Racine, Molière or La Fontaine, to see whether or not it gave them

[1] Stupidity.
[2] Polite society.
[3] Immediately.
[4] Disapprove.

pleasure. Literary judgments were for them founded not on reason, for that was the instrument of the pedants, but on the natural taste of the individual. It was for the 'honnêtes gens' to decide for themselves, not whether a work was in conformity with the rules, for they had no means of studying Aristotle and his commentators, but whether it possessed those indefinable qualities—that *je ne sais quoi* of which contemporary writers constantly speak—which a work of literature must have if it is to give pleasure.

L'art de plaire thus became the primary concern of French writers in the second half of the seventeenth century in all the different branches of literature. Not only were Racine and Molière and, more obviously still, La Fontaine influenced by the taste of polite society as formed in the *salons*, but other writers too in all the various types of literature. For the novelists, writing in a new genre for which there were no really accepted rules, this was natural enough, but it also affected other kinds of writing. The moralists of the age—La Rochefoucauld and La Bruyère in particular—did not attempt to compose logically constructed works, for that would be pedantic and unattractive to their readers; they sought instead to gain their interest and approval by dividing their work up into short maxims and reflexions with often no connected thread, to make books which one can dip into for half an hour or even a few minutes. Moreover, they strove to gain their readers' attention by carefully chiselled sentences which are masterpieces of compression and subtlety. To this La Bruyère added his famous portraits, the success of which made him give more and more space to them in the succeeding editions of *Les Caractères*. Even the sermon and the funeral oration, so popular with the high society of the time, at least when they were delivered by well-known preachers, bear traces of this desire to please the audience. True, Saint Vincent de Paul and his followers would have nothing to do with any concessions to the taste of their hearers; the aim of the preacher was to instruct, and there must be no compromise with the world. Yet many preachers—and among them some of the most famous of that age—accepted the fact that, in order to instruct, one must win the attention of one's congregation by the psychological insight and polished eloquence of one's sermons. Even in this sphere the influence of polite society can be detected.

So far we have stressed the influence exercised on seventeenth century French literature and even on the very language which was the instrument of the writers of the age, by the world of the court and the *salons*, the small section of the community which, if it was not the whole audience of the writers of the age, was at least the most important part of it. This is not to suggest that the great writers of the period were purely and simply the products of their age. Their genius raised them far above not only the literary occupations of the *salons*—the varied forms of society verse which flourished throughout the century, the portraits, *questions d'amour* and other literary games—but also above their lesser rivals in tragedy, comedy, poetry, the novel and the rest. It is these lesser writers who are more truly than the great men of genius the mirror of the age.

None the less, if a study of the literary background of seventeenth century France does not produce any cut-and-dried explanation of their genius, it is by no means a waste of time. To know something of the status of the writer in seventeenth century France, what sections of the community his works were written for and what influence this audience exercised on the literature of the age, is to come a step nearer appreciation of the great writers themselves. In all sorts of ways their works were influenced by the outlook of their contemporaries. Even such matters as their choice of subjects or their use of language were conditioned by the interests and aspirations of their audience. In the space available only the briefest outlines of that influence can be suggested; yet that should suffice to provoke further thought on the subject and to lead to a deeper understanding of the literary masterpieces of seventeenth century France.

CHAPTER IX

THE YEARS OF DECLINE, 1685-1715

THE personal reign of Louis XIV lasted for fifty-four years. For roughly half that period his affairs prospered At home he raised the power of the monarchy to untold heights, while abroad his armies met with victory after victory and secured for France a dominant position in Europe. During the second half of the reign economic distress combined with defeats in the field lowered the King's popularity at home and reduced his prestige and power in Europe. This change from prosperity to adversity was not a sudden happening to which a precise date can be conveniently assigned. 1685 is only a convenient approximation for the watershed which divided success and glory from failure and growing unpopularity.

The young King of twenty-three who took over the reins of power in 1661 had developed by 1685 into a man past the prime of life, increasingly under the influence of his confessor, and since 1683 secretly married to Mme de Maintenon, who succeeded in reclaiming him from the wild life of his earlier years and leading him into the paths of piety. The great ministers and generals of the reign were almost all dead by this time; their successors often proved incapable of solving the serious problems which confronted them as the domestic, diplomatic and military situation of the country gradually became more difficult.

As the years passed, the middle-aged King gradually grew into an old man, saddened not only by military defeats and by growing domestic difficulties, but also by the sudden deaths of so many members of his own family in the direct line of succession to the throne. The Dauphin, his only son, died in 1711, followed a year later by the Duc de Bourgogne, his eldest grandson and the new heir to the throne, who six days before had lost his wife, a great favourite with the old King. The elder son of the Duc de Bourgogne died in the same year at the age of five, and the only heir in the direct line left was a sickly child of two, the future Louis XV.

In the years immediately following the Treaty of Nimeguen (1678) Louis had been at the height of his power in Europe. For the moment there was no concerted resistance to his annexation of various towns and territories on France's eastern frontiers, even when this operation was carried out in time of peace. The repressive policy of Louis towards French Protestantism which culminated in the Revocation of the Edict of Nantes in 1685, had important international repercussions; indeed it may be said to have helped to precipitate the decline in France's position in Europe which marks the second half of Louis's personal reign. Coming as it did on top of his aggressive foreign policy, it helped to unite the greater part of Europe against him. After the Protestant states—Holland, Brandenburg and Sweden (though not England, which was still governed by James II)—had formed alliances, the Emperor, Spain, Savoy and various German states joined together to resist the aggressive designs of France and formed in 1686 the League of Augsburg. Two years later Louis endeavoured to forestall the action of his enemies by invading Western Germany, and thus precipitated the War of the League of Augsburg which was to last until 1697.

In this struggle France had to face the combined forces of the Emperor, Spain, various German states, Sweden, Savoy, Holland and, with the Revolution of 1688 and the arrival of William of Orange on the scene, England. In the opening stages of the war Louis attempted to put James II back on his throne, but with the Battle of the Boyne in 1690 his plans were finally frustrated. On the Continent the French armies met with more success, though the opening years of the war were inconclusive. Yet, despite the fact that both sides were anxious to conclude peace, the war dragged on until 1697 when it was brought to a close by the Treaty of Ryswick. This treaty formed a decided contrast with the Treaty of Nimeguen some twenty years earlier. Internal difficulties compelled Louis to make serious concessions: to give up Lorraine, as well as several fortresses on France's eastern and north-eastern frontiers which had been ceded to her at Nimeguen, and to recognize William of Orange as King of England, which meant withdrawing support from James II. Under the leadership of William of Orange England had stood at the head of the coalition of the powers which had set a barrier to French ambitions in Europe. This war marks the beginning of the long struggle between England and France which was to last for a hundred years and more. Throughout the eighteenth century there was bitter rivalry between the two countries—a rivalry produced above all by a clash of commercial and colonial ambitions.

The Treaty of Ryswick was merely a truce in the struggle between France and her neighbours. The immediate cause of the renewal of hostilities was the question of the fate of the throne of Spain and also of the numerous Spanish possessions both in Europe and the New World after the impending death of the King of Spain who had no children to succeed him. Among the numerous claimants to his throne and possessions were the Emperor and Louis, the latter on behalf of his son or one of his grandsons. England and Holland were both interested in preventing all the possessions of Spain from falling into the hands either of the Emperor or Louis, since either would then be all-powerful in Europe. In 1700 Louis concluded an agreement with England and Holland, though not with the Emperor, to divide the Spanish possessions between the two rival families. However, the dying King of Spain, indignant at this division of his territories, made a new will bequeathing all of them to the Duc d'Anjou, the second grandson of Louis XIV.

When the news of the death of the King of Spain and of this will reached Versailles in November 1700, Louis decided after some hesitation to go back on his agreement with England and Holland and to accept the throne of Spain for his grandson. War with the rest of Europe was precipitated by his tactless behaviour at this point. Despite the clause in the King of Spain's will which required that his successor should renounce all his rights to the French throne, he issued a declaration maintaining all his grandson's claims, and also began interfering in Spanish possessions, particularly the Spanish Netherlands. To the resentment of English traders at having the door of Spanish markets in the New World shut in their faces, he added the fresh provocation of proclaiming the Pretender King of England on the death of James II in 1701.

The War of the Spanish Succession which broke out in the following year was a struggle between the Grand Alliance of England, Holland, the Empire and various German states, and France, supported by Spain, which proved a negligible quantity. England and Holland were masters of the sea, and on land the Allies were able to put large armies into the field. Thanks to the generalship of Marlborough and Prince Eugene, the opening years of the war were disastrous for Louis. The invincible French armies were severely battered at Blenheim (1704) and Ramillies (1706); and two years later, after another victory at Oudenarde, the Allied armies invaded France and captured Lille. In 1709, after a terrible winter of cold and famine, the exhausted state of France forced Louis to seek peace terms. The sorry plight of the country is summed up in the following letter of the *Contrôleur général* to the King:

> Les armées ne peuvent être bien payées, les vivres et la subsistance des troupes n'ont pu être assurés dans des temps aussi malheureux: on a été à la veille de manquer entièrement et de craindre les plus terribles révolutions. . . . La mauvaise disposition des esprits de tous les peuples est connue. Depuis quatre mois, il ne s'est passé de semaine sans qu'il y ait eu quelque sédition . . . A tous ces maux il n'est possible de trouver des remèdes que par une prompte paix.

Yet despite the desperate economic state of the country and rising discontent, the terms offered by the Allies were so humiliating—Louis was even required to help to drive his grandson from the throne of Spain—that he could not bring himself to accept them. Then French fortunes changed for the better, thanks partly to dissensions among the Allies and especially to a change of government in England where the Whigs, who wished to pursue the war to the end, were replaced by the Tories who were anxious for peace, and in 1713 at the

Treaty of Utrecht Louis was able to make peace on much more favourable terms than could have been dreamed of four years earlier. His grandson remained on the throne of Spain, though he did not keep all the Spanish possessions, and despite her defeats, France managed to keep her frontiers of 1697 intact. Even so the military events of the War of the Spanish Succession were in striking contrast to those of the earlier wars of the reign: it was something new for Louis to see large French armies broken and France invaded, to be urged to flee from Paris, to find the country exhausted and to have to sue for peace.

The almost incessant wars of the last twenty-five years or so of his reign brought heavy increases in the burden of taxation inside France. Not only were old taxes increased, but new ones had to be introduced in order to keep the French armies in the field. On paper the new direct taxes—the *capitation* (1695) and *dixième* (1710)—were to apply to all classes of society, but, as usual, the main burden fell on the peasants. Successive *Contrôleurs généraux* lived from hand to mouth by a series of expedients—by loans (very often forced loans), lotteries, the issue of government bills and paper-money and by the sale of more and more official posts. By the last part of the reign the market for these was so saturated that people had to be bullied into taking them, and they were really no more than forced loans. The sale of titles was also used to raise the wind (five hundred were sold in the record year, 1696) and finally the government had recourse to depreciation of the coinage, which had most unfortunate effects on trade.

All these expedients barely enabled the Treasury to get through the critical war years, and by the end of the reign the state was virtually bankrupt. The net revenue for 1715 was 74 millions, and the expenditure 119 millions. Debts, the payment of which had fallen due, amounted to 430 millions, and several years' revenue had been mortgaged in advance. Thus Louis XIV left a shocking financial legacy to his successor.

This crippling burden of taxation fell on a country at a time of economic depression. It was a period of continuing low prices for corn, broken only by high prices in years of bad harvest; they rocketed, for instance, in 1708 and 1709 when famine caused intense suffering and many deaths. As foreign markets were cut off by the wars, wine prices remained extremely low, and wine-growers, a most important class, were very badly off. The situation of the peasants, especially the poorer ones, further deteriorated, and landowners were also sorely affected by the crisis in agriculture. According to Vauban, writing in 1707, the income from agricultural land had fallen by a third since 1661, and rents and the value of land had fallen in proportion.

The intense sufferings of the peasants in these years of low prices and high taxation, combined with periods of bad harvests and famine, led to sporadic revolts. In the province of Quercy in the South-West of France there was a revolt in 1707 and another in the black year of 1709. As usual, these revolts were brutally suppressed, and yet we see from a letter to the *Contrôleur général* that the *Intendant* was thoroughly scared by the volume of discontent in the province:

> Les auteurs de tous les tristes mouvements [1] du Quercy ne seraient pas difficiles à trouver, ayant tous leurs noms bien écrits dans mon portefeuille; mais ils sont en si grand nombre qu'il serait dangereux d'en vouloir faire des exemples, sans s'exposer à renouveler ces terribles désordres . . . Je ne saurais penser sans frémir que j'ai vu trente mille hommes armés en Quercy, Cahors assiégé pendant dix jours, et moi investi dans ma chaise [2] par un détachement de cette bonne compagnie, dont je me tirai par miracle. (Boislisle, *Correspondance des Contrôleurs généraux*, iii. 87.)

Graphic accounts of famine and desperate poverty continue to occur in official documents even nearer the end of the reign, as in this account of conditions in Anjou in May 1713:

> Cette province est dans une misère effroyable par la disette des blés. La moitié des gens de la campagne manquent de pain; il en est déjà mort un grand nombre de faim. Plusieurs gentilshommes quittent leurs maisons parce qu'ils y sont assiégés d'une multitude de pauvres qu'ils ne peuvent soulager, faute de blé . . . L'espérance d'une bonne récolte nous manque. Avec cela, le prix des bestiaux, qui nous donnait quelque soulagement, est

[1] Revolts. [2] Coach.

> beaucoup diminué . . . Cette triste situation nous rend insensibles à la joie que nous devrions avoir de la paix, et l'espérance qu'elle pourra diminuer nos maux n'est pas capable de diminuer la douleur que nous souffrons de notre état présent . . . Depuis soixante ans que je connais la campagne, elle est dépeuplée au moins d'un tiers; il y a plusieurs métairies abandonnées, et presque toutes sont mal cultivées, faute d'hommes . . . (*Ibid.*, iii. 490.)

In the same month the *Intendant* wrote from Limoges:

> . . . L'on a trouvé quelques paysans morts dans leurs vignes; je puis vous assurer aussi qu'il est mort une vingtaine de personnes dans cette ville, qui, dans l'espérance d'y trouver quelque charité, ont fait effort pour s'y rendre, et sont morts en arrivant dans des granges que M. l'évêque de Limoges a fait louer pour les retirer. Des personnes dignes de foi m'ont assuré aussi qu'il y a quelques paroisses où les paysans broutent l'herbe dans les prés, comme les bestiaux; d'autres, où ils font de la bouillie de cendre; d'autres où ils se nourrissent de racine de fougère; et, en général, la misère est fort grande. (*Ibid.*, iii. 492.)

No doubt such hard conditions of life were not to be found everywhere in France at the same time, but it is none the less clear that the reign of Louis XIV ended, as it had begun, with bitter suffering for many of the peasants.

There was similar distress and discontent among the workers in the towns, where, owing to the import of raw materials being hindered by the wars, there was considerable unemployment. This drove many workers to emigrate in search of work to such countries as Italy and the Low Countries. Wages were low, and employers, with the backing of the authorities, refused to raise them despite the steep rise in the cost of food in the years of bad harvests. In the very black years of 1708 and 1709 the price of bread rose in Paris to 8 *sous* a pound, a day's wage in many trades. The result was bread-riots in Paris, and bands of hungry people even demonstrated in front of the Palace of Versailles. The whole country swarmed with beggars, and there was heavy mortality both in town and country.

Naturally not all classes suffered equally in these black years.

If the nobles, as landowners, often felt the pinch, other sections of the upper classes were not affected in the same way. There were still wealthy merchants and shipowners, but above all bankers and tax-farmers prospered. The Treasury's desperate need for money enriched in particular *financiers* like the famous Samuel Bernard. Their hastily acquired wealth, often flaunted before the rest of the community, led to their intense unpopularity, reflected in the bitter satirical comedy of Lesage, *Turcaret* (1709).

The economic situation of the country in the last thirty years of the reign of Louis XIV was scarcely improved by the increasing persecution of the Huguenots, culminating in 1685 in the Revocation of the Edict of Nantes which had given the Protestants certain rights and a definite place in the community. The Revocation was based on the fiction that, since the greater part of the Huguenots had been converted to Catholicism—often by the most violent and cruel means—the Edict now had no point. It was a sign of the despotic character of the rule of Louis XIV that he should imagine it to be within his powers as King by Divine Right to 'convert' his Huguenot subjects to the State religion. In a letter written just before the Revocation he showed that he had no doubts in the matter: 'Je ne peux douter que c'est la volonté divine qui se veut servir de moi pour remettre dans ses voies tous ceux qui sont soumis à mes ordres.'

The Revocation was greeted with applause by French Catholics, but there is no question that its economic consequences were serious for France. The persecution of the Huguenots drove thousands of them into exile. Some estimates of the numbers involved would appear to be wildly exaggerated; altogether there were perhaps about a million Huguenots in France, and a reliable guess would probably be that some 200,000 left the country. Yet owing to the fact that they had gradually been excluded from official posts and the liberal professions, the refugees included large numbers of merchants, manufacturers and skilled workmen, and their emigration, while it aided the economic development of such Protestant countries as Holland, Prussia and England, meant a decided

loss to France. Writing five years after the Revocation, a foreign envoy declared:

> L'affaire de la persécution des gens de la Religion [1] en France n'a pu encore que contribuer considérablement à appauvrir le royaume, à ruiner le négoce, à affaiblir le commerce, à diminuer les revenus, surtout dans les provinces maritimes et d'ailleurs qui étaient les plus remplies des gens de la Religion, comme en Normandie, en Poitou, en Aunis, Languedoc, Guyenne et autres, et ce par la retraite d'un grand nombre de bons et fidèles sujets du Roi, par la perte de gens habiles en toutes sortes de professions, pour la guerre, pour la marine, pour les manufactures, pour les métiers, par le transport de grandes sommes d'argent, qu'ils ont portées hors du royaume, par la misère, la défiance, la contrainte des gens de la Religion ou *nouveaux convertis*, comme on les appelle, restés en France sans y être satisfaits de leur condition, et plutôt avec des vues qui y sont bien opposées. (Ézéchiel Spanheim, *Relation de la Cour de France*, p. 555.)

In face of these consequences of its policy even the French government had a moment of hesitation at the end of the War of the League of Augsburg, and consulted with the *Intendants* and Bishops about the policy it should adopt. The replies received showed a great division of opinion, for some advocated milder treatment of the Huguenots. In its instructions to the *Intendants* the government ordered them to use a milder policy. However, this phase was short-lived, and persecution continued to the end of the reign. One of its consequences was a Huguenot rising in the Cévennes, in Languedoc, which broke out in 1702, and for several years diverted from the front troops which could well have been used elsewhere. Though this rising was eventually suppressed, Protestantism, despite the sufferings of its adherents, had still not been wiped out in France, except on paper. Louis's policy of persecution had failed.

In the second half of the personal reign of Louis XIV the new rationalist, scientific outlook which was to produce a revolution in men's ideas in religion and philosophy through the writings of men like Voltaire and the Encyclopaedists, was already being worked out, and beginning, cautiously and surreptitiously, to undermine religious orthodoxy. If the story of

[1] *La Religion prétendue réformée.*

these changes in men's religious and philosophical ideas does not fall within the scope of this book, a few words must be given to the increasing discontent with social and political conditions in the France of these years.

Too much should not perhaps be made of the political writings of the exiled Huguenots, especially as there is no means of knowing how much they influenced opinion inside Catholic France. The most interesting and effective of their writings was the *Soupirs de la France esclave qui aspire après la liberté* (1689). Although outwardly from the pen of a Catholic, this book is generally attributed to the exiled Protestant pastor, Jurieu.

The author of this bitter denunciation of absolutism paints in vivid colours the grievances of all sections of the community under the existing system of government. He contrasts the tyranny under which the nation groans with the liberty enjoyed by neighbouring countries, especially England which had just cast off its chains in the 'Glorious Revolution'. The cause of all the sufferings of the French people is simply the tyrannical rule of Louis XIV:

> C'est la puissance despotique et le pouvoir arbitraire, absolu et sans limites que les rois de France s'attribuent et que Louis XIV a exercé, et exerce, d'une manière à faire trembler tous les pays qui ont des rois.

There follows a violent denunciation of the theory of the Divine Right of Kings:

> Le Roi de France ne se croit lié par aucunes lois; sa volonté est la règle du bon et du droit; il croit n'être obligé à rendre compte de sa conduite qu'à Dieu seul; il se persuade qu'il est le maître absolu de la vie, de la liberté, des personnes, des biens, de la religion et de la conscience de ses sujets. Maxime qui fait frémir et qui saisit d'horreur, quand on en considère les conséquences, et que sous ses yeux on [en] voit les suites présentes! (pp. 29-30.)

The *Soupirs de la France esclave* is far from being an entirely negative work. The author seeks a remedy for present ills in a return to the institutions which existed in France before absolutism had won the day. While it is true that some of his history is dubious, in appealing to French traditions of liberty he puts forward in the clearest possible terms the case for a monarchy with limited, and not absolute power. If he considers that it would not be necessary for the French to go as far as the English had in their recent Revolution, he maintains that it is urgently necessary to 'contenir les rois dans les justes bornes de leur puissance' (p. 175).

Much more interesting and significant is the growth of discontent inside France itself in these same years after 1690. Occasional glimpses of disaffection are contained in various contemporary *chansons*, such as the one which circulated in Dijon in 1709 and which reflects most unfavourably on Louis, the Dauphin, and his grandson, the Duc de Bourgogne—indeed on the whole régime:

Le grand-père est un fanfaron,
Le fils un imbécile,
Le petit-fils un grand poltron.[1]
Ohé! la belle famille!
Que je vous plains, peuples français,
Soumis à cet empire,
Faites ce qu'ont fait les Anglais,
C'est assez vous le dire.

Too much should not be made of such lampoons. It is much more interesting to study the two writers who criticized the workings of the whole taxation-system in France in this period, Boisguilbert and Vauban. Boisguilbert, who held an important judicial position in Rouen, bombarded the *Contrôleur général* and Treasury officials with proposals for reforming the existing system of taxation, and when they refused to listen, published surreptitiously his *Détail de la France* (1695), followed a decade later by *Le Factum de la France*. Boisguilbert diagnosed the economic troubles from which France was suffering as a crisis of under-consumption, brought on by the iniquitous methods by which the *taille* and indirect taxes were levied. The remedies which he proposed were the abolition of internal customs-barriers and the *aides*, and a fair method of assessing

[1] He had failed to distinguish himself when sent to command one of the French armies.

the *taille*. This would have meant making everyone, rich and poor, contribute according to his wealth: 'Quand Dieu a commandé de payer des tributs aux princes, il a prétendu parler à tout le monde, et non pas aux misérables et aux indéfendus seulement, qui ne s'en pouvaient exempter'. (*Détail de la France*, p. 221.)

Though both these works went through several editions, Vauban was probably more influential as a critic of the taxation-system because of his immense prestige as the great engineer of the wars of Louis XIV. It is significant that in the last part of the reign a great soldier who owed his whole position as *maréchal de France* to Louis XIV, should have been moved to pen, and at last even to print, a work which bitterly denounced the injustices of the existing taxation system, and even to raise his voice in favour of the neglected and despised common people:

> Je me sens encore obligé d'honneur et de conscience de représenter à Sa Majesté qu'il m'a paru que de tout temps on n'avait pas eu assez d'égard en France pour le menu peuple, et qu'on en avait fait trop peu de cas. Aussi c'est la partie la plus ruinée et la plus misérable du royaume; c'est elle cependant qui est la plus considérable par son nombre et par les services réels et effectifs qu'elle lui rend. (*Dîme royale*, p. 17.)

Vauban was no revolutionary. He was profoundly devoted to Louis XIV and the monarchy; and yet he was moved by the conditions which he had observed in his travels through France throughout his long career to submit to the King a detailed criticism of the existing system of taxation and to propose a new one in its place. All his efforts to persuade the King and his ministers to adopt his system having failed, in 1707, at the age of seventy-four, he had 300 copies of his *Dîme royale* printed and began to distribute them among his friends. The work was immediately banned by the authorities, and Vauban died a few days later. The great principle underlying his book was that the main burden of taxation should no longer fall on the poorer classes. Since the King owes protection to all his subjects, rich and poor, high and low, there exists, declares Vauban, 'une obligation naturelle aux sujets de toutes conditions,[1] de contribuer, à proportion de leur revenu ou de leur industrie, sans qu'aucun d'eux s'en puisse raisonnablement dispenser'. (*Ibid.*, p. 23.) Despite—or because—of the ban on the *Dîme royale*, it secured a wide circulation, thirteen or fourteen editions appearing between 1707 and 1709. It was significant that, even under absolutism when such matters were not the concern of the private citizen, however exalted, men like Boisguilbert and Vauban should begin to probe the most sensitive spot in the body politic—the financial chaos of the Monarchy, which in 1789 was to be the immediate cause of its collapse. Moreover, when both men failed to convert the authorities to their views, they sought to appeal to public opinion by publishing their works.

Another centre of discontent in this period was to be found among a minority of the court aristocracy who danced attendance upon the King at Versailles. Not all of them were content with their state of abasement under absolutism. Some looked back with longing to the age when their ancestors had enjoyed considerable power in the State, before Kings chose as their ministers low bourgeois fellows and confined the aristocracy to a purely decorative function. The most interesting member of this small group of discontented great noblemen was the Duc de Saint-Simon (1675-1755), the author of the famous memoirs which cover the latter part of the reign of Louis XIV and the period of the Regency which followed. Although Saint-Simon's dukedom was a relatively new affair—it was conferred on his father by Louis XIII for not very distinguished services—his political ideas were largely inspired by his fanatical attachment to the prerogatives of his caste, the *ducs et pairs*. Yet he was not altogether lacking in a broader outlook, for he felt a genuine sympathy for the sufferings of the masses in these black years of the reign, as we see from the following eloquent passage in his *Lettre anonyme au Roi* (1712):

> Quel compte, Sire, et pardonnez à ma tendresse pour vous si elle s'échappe, quel compte qu'un règne de soixante et dix ans,

[1] All ranks.

> pour soi tout seul en toutes manières, et jusqu'aux adversités mêmes par lesquelles Dieu essaie de vous rappeler à lui; quel compte que tant de fleuves de sang dont vos ministres vous ont fait inonder l'Europe: quel compte que tant d'autres déluges d'un sang d'une autre espèce, mais non moins réel, je veux dire de tant de trésors que ces ministres vous ont fait répandre, et qui vous ont réduit, à force d'en répandre, de les rechercher jusque dans les os de vos sujets, dont la nudité et la défaillance rend les champs incultes, tarit l'espèce du bétail et ne laisse plus en proie aux durs exacteurs des impôts que les restes de leurs maisons délabrées dont ils démontent la charpente pour être vendue à vil prix! Ce ne sont point, Sire, des figures et des exagérations. Et si votre Majesté les regarde comme telles, autre compte, Sire, plus terrible que tous les autres que vous vous préparez. (*Écrits inédits*, iv. 52-53.)

Yet it would not be unjust to Saint-Simon to trace the main part of his discontent with the existing form of government to the fact that, through the development of absolutism, the aristocracy and particularly its most exalted members, the *ducs et pairs*, had been stripped of all power in the State. His ideal was a Royal Council, composed of five ministers, who would all be members of the *noblesse d'épée*, with a series of Councils to run the different departments of State in place of the bourgeois *Secrétaires d'État*. Saint-Simon's system was thus essentially feudal in inspiration since it sought to give back power in the State to the great nobles.

A more important figure behind the scenes during the last twenty-five years of the reign was Fénelon, who in 1689 became tutor to Louis's grandson, the Duc de Bourgogne, and six years later was appointed Archbishop of Cambrai. In 1697 he was exiled to his diocese for his unorthodox theological views, but he continued to keep in touch with his pupil and with his entourage at Versailles. In 1711 on the death of his father, the Dauphin, the Duke became heir to the throne, and as Louis was now seventy-two, there seemed every possibility that Fénelon would become Prime Minister when his pupil ascended the throne. However, the Duke died only a year after his father, and Fénelon himself, still in exile, died in 1715, shortly before Louis XIV.

One of the most famous of his writings in these years is his *Lettre à Louis XIV* (1694) which severely criticizes both the character and policies of the King. Beginning with the war with Holland in 1672, his unjust ambitions, Fénelon tells him, have led to endless wars and devastation:

> Tant de troubles affreux qui ont désolé toute l'Europe depuis plus de vingt ans, tant de sang répandu, tant de scandales commis, tant de provinces saccagées, tant de villes et de villages mis en cendres, sont les funestes suites de cette guerre de 1672. (*Écrits et lettres politiques*, p. 147.)

In the midst of these almost incessant wars, Fénelon goes on in an eloquent passage, his peoples have been reduced to poverty and suffering:

> Cependant vos peuples, que vous devriez aimer comme vos enfants, et qui ont été jusqu'ici si passionnés pour vous, meurent de faim. La culture des terres est presque abandonnée, les villes et la campagne se dépeuplent; tous les métiers languissent et ne nourrissent plus les ouvriers. Tout commerce est anéanti . . . Au lieu de tirer de l'argent de ce pauvre peuple, il faudrait lui faire l'aumône et le nourrir. La France entière n'est plus qu'un grand hôpital [1] désolé et sans provision. (*Ibid.*, pp. 149-50.)

The *Lettre au Roi* is justly famous for its eloquence and brutal frankness, but it is a moral certainty that it was never sent to Louis. It was clearly impossible in the 1690's to change his ideas, but in his grandson Fénelon had a pupil who seemed more likely to make use of his advice. Among the writings which he composed for the Duc de Bourgogne was the famous novel, *Télémaque*, which fell into the hands of a publisher who brought out the first edition of the work in 1699. The book scored an immediate success, and as many as sixteen editions appeared in that year, though it did not make the exiled Fénelon any more popular with the King. The instruction in kingship which the young Télémaque receives from Mentor is based on a very different conception of monarchy from that held by Louis XIV. His parting words to Télémaque both reject Louis's attitude to his functions as King and put forward

[1] Poor-house.

a new ideal: 'N'oubliez jamais que les rois ne règnent point pour leur propre gloire, mais pour le bien des peuples.' From the pages of *Télémaque* emerges a picture of an ideal king, living in peace with his neighbours and pursuing at home a policy which brings happiness and prosperity to his subjects by encouraging agriculture, discouraging luxury and listening to the advice of wise and virtuous counsellors.

Télémaque, however, confines itself by its very nature to generalities. If we want to see what practical changes Fénelon and the circle round the Duc de Bourgogne at Versailles wished to introduce, we must refer to a document drawn up in 1711, called *Les Tables de Chaulnes*. Fénelon and his associates were determined to destroy absolutism and the administrative machine on which it rested. Almost every reform which they propose has in view the restoration of the power of the *noblesse d'épée* and higher clergy. Thus, while they wished to revive the *États Généraux*, they allowed only one representative of the *tiers état* from each province, against two representatives of the privileged orders. Like Saint-Simon, Fénelon and his group looked to the past rather than to the future. Their programme was one of feudal reaction; they were, no doubt, opposed to absolutism, but in most of the reforms which they advocated they sought to further the interests of a caste, the *noblesse d'épée*.

Yet, though it is unhistorical to see in writers like Fénelon or Saint-Simon precursors of the French Revolution, it is none the less clear that in the last twenty-five years or so of the reign of Louis XIV absolutism was weighed in the balance and found wanting. If hostility to absolutism was the attitude of only a small minority in these years, quite a number of criticisms of the government of Louis XIV and its taxation policy appeared in print and secured a wide circulation. The contrast with the earlier period of the reign when such criticism was driven underground is striking.

The end of this 72-year reign came in September 1715. Since the 1680's the position of France had been greatly weakened. Abroad the expansionist policy of Louis XIV had suffered severe setbacks. At home the finances were in disorder, the economic position of the country had deteriorated, while the attempt to impose religious uniformity on Huguenots—and also on recalcitrant Catholics—had been a failure. To his successor, a boy of five, Louis XIV left grave and almost insoluble problems—financial, economic and political. His own failure to solve them had led to increasing discontent in the last years of the reign. Criticism of absolutism was widespread and in his last years penetrated even to Versailles where Louis had isolated his government and court from the rest of the nation. The main problem which he left his successor was how to adapt the institutions of the Monarchy to the needs of a rapidly changing society in which trade and industry were becoming ever more important, and the privileged orders with whose existence the Monarchy seemed to identify itself, more and more out of touch with the rest of the nation. This was to prove an impossible task, and the absolutism which Louis had carried to its highest point, was finally destroyed in France only three-quarters of a century after his death.

SOME SUGGESTIONS FOR FURTHER READING

I. Social and Political Background

J. Boulenger, *Le Grand Siècle*, Paris (Hachette), n.d.

M. Crouzet (editor), *Histoire générale des civilisations*, Vol. IV. *Les XVIe et XVIIe siècles*, by R. Mousnier. Paris (Presses Universitaires), 1956, 2nd edition.

P. Goubert, *Louis XIV et vingt millions de Français*, Paris (Hachette), 1965.

E. Magne, *La vie quotidienne au temps de Louis XIII*, Paris (Hachette), 1942.

G. Mongrédien, *La vie quotidienne sous Louis XIV*, Paris (Hachette), 1948.

L. Méthivier, *Louis XIV*, Paris (Collection "Que sais-je?"), 1950.

L. Halphen & P. Sagnac (editors), *Peuples et Civilisations: Histoire générale* (Presses Universitaires). Henri Hauser, *La prépondérance espagnole (1559-1660)*, 3rd edition, Paris, 1948. P. Sagnac & A. de Saint-Léger, *Louis XIV (1661-1715)*, 2nd edition, Paris, 1944.

G. Pagès, *La Monarchie d'Ancien Régime*, Paris (Collection "Armand Colin"), 1928.

Naissance du Grand Siècle: La France de Henri IV à Louis XIV (1598-1661), Paris (Hachette), 1948.

R. Mandrou, *La France aux XVIIe et XVIIIe siècles*, Paris (Collection "Nouvelle Clio"), 1967.

M. Reinhard (editor), *Histoire de France*, Paris (Larousse), 1954, 2 vols. Vol. I, *L'Age classique (1598-1715)*, by R. Mousnier.

P. Sagnac, *La Formation de la Société Française Moderne*, Vol. I. *La Société et la Monarchie Absolue (1661-1715)*, Paris (Presses Universitaires), 1945.

H. Sée, *Histoire économique de la France*, Vol. I. *Le moyen âge et l'ancien régime*, Paris (Armand Colin), 1939.

V. L. Tapié, *La France de Louis XIII et Richelieu*, Paris (Flammarion), 1952.

II. The Literary Background

A. Adam, *Histoire de la littérature française au XVIIe siècle*, Paris (Domat), 1948-56, 5 vols.

F. Brunot, *Histoire de la langue française*, Vols. III & IV, nouvelle édition, Paris (Armand Colin), 1966.

G. Lanson (editor), *Choix de lettres du XVIIe Siècle*, Paris (Hachette), n.d.

J. Lough, *Paris Theatre Audiences in the Seventeenth and Eighteenth Centuries*, London (Oxford University Press), 1957.

G. Mongrédien, *La Vie Littéraire au XVIIe Siècle*, Paris (Tallandier), 1947.

Les Précieux et les Précieuses, Paris (Mercure de France), 1939.

D. Mornet, *Histoire de la littérature française classique*, Paris (Armand Colin), 1940.

G. Reynier, *La Femme au XVIIe Siècle*, Paris (Tallandier), 1929.

P. J. Yaroow, *A Literary History of France: Vol II. The Seventeenth Century, 1600-1715*, London (Benn), 1967.

The following works which are frequently quoted from in this book are well worth reading :

La Bruyère, *Les Caractères*.
Saint-Simon, *Mémoires*.
Mme de Sévigné, *Lettres*.

They are available in a variety of annotated editions.

INDEX OF AUTHORS QUOTED

The editions listed are not necessarily the earliest, but are those referred to in the text

P. Corneille, *Œuvres*, ed. Marty Laveaux, Paris, 1862-8, 12 vols., 181, 183, 187, 190.

Correspondance des Contrôleurs généraux des finances avec les intendants des provinces, ed. A. de Boislisle, Paris, 1874-97, 3 vols., 35, 41, 273-4.

R. Cotgrave, *A French-English Dictionary*, 2nd edition, London, 1650, 246-7.

A. de Courtin, *Nouveau traité de la civilité qui se pratique en France parmi les honnêtes gens*, 13th edition, Paris, 1700, 200-1.

V. Cousin, *Madame de Sablé*, Paris, 1882, 195.

G. Delamothe, *The French Alphabet*, London, 1639, 246.

Dictionnaire de l'Académie Française, Paris, 1694, 2 vols., 254-5.

Fénelon, *Écrits et lettres politiques*, ed. C. Urbain, Paris, 1920, 282.

Fléchier, *Mémoires sur les grands jours d'Auvergne en 1665*, ed. A. Chéruel, Paris, 1856, 68-9, 96.

Furetière, *Poésies diverses*, ed. I. Bronk, Baltimore, 1908, 190.
Le Roman bourgeois, ed. E. Fournier, Paris, 1854, 218-19.

A. Gasté, *La Querelle du Cid*, Paris, 1898, 177.

Gourville, *Mémoires*, ed. A. Lecestre, Paris, 1894-5, 2 vols., 77-8.

Abbé Goussault, *Réflexions sur les défauts ordinaires des hommes*, Paris, 1695, 228.

Paul Hay du Châtelet, *Traité de la politique de France*, Cologne, 1677, 16-17.

Victor Hugo, *Les Contemplations*, Paris, 1856, 2 vols., 257-8.

Claude Joly, *Recueil de Maximes véritables et importantes pour l'institution du Roi*, Paris, 1653, 128-9.

Guy Joly, *Mémoires*, Amsterdam, 1718, 2 vols., 130.

La Bruyère, *Œuvres complètes*, ed. G. Servois, Paris, 1865-1912, 3 vols., 4, 32-3, 47, 50, 53, 56-7, 66, 76, 80-1, 97-8, 102, 163, 169-70, 192-3, 217.

Mme de La Fayette, *Mémoires de la cour de France pour les années 1688 et 1689*, Amsterdam, 1731, 170.

La Fontaine, *Œuvres*, ed. H. Régnier, Paris, 1883-92, 11 vols., 17, 31, 263.

M. Langlois, *Madame de Maintenon*, Paris, 1932, 170-1.

Mme de La Suze & P. Pellisson, *Recueil de pièces galantes en prose et en vers*, Trévoux, 1725, 4 vols., 239.

Jean de Préchac, *Le Voyage de Fontainebleau*, Paris, 1678, 194.

Racan, *Œuvres complètes*, ed. T. de Latour, Paris, 1857, 2 vols., 202, 206, 215-16, 256.

Jean Racine, *Œuvres*, ed P. Mesnard, Paris, 1865-70, 8 vols., 135, 221, 243, 256-7, 262.

Louis Racine, *Mémoires sur la vie de Jean Racine* (in Jean Racine, *Œuvres*, Vol. I), 177n., 194, 249.

Rapin, *Réflexions sur l'éloquence* (in *Les Comparaisons des grands hommes de l'antiquité*, Paris, 1684, 2 vols.), 255.

Mathurin Régnier, *Œuvres complètes*, ed. J. Plattard, Paris, 1930, 184.

Cardinal de Retz, *Œuvres*, ed. A. Feillet etc., Paris, 1870-1920, 11 vols., 93, 125, 127, 128.

Richelieu, *Mémoires*, Paris (*Société d'Histoire de France*), 1908-31, 10 vols., 114.

Testament politique, ed. L. André, Paris, 1947, 118-19, 120-1, 124.

Saint-Évremond, *Œuvres*, s.l., 1751, 9 vols., 203, 260-1.

Marquis de Saint-Maurice, *Lettres sur la cour de Louis XIV* (*1667-1673*), ed. J. Lemoine, Paris, 1910-12, 2 vols., 144, 146.

Saint-Simon, *Écrits inédits*, ed. P. Faugère, Paris, 1880-95, 8 vols., 280-1.

Mémoires, ed. A. de Boislisle, Paris, 1879-1930, 43 vols., 81, 85, 93-6, 146-7, 162, 165-6, 167-8.

Jacques Savary, *Le Parfait Négociant*, Paris, 1675, 2 vols., 38, 40.

Scarron, *Œuvres*, Paris, 1786, 7 vols., 186, 187.

Georges de Scudéry, *Ligdamon et Lidias*, Paris, 1631, 193.

Madeleine de Scudéry, *Clélie, histoire romaine*, Paris, 1654-60, 10 vols., 228-9, 238-9.

Mme de Sévigné, *Letters*, ed. Monmerqué & P. Mesnard, Paris, 1862-6, 14 vols., 33-4, 46-7, 61-2, 63, 64-5, 72-3, 76, 78-9, 82-5, 98, 101-2, 143, 148, 149, 150, 151, 160, 168-9, 172, 236-8, 265.

Les Soupirs de la France Esclave qui aspire après la liberté, Amsterdam, 1689, 277-8.

E. Spanheim, *Relation de la cour de France en 1690*, ed. E. Bourgeois, Paris, 1900, 91, 137-8, 139-40, 147, 149, 276.

Tallemant des Réaux, *Historiettes*, ed. G. Mongrédien, Paris, 1932-4, 8 vols., 46, 52, 69, 74, 110, 177, 182, 193-4, 223-5.

INDEX